PRAGMATISM AND METHODOLOGY

T0381539

Taking a pragmatist approach to methods and methodology that fosters meaningful, impactful, and ethical research, this book rises to the challenge of today's data revolution. It shows how pragmatism can turn challenges, such as the abundance and accumulation of big qualitative data, into opportunities. The authors summarize the pragmatist approach to different aspects of research, from epistemology, theory, and questions to ethics, as well as data collection and analysis. The chapters outline and document a new type of mixed methods design called "multi-resolution research," which serves to overcome old divides between quantitative and qualitative methods. It is the ideal resource for students and researchers within the social and behavioral sciences seeking new ways to analyze large sets of qualitative data.

ALEX GILLESPIE is Professor of Psychological and Behavioral Science at the London School of Economics and Political Science and Visiting Professor II at Oslo New University. He is an expert on communication, especially divergences of perspective, misunderstandings, internal dialogues, distrust, and problems in listening. He uses a variety of research methods and has developed several methodological tools.

VLAD GLĂVEANU is Professor of Psychology at Dublin City University, and Visiting Professor II at the Centre for the Science of Learning and Technology, University of Bergen. He is a leading expert in the fields of creativity, imagination, wonder, collaboration, and culture research, as well as the Founder and President of the Possibility Studies Network and Editor of *Possibility Studies & Society* (SAGE).

CONSTANCE DE SAINT LAURENT is Assistant Professor of Sociotechnical Systems at National University of Ireland, Maynooth. She works on trust in technology as well as on the impact of technology and societal changes on people and organizations. She has previously carried out research on social media, misinformation, collective memory, and representations of alterity, some of which has been published in the open access book *Social Thinking and History: A Sociocultural Psychological Perspective on Representations of the Past* (2021).

PRAGMATISM AND METHODOLOGY

Doing Research That Matters with Mixed Methods

ALEX GILLESPIE

London School of Economics and Political Science

VLAD GLĂVEANU

Dublin City University

CONSTANCE DE SAINT LAURENT

National University of Ireland, Maynooth

CAMBRIDGE
UNIVERSITY PRESS

Shaftesbury Road, Cambridge CB2 8EA, United Kingdom

One Liberty Plaza, 20th Floor, New York, NY 10006, USA

477 Williamstown Road, Port Melbourne, VIC 3207, Australia

314–321, 3rd Floor, Plot 3, Splendor Forum, Jasola District Centre, New Delhi – 110025, India

103 Penang Road, #05–06/07, Visioncrest Commercial, Singapore 238467

Cambridge University Press is part of Cambridge University Press & Assessment, a department of the University of Cambridge.

We share the University's mission to contribute to society through the pursuit of education, learning and research at the highest international levels of excellence.

www.cambridge.org
Information on this title: www.cambridge.org/9781316516140

DOI: 10.1017/9781009031066

Published with the support of the Swiss National Science Foundation

First published 2024

A catalogue record for this publication is available from the British Library

A Cataloging-in-Publication data record for this book is available from the Library of Congress

ISBN 978-1-316-51614-0 Hardback
ISBN 978-1-009-01378-9 Paperback

For Alice, Arlo, Arthur, Lyla, and Zoé.

Contents

Preface

There is nothing as practical as a good theory.

Lewin (1943, p. 118)

The idea that theory should be practical is both obvious and surprising. It is obvious because the avowed aim of science is to create knowledge to empower human activity (Bacon, 1620). However, theory is often associated with abstruse terms and obscure concerns (Tourish, 2020). Kurt Lewin's (1943, p. 118) maxim that "there is nothing as practical as a good theory" has gone from being cited about ten times a year in the 1990s to nearly fifty times a year recently (McCain, 2015). This upsurge betrays the challenge of creating robust and insightful theories in social science that are also useful.

Developing useful knowledge is challenging because theory that is *too* practical is quickly criticized for being unsurprising, lacking intellectual depth, and merely repackaging common sense. While it is easy to do something useful (e.g., help someone, cook a meal), it is much more challenging to create helpful knowledge. Creating useful knowledge entails synthesizing prior experience and applying it to an unknown future. It means going beyond what is already done, opening the future up to more purposive human action, and, in short, expanding human agency. In this sense, useful knowledge aims to empower human action, to make the consequences of human action expected, and to avoid unwanted surprises.

We propose that pragmatism, especially as developed by the early American pragmatists (Charles Sanders Peirce, John Dewey, Jane Addams, William James, and George Herbert Mead), provides a helpful way to think about methodology in social research. It provides timely conceptions of epistemology, theory, research questions, and data that can address our current concerns. It can help us make useful knowledge that is neither naïvely realist nor impotently critical, and it can help us address the current challenges and opportunities of both big and small data.

There is an irony in the consequences of pragmatism. As an approach, it is avowedly against abstraction and abstruse theory. It argues for starting and ending with the problems of living. But the consequences of pragmatism have been mainly theoretical and philosophical rather than practical. Despite pragmatism contributing to diverse domains (Allemang et al., 2022; Ansell & Boin, 2019; Craig, 2007; Kaushik & Walsh, 2019; Kelly & Cordeiro, 2020) and being foundational to mixed methods research (Morgan, 2014a), there have been few systematic attempts to translate the philosophy of pragmatism into a consistent methodology. This book aims to bridge this gap in pragmatist scholarship by outlining the consequences of pragmatism for social research.

From a pragmatist standpoint, knowledge should be effective, insightful, and emancipatory in its consequences. We have written this book not to contribute to pragmatist philosophy but to develop pragmatism's fruitful consequences for social research methodology. Traditionally, methods in the social sciences have been caught between realist (often quantitative) and relativist (often qualitative) tendencies. We use pragmatism to chart a course between these extremes and to produce knowledge that is both useful and critical. To this end, the book provides an end-to-end pragmatist approach to knowledge creation, spanning epistemology, theory, question creation, and the nature of data, methods of analysis, and ethics.

We are social and cultural psychologists focused on studying human activity in context, enabled by both knowledge and technology. Indeed, we use this basic orientation to understand social research activity as also being enabled by knowledge (e.g., theories, epistemology, research questions) and technology (e.g., questionnaires, interview techniques, and computational algorithms). While many of our examples pertain to social and cultural psychology, the ideas presented are broader and, we believe, have applicability across the human sciences. Specifically, this book aims to contribute to three broad debates.

1) *Rehabilitating the value of useful knowledge.* The so-called paradigm wars in social science have had consequences beyond academia, providing resources for "post-truth" politics. The paradigm wars related to debates between realism and relativism (often termed "constructionism"), focusing on the extent to which scientific knowledge is true versus being a human construction (Bryman, 2008). Unhelpful oppositions were created: science versus critique, realism versus relativism, and objectivity versus subjectivity. Nuanced arguments on both the realist side (Hacking, 1999) and the constructionist side (Berger & Luckmann, 1967) were oversimplified. Extreme and unrepresentative positions emerged on both sides. On the

realist side, qualitative analysis was shunned as unscientific, and on the constructionist side, quantitative analysis was resisted as naïve, uncritical, or even oppressive. Nevertheless, despite being uncommon positions, these extremes undermined science within the public domain (Onwuegbuzie & Leech, 2005) and sowed seeds of doubt that enabled inconvenient facts to be dismissed and "alternative facts" to thrive (Cooke, 2017, p. 211).

A pragmatist approach to social research acknowledges the stubborn resistance of facts and also the subjectivity and contextuality inherent in all knowledge. We argue that this approach can provide both the basis for creating common ground around effective knowledge while also avoiding science as an ideology beyond critical questioning.

2) *Mixing methods.* The paradigm wars drove an unhelpful wedge between qualitative and quantitative methods that had previously worked synergistically (Morgan, 2007). It was argued that qualitative and quantitative methods pertained to fundamentally different, incommensurable, epistemological frameworks (Filstead, 1979) and were "competing paradigms" (Guba & Lincoln, 1994, p. 105). While separating qualitative methods from quantitative methods enabled qualitative methods to mature independent of a quantitative framing, it had the unfortunate consequence of undermining mixed methods research. Indeed, it even became seen as potentially philosophically naïve to try and combine them (Denzin, 2012).

A pragmatist approach argues that qualitative and quantitative methods can be combined and, moreover, that they *should* be combined. Quantitative methods provide breadth, and qualitative methods provide depth. If both add value, why choose one over the other? The choice is false: It is more rigorous to have both breadth and depth. Together, they can make social science more robust, insightful, and emancipatory. Moreover, we will argue that mixed methods research is necessary for addressing the challenges and harnessing the potential of big qualitative data.

3) *The challenge and potential of big qualitative data.* Qualitative research in psychology and related disciplines is at a crossroads. On the one hand, the field has substantially increased in terms of its thematic reach – the number of studies, journals, and textbooks. However, we are living through a qualitative data explosion, with an exponential growth of digitally recorded but unstructured text, image, audio, and video data. While these data are often termed "big data," they are also "qualitative data." Thus, somewhat ironically, at the extreme end of quantification (i.e., big data) is qualitative data (i.e., digital text, image, video). To tackle the challenges of these data, and to make the most of the opportunities they offer for social research, we need to integrate data science (i.e., quantitative and

computational) techniques with qualitative research techniques (Bazeley, 2017; Chang et al., 2021).

A pragmatist approach suggests a novel way of mixing big data and qualitative research techniques. We will argue not only for mixing qualitative and quantitative methods side by side but also for what we call multi-resolution research, where the same data are analyzed both qualitatively (to zoom in on details) and quantitatively (to zoom out on patterns). Such analysis is possible only by reconceptualizing raw data as affording a bidirectional transformation into both qualitative and quantitative forms. Such bidirectional transformations enable a continual moving back and forth between qualitative and quantitative facets *of the same dataset*.

Overall, we argue that a pragmatist approach to methodology can address the challenge of creating useful knowledge, enhance the rigor and creativity of research, foster deeply integrated qualitative and quantitative methods, and avoid overly simplistic oppositions between realism and relativism. Pragmatism's guiding insight is to consider the consequences of knowledge. This enables a realist-type analysis of the effectiveness of knowledge combined with a constructionist-type critique of who benefits from that effectiveness. The chapters in the book step through pragmatism (Chapter 1), epistemology (Chapter 2), theory (Chapter 3), research questions (Chapter 4), data collection and curation (Chapter 5), mixed methods research (Chapter 6), multi-resolution research (Chapter 7), ethics (Chapter 8), and the role of social research in enhancing human possibility (Chapter 9). The aim is to propose pragmatism as a coherent, flexible, and robust framework for creating useful knowledge that can enhance society.

Finally, in preparing this book, and in the many years of discussion that led to this book, we would like to acknowledge the intellectual support of our colleagues, including Flora Cornish, Kevin Corti, Ioana Literat, Mark Noort, Tom Reader, and Tania Zittoun. This book has been supported financially by two grants from the Swiss National Science Foundation (51NF40-205605 via "nccr – on the move" and P400PS-180686).

CHAPTER I

Pragmatism

A pragmatist ... turns away from abstraction and insufficiency, from verbal solutions, from bad *a priori* reasons, from fixed principles, closed systems, and pretended absolutes and origins. He turns towards concreteness and adequacy, towards facts, towards action, and towards power. That means the empiricist temper regnant, and the rationalist temper sincerely given up. It means the open air and possibilities of nature, as against dogma, artificiality and the pretence of finality in truth.

James (1907, p. 51)

An originating insight for pragmatism was Charles Sanders Peirce's (1878) argument that the truth of an idea is found in its consequences. Specifically, what we call "true" is knowledge that yields the expected outcome. This paradigmatic insight was developed in America by John Dewey (especially in psychology, education, and art; Dewey, 1922, 1934, 1958), William James (especially in psychology and philosophy; James, 1890, 1907), George Herbert Mead (especially in social psychology; Mead, 1913, 1925), and Jane Addams (especially in activism and social work; Addams, 1990, 2002). These heterogeneous scholars were united in believing that science, within the context of democracy, could improve society. Instead of searching for absolute truths, independent of humans, they wanted society to take responsibility for creating knowledge that would enrich humanity.

Pragmatism can be challenging to understand because it resists the languages of both realism and skepticism. It mixes a hard-headed focus on facts with social values, especially democracy. How can knowledge be underpinned by both truth (thought to be independent of humans) and values, such as democracy (clearly not independent of humans)? It achieves this by reconceptualizing the subject–object (subjectivity–objectivity, relativism–truth) dichotomy. This dichotomy is so fundamental to our thinking that, sometimes, pragmatism can seem contradictory. For example, in the opening quotation James, on the one hand, looks away from final truths but, on the other hand, looks "towards facts." This is possible because pragmatism takes time very seriously. Facts are in the past, things that happened, that cannot be undone; knowledge leans into the future and will become a fact only after its consequences are realized. From a pragmatist standpoint, truths outside of time are an illusory "quest for certainty" (Dewey, 1929). The idea of a timeless truth fails to distinguish what has happened from what might happen, and it thus suppresses our responsibility for what will happen.

In this chapter, we introduce pragmatism. First, we situate pragmatism within a process paradigm that emphasizes temporality and change, and we contrast this with approaches that prioritize timeless things. We discuss both the criticisms of pragmatism (that it is relativistic, uncritical, and behaviorist) and the benefits of pragmatism (that it enables multimethod research, creates useful knowledge, and helps generate novel theories). Finally, we distill pragmatism into eight propositions. The eight subsequent chapters will develop the implications of each one of these propositions for methodology in the social sciences.

1.1 Paradigms: "Things" or "Processes"?

According to Thomas Kuhn (1962) all sciences are embedded in paradigms that are more or less implicit. These paradigms are sets of assumptions, articles of faith, root metaphors, and themata that are taken for granted (Holton, 1975). Paradigms demarcate discontinuities in knowledge. If ideas fit harmoniously together, they are part of the same paradigm. Moving from one paradigm to another is discontinuous and often abrupt. Such paradigm shifts, or scientific revolutions, are stimulated by the accumulation of anomalies. Anomalies are observations or logical contradictions that are difficult to explain within a given paradigm. All paradigms have anomalies, and the tendency is to overlook them and focus on the affordances and successes of the paradigm (Kuhn, 1962). However, anomalies are the seeds of progress.

Ivana Marková (1982) has used the Kuhnian concept of paradigm to characterize two fundamental paradigms in psychology and the broader social sciences. The first is a mechanistic paradigm within which the world comprises "things" that subsequently enter into interactions. The second is a process paradigm within which the world comprises interactions (or experiences) and only subsequently are these decomposed into "things." Marková calls these the Cartesian and Hegelian paradigms after their respective ancestors.

1.1.1 The Cartesian Paradigm

The French philosopher René Descartes (1641) laid the foundations for the mechanistic and deterministic paradigm. He argued that there are two separate ontological realms: *res extensa* and *res cogitans*. *Res extensa* pertains to all that is extended in three-dimensional space, while *res cogitans* refers to all the things that appear in the mind (e.g., thought, internal dialogue, and imagery) and rational thought (e.g., Pythagoras' theorem, mathematics). Unlike *res extensa*, *res cogitans* does not have any extension in three dimensional space.

Descartes' (1641) dualistic ontology isolated the cognitive and spiritual element within *res cogitans*, thus enabling scientists to study *res extensa* in purely mechanical terms. This separation had the benefit of isolating the soul, and thus religion, and freeing scientists up to study the natural world unencumbered by religious doctrine. It laid the foundations for material determinism: the idea that everything that has happened and will happen in the material domain is merely the unfolding of a mechanical system. Pierre-Simon Laplace (1814, p. 4) described material determinism as follows:

> We ought then to regard the present state of the universe as the effect of its anterior state and as the cause of the one which is to follow. Given for one instant an intelligence which could comprehend all the forces by which nature is animated and the respective situation of the beings who compose it – an intelligence sufficiently vast to submit these data to analysis – it would embrace in the same formula the movements of the greatest bodies of the universe and those of the lightest atom; for it, nothing would be uncertain and the future, as the past, would be present to its eyes.

Laplace's arresting idea was that the entire universe is like a mechanical clock – fully determined by its starting position. Thus, everything, from exploding stars to the sentences on this page, is the inevitable ticking of the mechanical universe set in motion at the start of time.

Descartes' sharp separation between *res extensa* and *res cogitans* led, on the one hand, to the rationalistic study of ideas without extension (mathematics, geometry, logic, etc.) and, on the other hand, to the empirical sciences of things with extension (physics, biology, chemistry, etc.). Although rationalism and empiricism are often opposed (because they disagree on whether truth comes from ideas or observations), they are both mechanistic ontologies: They start with things (empirical or logical), and all interactions are secondary.

For Descartes, Truth is timeless. True logical relations do not change with time. For example, the laws of geometry are unchanging. Equally, the human mind, he argued, does not develop. The human soul, Descartes wrote, is always conscious in any circumstance – even in a mother's womb. Furthermore, logical relations between objects in the world, in so far as they are True, must be True for all time. Descartes' ideas carry forward Plato's allegory of the cave: that human experience is like the shimmering colorless shadow of an intricate three-dimensional object cast upon a cave wall by a flickering fire. Plato termed the posited Truth behind experience "natural kinds" – these are the objects that underly human experience. While experience is fallible, natural kinds are perfect and outside of time.

Much contemporary social research is within the Cartesian paradigm (Farr, 1997; Marková, 1982). This paradigm aims to identify, define, and measure "variables" (i.e., things). Only secondarily are these variables related to one another (e.g., correlations, experiments). The metaphor is Laplace's clockwork universe, with the variables being the cogs ticking onward through cause–effect relations. When change occurs, the Cartesian paradigm searches for causal cogs. The assumption is that the change needs explanation, but the variables do not – they are taken for granted.

One anomaly in the Cartesian paradigm is development. While there are many methodologies for assessing initial states and outcomes, there are fewer methodologies for assessing what happens in between (Valsiner, 2006). The relations between independent and dependent variables are described with probabilistic statistics, but what actually occurs within any given situation is not an abstract probability. Probabilistic statistics obscure variance, thus blending various underlying processes into a single abstract and possibly nonexistent curve of probability (Fisher et al., 2018; Hayes et al., 2019). Even asking questions about what happened in a given case between input and output becomes challenging. Studying a single case is seen to be foolish because, within this paradigm, a single case does not form a probability. Thus, the actuality of an event (i.e., the case of what actually happened – a fact in pragmatist terms) is secondary to an abstraction that never occurred (i.e., the statistical model). Indeed, cases that do not fit the model (i.e., outliers) are deviations to be removed. This subordination of the actual to the abstract model is deeply antipragmatist; pragmatism puts events first and treats theories, and knowledge more generally, as fallible abstractions.

A second anomaly of the Cartesian paradigm arises in the domain of psychology. Psychology is the science of mind and behavior, with the "and" revealing the Cartesian split (Farr, 1987). On the one hand, psychology operates with an ontology of *res extensa*, for example, when studying the neuroscience of the brain or the predictability of human behavior. On the other hand, it operates with an ontology of *res cogitans*, for example, when studying the phenomenology of human experience or the psychological dynamics of self-reflection. This oversharp separation between the mind and the world led to a psychology of mind disconnected from the body (Damasio, 2006) and from other minds (Gillespie, 2006a). The mind was marooned, cut adrift from the material and social world.

Although Descartes is too often oversimplified and blamed for the ills of contemporary thinking (Baker & Morris, 1996), his ideas did lay the groundwork for a paradigm that separates the mind from the body and foregrounds things over processes. The peculiarity of this Cartesian paradigm becomes more apparent when contrasted with the alternative, a paradigm that foregrounds processes over things.

1.1.2 The Hegelian Paradigm

The Hegelian paradigm gets its name from the German philosopher Georg Wilhelm Friedrich Hegel (1807), an early and celebrated proponent of processes. Specifically, Hegel theorized "things" as being secondary to processes, as arising within "the life of the whole":

> The bud disappears in the bursting-forth of the blossom, and one might say that the former is refuted by the latter; similarly, when the fruit appears, the blossom is shown up in its turn as a false manifestation of the plant, and the fruit now emerges as the truth of it instead. These forms are not just distinguished from one another, they also supplant one another as mutually incompatible. Yet at the same time their fluid nature makes them moments of an organic unity in which they not only do not conflict, but in which each is as necessary as the other; and this mutual necessity alone constitutes the life of the whole. (Hegel, 1807, p. 2)

Is the oak tree superior to the acorn? Which comes first? Which is right? According to Hegel, these questions do not make sense because both are phases of the same process. However, although they are parts of the same process, the acorn and the oak tree are not equivalent. There is genuine nontautological growth and transformation. Hegel wrote, somewhat flippantly, that mathematics was boring because it was all tautology; every discovery was given in advance in the axiomatic assumptions of mathematics. Equally, a mechanical clockwork universe, like mathematics, does not grow or develop; it merely rearranges. In contrast, Hegel was interested in qualitative transformation and the emergence of nontautological novelty.

Hegel's philosophy was notoriously abstract (and, in that sense, deeply unpragmatist; James, 1882). But he needs to be understood in his historical context as trying to describe systems evolving before Darwin, systems theory, or ecological thinking. Dewey (1910b) saw in Darwin a concrete instantiation of Hegel's process philosophy, and by combining Hegel and Darwin, he arrived at a naturalistic conception of the human mind and society undergoing continual change. That is to say, the mind and society are not outside of nature but part of it – responding, adapting, and acting within the ecology of nature. In contrast to the mechanistic stimulus–response psychology of his time, Dewey (1896) argued that perception, cognition, and action form a dynamic system of adjustment. He rejected the idea that the mind is a subjective domain observing the objective domain. He replaced this Cartesian idea with a pragmatist conception of the mind as the means through which we reconstruct our relation to the world to enable action to proceed.

Every philosophy has to start with something. Plato began with a timeless Truth "behind" human experience. Descartes began with the unquestionable Truths of rationality and geometry. Laplace began with the idea of a clockwork universe in motion. In contrast, pragmatism begins with human activity – everyday actions and experiences that comprise the world as we know it. Within ostensibly mundane daily activities, humans are in a dynamic processual relation to the world. Within daily activities, knowledge is successfully created and used, and the debate between timeless Truths and solipsistic skepticism dissolves (James, 1912). While Plato and Descartes chose to build their systems of knowledge on something outside human experience, pragmatism chooses to build knowledge from within the experience of mundane human interaction. Human experience arises when we interact with the world or other people.

The idea of taking interactions (or processes) as foundational, as the basic unit of analysis, is not unique to pragmatism. It is evident in a range of domains, including studies of language, evolutionary and ecological theory, and complex systems theory.

In terms of language, Bakhtin's (1981) contributions are clearly within a process philosophy. He conceptualized language and texts as living, dynamic, and contextual. A paradigmatic orientation is especially evident in Bakhtin's (1986) criticism of Saussure. Saussure (1916) sought the structure of language (*langue*) "behind" the concrete manifestations of talk (*parole*). For Saussure, the aim was to identify the abstract rules that could explain language use in everyday life. More recently, Chomsky (1995) has sought to identify a universal grammar underlying all human languages.

In contrast, Bakhtin, operating within a process paradigm, argued that *langue* was an abstraction, and instead, the bedrock reality of language was *parole* – how language is used in daily life and how it varies between contexts (Linell, 2009). Everyday language use, Bakhtin argued, is not a pale reflection of a more abstract Truth; rather, it is language in process – grounded in the past, adapting to new contexts, and becoming the language of tomorrow.

In terms of evolutionary and ecological theory, process philosophy is pervasive, if often implicit. This point was made in philosophy by Dewey (1910b) and was developed in psychology by Werner (1957), among others. Where Hegel had the idea of things evolving and changing, Darwin's theory of evolution by natural selection made the idea of evolution concrete; it showed how species, and even humans, were within a process of change. More recently, Deacon (2011) contrasts engineering logic (a Cartesian paradigm that builds things up from parts) with organic (biological) logic (a Hegelian paradigm in which the parts are differentiated within a functional whole). Humans, Deacon argues, are not created by assembling hearts, lungs, and limbs together – like Frankenstein's creation. Human life begins with cell differentiation and the progressive specialization of cells, which functionally differentiate within the whole of the emerging organism. The "parts" of an organism, like the parts of an ecosystem, become what they are through their functional role within the larger system.

Finally, complexity theory studies complex, especially dynamic, systems (Byrne & Callaghan, 2013). It is closely related to evolutionary and ecological thinking, but it takes more inspiration from mathematics (Kauffman, 1996). It is often applied beyond biology, for example, to understand cellular automata, turbulence, and weather systems. Increasingly, it is used to understand human psychological (Guastello et al., 2008) and societal phenomena (Page, 2015). The basic idea is that numerous elements interacting produce higher-level phenomena that are more than the sum of the elements (e.g., rivers are more than water molecules, the mind is more than the cortex, and society is more than individuals). Complex systems have emergent phenomena, such as attractors (e.g., a whirlpool), and qualitative phase shifts (e.g., water becoming ice). Complexity theory is an example of a process paradigm because these higher-level phenomena emerge from the interactions of component elements.

Pragmatism has an affinity to any tradition that emphasizes "processes" over "things" and takes change and development seriously – whether it is the development of language systems, biological systems, or any other complex systems. The elements can be diverse (words, people, species), but they are all situated within larger systems (language, societies, ecosystems). The key is that the elements are not timeless but developing; not definable in isolation but definable in terms of their functional role within the system; and not hidden "behind" what is going on but are what is going on.

1.2   Pragmatism: Knowledge within Human Activity

Early American pragmatism was a response to relativism (or skepticism), which itself was a response to naïve realism. From a realist standpoint, Truth is independent of humans: timeless, hidden "behind" the blooming buzzing confusion of experience awaiting "discovery." The skeptical reaction to this is that humans "construct" knowledge; it is created through social and discursive processes and ceases to exist when the supporting social processes wane. History, the skeptics observe, is littered with the vestiges of so-called timeless truths, each bound to a civilization, culture, or research paradigm.

Pragmatism is often misunderstood because it transcends this debate between realism (there are infallible timeless Truths) and skepticism (all knowledge is uncertain). It is unusual because it subscribes to both fallibilism and antiskepticism (Putnam, 1995). It agrees with the skeptics: There is no guarantee that any theory is timeless and will not need revision. But it also agrees with the realists: Just because knowledge can be doubted, it does not mean that all knowledge should be doubted equally.

Pragmatism proposes that knowledge is neither purely a function of the world (realism) nor of humans (skepticism). Instead, knowledge is an *interaction* between humans and the world. The term "pragmatism" comes from the Greek *pragma* meaning "deed" or "action." The core pragmatist idea is that the opposition between subject and object, or representation and reality, should be replaced with activity and experience (which binds the subject and object together). Pragmatism is a process paradigm because it starts with the dynamics of experience and activity.

To understand how pragmatism can be both fallibilist and antiskeptical, it is necessary to return to the subject–object dualism. Descartes institutionalized this dualism, which now permeates the social sciences and modern thinking (Latour, 1993). However, it is a loaded and oversimplistic opposition that leads us to pigeonhole theories as belonging to either the subject or the object side of the dualism. It creates a host of anomalies, especially for psychology, which aims to be an objective science of subjectivity.

1.2.1 Beyond Subject and Object: The Truth Is in the Future

At the heart of pragmatism is a reconceptualization of Descartes' infamous distinction between subject (*res cogitans*) and object (*res extensa*). This distinction is central to a correspondence theory of Truth: Does the image in the mind of the subject mirror the object out in the world? Such a "mirror theory" of truth pervades naïve realism (Rorty, 1981). Pragmatism reconceptualizes the distinction between subject and object and, in so doing, reconceptualizes the nature of truth.

Although the Cartesian separation between subject and object looks clear-cut, in practice it is messy. Dewey (1905, p. 230) identifies this anomaly using the example of awakening to a scary sound:

> I start and am flustered by a noise heard. Empirically, that noise is fearsome; it really is, not merely phenomenally or subjectively so. That is *what* it is experienced as being. But, when I experience the noise as a *known* thing, I find it to be innocent of harm. It is the tapping of a shade against the window, owing to movements of the wind. The experience has changed; that is, the thing experienced has changed not that an unreality has given place to a reality, nor that some transcendental (unexperienced) Reality has changed, not that truth has changed, but just and only the concrete reality experienced has changed.

This seemingly innocuous example poses a problem. Is the scary perception subjective, while the chaffing shade is objective? The problem is that the frightening perception did not feel subjective in the moment. And what if there really was a burglar at the window? Then, would the chaffing shade now become subjective? Dewey's point is that assigning experiences to subjective or objective domains is unhelpful and muddled because the raw experience, in the moment, is equally real in all cases.

> [There] is no reason for assuming the content of one [experience] to be exclusively 'real' and that of others to be 'phenomenal'[.] [W]e have a contrast, not between a Reality, and various approximations to, or phenomenal representations of Reality, but between different reals of experience. (Dewey, 1905, p. 227)

Dewey argues that the first experience (the scary noise) is no less real than the second (the chaffing shade); both empirical experiences are equally real experiences. What differentiates them is in the future (whether there was anything more than the chaffing shade). As experiences accumulate, one experience may supersede the other at the level of understanding, as a theory of the world, setting an expectation for how to act next – which in turn may be superseded (see Chapter 2).

We often use the term "subjective" to talk about an action that has become uncertain, where expectation has been surprised. Within this disruption, the path of action is no longer obvious, decisions have to be made, and options have to be weighted against one another (e.g., to go back to sleep or to investigate the noise). In such scenarios, what seems objective at time one becomes subjective at time two and vice versa. Thus objectivity and subjectivity cannot exist side by side in different ontological realms; instead, they are sequentially related as different phases of human activity, with the former being a taken-for-granted activity and the latter being an activity that has become problematic. The critical point is that both subject and object become differentiated within the activity.

Another anomaly of the subject–object dualism can arise between people (Mead, 1932). Consider a neuroscientist examining the brain of a patient using an advanced scanner. The screen shows the topography of the brain, where the blood flows, and thus the loci of cognitive activity. It is seductive to conceptualize this as the "real" or "objective" basis of the patient's experience; or, put another way, what is real is the blood flow, while the patient's experience is merely subjective. But the anomaly arises when we take a step back: Is the neuroscientist's assessment of the scan also merely subjective? Is the blood flow merely a perception in the neuroscientist's brain? If so, this could only be detected by a second neuroscientist examining a brain scan of the first neuroscientist. But, again, this examination would be a mere subjective experience, and so on, *ad infinitum*. The point is that the patient's experience is as real as the neuroscientist's experience; the only difference is that they are in two different bodies coupled with a belief system that privileges one experience over the other.

Pragmatism reconceptualizes the subject–object dualism by taking a naturalistic stance. Building on the ideas of Darwin, pragmatism argues that all human activity (including mental activity) is part of nature (Dewey, 1922; Mead, 1932). Thinking and collective inquiry (e.g., science) are not outside of nature, observing it, but part of the interactions that comprise nature. The term "naturalism" denotes the fact that experience (including empirical observation) does not "give access to" nature but rather is part of nature (see Chapter 2). Thus, "experience" is not a subjective quality; *it is a real relation to the world that is part of the world*. This overcomes the problematic idea that the subjective is outside the objective, observing it.

Pragmatism's primary unit of analysis is interaction, variously called "acts" (Dewey, 1896), "experience" (James, 1912), "social acts" (Mead, 1912), "perspectives" (Mead, 1926), and "transactions" (Dewey & Bentley, 1946). These terms overcome the subject–object dualism because both subject and object are derivative of these experiences, acts, or transactions. An experience is holistic, and a conceptual act is required to differentiate subject and object within the experience. From the standpoint of an observer (either a third party or observing one's past self), it is tempting to say that subject and object meet in experience – that experience is a fusion of subject and object, a view on the object tainted by subjectivity. But from the standpoint of the experience, there is only that which is experienced. The experience is primary, and any differentiation of subject and object is secondary. Pragmatism is firmly rooted in the primary moment of experience – conceptualized as a dynamic moment of activity. For this reason it has been variously described as "immediate empiricism" (Dewey, 1905), "radical empiricism" (James, 1912), and "empirical naturalism" (Dewey, 1958).

The problem with trying to locate the experience in subjectivity (*res cogitans*) is that it gets marooned there; then all experience becomes merely subjective, and the anomaly of "objective" observation rises again. This leads to a foundational philosophical problem: How can we reliably know anything? The realist argues that we can distinguish what is "in the mind" from what is "in the world." The relativist counters that because things at time one are "in the world" and at time two are "in the mind" (e.g., spontaneous generation, phrenology), it must all be in the mind. The pragmatist makes a more fundamental point: Both the realist and the relativist are arguing the two sides of Descartes' problematic dualism. Pragmatism aims to transcend this dualism, and the associated anomalies. It does this by holding on to the "reality" (with a small "r") of experience while rejecting the spurious distinction between "timeless Reality" (with a capital "R") and human subjectivity.

Experiences are real; they can be expected or unexpected, desirable or undesirable. Believing that the wall one is walking toward is subjective will lead to a bruising encounter. This means that we can talk about false beliefs as beliefs that produce an unexpected outcome. False beliefs, just like true beliefs, are consequential, and it is the future consequences that will definitively distinguish them. Pragmatism eschews timeless Truth (with a capital "T") in favor of a future-oriented truth (with a small "t"). James (1907, p. 201) writes: "The truth of an idea is not a stagnant property inherent in it. Truth *happens* to an idea. It *becomes* true, is *made* true by events. Its verity *is* in fact an event, a process." In this sense, truth exists in the past; in the present is experience and in the future is uncertainty.

Rorty (1982, p. xxix) pointed out that the sentence "it works because it is true" is equivalent to the sentence "it is true because it works." He argued that this equivalence reveals that "truth" is nothing more nor less than the demonstration of truth. Truth is not inherent and timeless; it merely expresses confidence about the next test. Although abandoning the idea of a Truth independent of its testing might seem to be a step too far toward relativism, it is actually how science (in a positivist sense) proceeds. Pragmatism is essentially a formalization of science (e.g., postulating hypotheses and testing them) that, like science, subordinates all theories to the next test.

Knowledge, according to pragmatism, is a promise that is more or less justified. It does not abandon truth; it defers it. Pragmatism is an attempt to learn from past events, to extrapolate from the past toward a future that is unknown. And who would claim that the future holds no surprises? To talk about our theories being True and timeless is hubris in the face of infinity. To quote James (1907, p. 207) again: "Truth lives, in fact, for the most part on a credit system. Our thoughts and beliefs 'pass', so long as nothing challenges them, just as banknotes pass so long as nobody refuses them." But, just like the credit system, the edifice is unstable, and the parts are liable to collapse when the future that we expected is not the future that we get.

1.2.2 Starting from Where We Are

Every philosophy requires a starting point, and pragmatism starts from where we are. Descartes (1641) sought a single unquestionable Truth from which to rebuild all knowledge. He found his Archimedean point in his indubitable doubting ("*cogito, ergo sum*," "I think, therefore I am") and the rational Truths of mathematics (e.g., Pythagoras' theorem). Pragmatism, in contrast, does not have an Archimedean point of absolute certainty. Instead, it starts from the dense web of mini truths and practical realities that constitute everyday life. As Toulmin (1992, p. 179) wrote: "[T]he only thing we can do is make the best of starting with what we have got, here and now."

The naïve realist idea that there is a singular, beautiful, and timeless Truth waiting to be "discovered" behind human experience is seductive but blinding (Midgley, 2003). This beguiling idea is an assumption, not an empirical experience; it is grounded in metaphors (e.g., deterministic clocks, mirrors of truth, laws of nature) and allegories (such as the forms casting shadows on Plato's cave). Instead of building science upon such metaphors and allegories, pragmatism takes a more cautious approach, arguing that we should start with the empirical (i.e., experiential) reality of our situation, namely the here and now, including the bricolage of ideas, heuristics, and tools that have got us this far. Instead of building knowledge on some utopic but unknowable (and thus uncertain) foundation, pragmatism builds knowledge on the messy but familiar foundation of everyday life. Despite being imperfect, this web of practices has the advantage of being honed over millennia. Pragmatists celebrate this bricolage of mini truths and context-dependent heuristics. This is in stark contrast to Descartes, who sought well-planned and rational knowledge.

> The buildings undertaken and carried out by a single architect are generally more seemly and better arranged than those that several hands have sought to adapt, making use of old walls that were built for other purposes. Again, those ancient cities which were originally mere boroughs, and have become towns in process of time, are as a rule badly laid out, as compared with those towns of regular pattern that are laid out by a designer. (Descartes, 1637, p. 15)

Descartes wanted to use his Archimedean point of unquestionable Truth as a foundation for rebuilding all knowledge. He sought an orderly, internally consistent, and superficially "more seemly" body of knowledge. But nearly 400 years later, we still only have, as we have always had (and probably always will have), an unruly, context-dependent, and deeply organic bricolage of knowledge. While Descartes would be dismayed, pragmatists are unsurprised. We should evaluate knowledge not in terms of how well laid out it is but in terms of how empowering it is. What does it enable people to do?

The pragmatist approach has no grand ambition to reconstruct all knowledge. Instead, it seeks local fixes and incremental improvements. As Ansell and Boin (2019) describe, pragmatism aims to repair the ship while at sea. It respects what is and focuses on what is problematic. It evaluates knowledge piecemeal in terms of its function, consequences, and potential. The aim is only to improve upon the knowledge we have. This makes pragmatism deeply consonant with science. Science is not about making grand narratives, holding nonempirical assumptions as unquestionable, or seeking timeless Truths. Science uses empirical methods to solve problems, address predicaments, and develop useful knowledge; it is a method of continual refinement (Midgley, 2003).

Like the earth itself, human knowledge is suspended in space without foundations. But this does not detract from its remarkable, intricate, and contextual refinement. Knowledge grows, not by finding foundations but by continually challenging, revising, and weaving an ever-denser web. Knowledge grows because it is woven into the warp and weft of practical activity. It is tested and tuned each time we experience the consequences of our actions. Our knowledge is robust because it does not rely upon any singular foundation. It is a web spun by trillions of action-consequence loops, and like any web, there is no singular point of failure. Midgley (2003, p. 26) asks: Why do "we choose to represent the development of our knowledge always in terms of building," with the assumption of need-ing good foundations, "rather than, for instance, of an interaction with the world around us, leading to growth"?

For those in search of timeless Truths and indubitable foundations, the pragmatist paradigm can be unsettling. It can seem, James (1907, pp. 260–261) writes, that knowledge is "adrift in space, with neither elephant nor tor-toise to plant the sole of its foot upon. It is a set of stars hurled into heaven without even a centre of gravity to pull against." But knowledge from a pragmatist standpoint has an anchor, namely, human activity. Holding firm to human action, knowledge can be evaluated as effective or ineffec-tive, as insightful or mundane, and as empowering or disempowering.

1.2.3   Navigating Rupture and Surprise

The social world is not stable or timeless; history continues to be made, and knowledge must continue to adapt (Power et al., 2023). New technologies, societal challenges, and scientific breakthroughs disrupt our expectations. Technologies we take for granted did not exist a generation ago. Moreover, many of the challenges we face are partly a product of these technologies (e.g., climate change, inequality, and sedentary lifestyles). Consequently, many contemporary research questions could not have been asked a gen-eration ago (e.g., reducing polarization online, algorithmic bias, and the impact of social media on the formation of teenage identities). Given our dynamic social world, the idea of timeless Truths is, at best, simplistic and, at worst, risks blinding us to our responsibility for creating tomorrow's truths (and problems).

Pragmatism is well suited to understanding crises, ruptures, and uncer-tainty (Rorty, 1989). Indeed, it conceptualizes knowledge as a means for handling uncertainty (Dewey, 1929). Human knowledge aims to make the world predictable, explainable, and actionable (Ansell & Boin, 2019). The only facts we have are in the past; the future is an expectation await-ing disruption. What happens will establish the truth of our expectations. However, hindsight is of little use. Knowledge is a crystallization of past experiences and events that did happen, into extrapolations and general-izations that help us to navigate what might happen (Peirce, 1955). From a

made many contributions beyond philosophy to psychology, language, education, politics, policy, and ethics. In this book, we want to focus on the contribution that pragmatism can make to methodology in the social sciences.

So far, the contribution of pragmatism to methodology has been limited relative to its potential. To date, pragmatism has mainly been used to (1) justify mixed methods research, (2) legitimate the value of applied research, and (3) conceptualize how new theories develop.

1.4.1 Pragmatism and Mixed Methods

One of the main contributions of pragmatism to social research has been to provide a framework for combining qualitative and quantitative methods. Although these methods can be combined within realist and constructionist frameworks (Cassell et al., 2017), doing so risks introducing evaluative criteria that undermine one or the other method (Yardley & Bishop, 2017). For example, within a realist framework, qualitative data might be either overinterpreted as indicating causal relations or underinterpreted by overlooking how the data collection method (e.g., interview) constructed the responses. Within a constructionist framework, quantitative data can be dismissed as a mere experimental or historical artifact (Gergen, 1973), thus missing out on the opportunity for cautious generalization. The problem is that positivism and constructionism are skewed toward quantitative and qualitative methods, respectively. Thus, using one of these paradigms for both methodologies risks failing to avail of the unique contributions of each method.

Pragmatism can combine qualitative and quantitative research strengths and avoid subordinating one to the other (Morgan, 2007, 2014a; Yardley & Bishop, 2017). Instead of debating whether qualitative and quantitative methods are paradigmatically commensurable (e.g., Guba & Lincoln, 1994), a pragmatist approach focuses on what each methodological approach can do, what insight it adds, and what contribution it makes (Feilzer, 2010; Morgan, 2007). Thus, pragmatism provides mixed methods research with a flexible framework within which realist concerns about efficacy can be synergistically combined with constructionist concerns about social justice (Morgan, 2014a).

A more radical option for mixed methods is to move fluidly between positivism and constructionism – as advocated by dialectical pluralism (Johnson, 2017). This is the idea that all ontologies, epistemologies, methodologies, and ethical frameworks have value. Dismissing any based on logical incompatibility with prior commitments fails to avail of the breadth of ways of thinking about the given problem. Arguably, such open-mindedness toward potentially contradictory paradigms is pragmatic. A pragmatist, according to James (1907, p. 259), "is a happy-go-lucky anarchistic sort of creature" – and thus untroubled by mixing ontologies and epistemologies. But what distinguishes the pragmatist from the dialectical pluralist is the question: What does each perspective contribute to the problem at hand? Without this pragmatic focus on the consequences, a straddling of paradigms can cause problems. It can lead to mixed methods research where findings are siloed, or juxtaposed, with little synergy (Feilzer, 2010) – with each finding marooned in its own paradigm. There needs to be a point of integration; otherwise, anything goes, and all findings are equal. Integration is needed so that tensions can be transformed into synergies (Fetters & Freshwater, 2015a). According to pragmatism, integration occurs in the consequences, through each approach yielding its fruit.

1.4.2   Pragmatism and Applied Research

Pragmatism foregrounds applied research and has, unsurprisingly, had significant traction in domains addressing practical issues. It has been advocated in education (Biesta & Burbules, 2003), social work (Kaushik & Walsh, 2019), law (Patterson, 1990), crisis management (Ansell & Boin, 2019), organizational research (Kelly & Cordeiro, 2020), and health psychology (Allemang et al., 2022; Cornish & Gillespie, 2009). In each case, pragmatism validates the frontline challenges of intervening in the social world, provides practical ideas for improving practice, and draws theoretical sustenance from the practical problems addressed.

The traditional realist and constructionist paradigms build their knowledge on foundations outside of daily life, and as such, they sometimes view applied research as secondary to "fundamental" research. The idea is that these are the domains within which fundamental knowledge is merely "applied." However, from a pragmatist standpoint, it is the so-called applied domains of practice that are "fundamental." These varied and peculiar contexts are the reality of social life. From a pragmatist standpoint, evaluating a theory either in the abstract domain of logic or in the artificial domain of the laboratory is merely a starting point to the most robust test of knowledge; is it helpful in practice?

All knowledge is contextual, and the context that is most valued from a pragmatist standpoint is the context of activity outside the laboratory.

Theories that work only in the laboratory merely have the consequence of making careers for academics. Pragmatism aims to improve the human condition more broadly. This applied focus was most evident in the work of Addams (1990, 2002), who was awarded a Nobel Prize for her peace activism and made fundamental contributions to social work. She rejected a teaching position at the University of Chicago so that she could focus on providing adult education and empowering people in poverty (Knight, 2008).

Experimental research is currently grappling with the replication crisis (Shrout & Rodgers, 2018). This is the problem of experimental findings, especially in psychology, failing to replicate in other experimental contexts (Open Science Collaboration, 2015). But if findings cannot be replicated in experiments that are set up to be as similar as possible, then what hope is there of these findings having applicability in domains far removed from the controlled environment of a laboratory? There are many degrees of freedom in laboratory research (Wicherts et al., 2016), but how many more are there in the diverse geographic, historical, and sociocultural domains of practice?

A pragmatist approach cuts through these methodological concerns by arguing that the most rigorous test of a theory is not whether it works in the laboratory but whether it feeds forward to help people build the future they want (Power et al., 2023). In short, the real test of knowledge, from a pragmatist standpoint, is: Does it, even in some small way, enrich humanity? Specifically, what does it enable people to do? And, more critically, what does it enable people to do to one another?

The pragmatist celebration of applied contexts is not a repudiation of theory: Theory is our best preparation for an uncertain future, enabling action in tried and tested domains, and serving as a resource in contexts unknown. Empowering, enriching, and useful theory is the goal of social science. The point is that applied contexts are the most fertile soil for generating empowering and enriching theory. In contrast, building theory from knowledge created in nonapplied domains, in artificial or highly peculiar domains, is likely to produce knowledge that does not generalize, that increases, rather than reduces, surprise in the domains of daily life.

1.4.3 Pragmatism and Abduction

Pragmatism has also contributed to conceptualizing how new ideas come about. New ideas are the basis of both small and large, incremental and paradigmatic, scientific advances (Galenson, 2008; Kuhn, 1962). Yet there is a surprising dearth of theorizing about where new ideas come from. Most research methodology focuses on answering research questions or testing hypotheses. Few methodology textbooks have a section, much less a chapter, on creating new ideas (but see Crano et al., 2014). And there are only a handful of articles and books on theory creation (Jaccard & Jacoby, 2020; McGuire, 1997; Tavory & Timmermans, 2014). This neglect was institutionalized by Popper's (1934) harsh separation between the context of discovery (i.e., how an idea comes about) and the context of justification (i.e., how it can be evidenced). Popper argued that there can be no method, or procedure, for the discovery, only for justification. Thus, the context of discovery was essentially excluded from methodology.

Pragmatism, as we have outlined, is a thoroughly processual paradigm. It foregrounds development, change, and adaptation. Accordingly, it embraces the challenge of theorizing the context of discovery – to provide insight into the emergence of new ideas. From the early writings of Peirce (a person hesitating how to pay for a taxi; 1878) and Dewey (a child reaching for a flame; 1896), there was an idea that conflicting responses to stimuli could lead to novel ideas and paths of action. The assumption is that thought and action are typically in a tight functional loop, with little self-reflection or novelty. But, sometimes, action is halted, the consequences are not what was expected. In these moments, cognitive effort aims to reconstruct a new viable path of action. Practical, cultural, and experiential resources are mobilized to create a new path of action (Gillespie & Zittoun, 2010). It follows from this that in the research domain diverse theoretical frameworks and methodological tools can act as resources to create and imagine new paths for research.

One concrete attempt to use pragmatism to conceptualize the emergence of new ideas is abductive analysis (Tavory & Timmermans, 2014). Abduction is a concept developed by Peirce (1955) to denote the mode of inference that goes beyond summarizing data (induction) and logically extrapolating from theory (deduction) and instead entails a reasonable guess that leaps toward a new theory. An abductive insight brings something to the data; it posits something new that, if it were the case, would provide an improved explanation. Abductive inference is fostered through in-depth engagement with applied domains, using mixed methods, and being attuned to tensions within the data (more on this in Chapter 7). The key point is that pragmatism, as a process paradigm, provides a framework and practical suggestions for testing theory (i.e., via consequences) and generating theory (i.e., via abduction).

1.5   Pragmatist Propositions

It is ironic that pragmatism, which champions the practical consequences of knowledge, has been most influential in philosophy and social theory (Goodman, 1995; Joas, 1993; Rorty, 1981; West, 1989). Aside from contributing to mixed methods research (Morgan, 2014a), pragmatism has had little consequence for mainstream social research. We aim to address this gap by proposing an end-to-end pragmatist approach to research methodology in the social sciences.

To build this bridge from pragmatism to methodology, we advance eight propositions. Although these propositions are rooted in pragmatism, they do not intend to be a general distillation of pragmatism. Instead, these propositions aim to identify the consequences of pragmatism for social science methodology. The following briefly outlines each proposition, and the subsequent eight chapters will elaborate upon each proposition in turn.

1) *Truth is in its consequences.* This is the fundamental pragmatist insight (Peirce, 1878), which, when worked through, has broad implications for methodology. This proposition insists that truth is always tied to human interests, which in turn implies that truth can never be completely separate from human values. In Chapter 2 we unpack this principle, showing how pragmatism is neither naïvely realist nor relativist but instead provides a flexible paradigm through which useful and ethical knowledge can be created.

2) *Theories are tools for action.* Rather than theories being "mirrors" of nature, pragmatism argues that theories enable us to interact with nature. Theories synthesize past experiences into semiotic tools that empower action in the face of an uncertain future (Peirce, 1955). Chapter 3 develops the idea that theories are "made," not "found," and, as such, are always "for humans." It follows that some theories in social science can be criticized for serving some groups more than others. But this does not mean that all theories are equal. Theories can be evaluated and compared in terms of their consequences.

3) *Research is as much about creating questions as answering questions.* A pragmatist approach bypasses the debate between qualitative and quantitative paradigms, arguing that qualitative and quantitative methods are useful for answering different questions. In Chapter 4, we introduce a pragmatist typology of research questions, or purposes, arguing that mixing qualitative and quantitative questions is often necessary for tackling real-world issues. Finally, we introduce pragmatic heuristics for generating research questions.

4) *Data are always transformations.* Data are often conceptualized
   as a thing, with more seeming to be better. However, all data are
   contextual and embedded, and they require transformation to
   become useful for research. Moreover, the significance of the data
   varies depending on the theories or expectations we have. Some data
   reinforce expectations, while other data thwart them. In Chapter 5,
   we unpack this proposal that data require transformation to become
   a bridge between what happened (raw data) and the expectation
   (theory). Specifically, we examine the different ways of eliciting and
   curating data in the context of the rise of big qualitative data.

5) *Qualitative and quantitative methods are synergistic.* Qualitative and
   quantitative methods can be combined synergistically precisely
   because they address different research questions. If they each
   answered the same questions, they would be duplicative; instead,
   each adds a different value. Chapter 6 shows how qualitative and
   quantitative questions can be combined and recombined to yield
   creative synergies. These different approaches are integrated by being
   anchored to a given problem; each approach is compared, evaluated,
   and integrated in terms of what it contributes to the given problem.

6) *Big qualitative data can be recursively restructured to enable both
   qualitative and quantitative analyses.* A common criticism of mixed
   methods research is that there is a lack of integration between the
   qualitative and quantitative methods (Bazeley & Kemp, 2012); the
   qualitative and quantitative components run in parallel. In Chapter
   7 we propose "multi-resolution research" as an approach to research
   that integrates qualitative and quantitative methods by anchoring
   them both in the same dataset. The idea is to use big qualitative
   datasets and then recursively transform them into excerpts (for
   qualitative analysis) and numbers (for quantitative analysis). Moving
   back and forth between qualitative and quantitative transformations
   of the same data, we argue, can increase rigor and support abductive
   theory generation.

7) *Social research creates both power and responsibility.* A pragmatist
   approach to social research significantly broadens the role of ethics.
   Traditionally, research ethics pertains to data collection (e.g.,
   ensuring consent, right to withdraw) and data storage (e.g., data
   protection, anonymization). In Chapter 8 we use pragmatism to
   expand beyond these concerns to consider the interests motivating
   the research, participation in setting the research agenda, and the
   consequences of the knowledge produced. Giving up on the idea

that theories are neutral "mirrors" of nature forces researchers to take more responsibility for the questions they choose to address and the knowledge they create.

8) *Social research should aim to expand human possibility.* What is the purpose of social research? Is it to "find" truths? To document the truth "'behind" the messiness of life-as-we-find-it? A pragmatist approach rejects such suggestions and instead argues that social research is an act of world-making (Gergen, 2015) – even if only in a small way. The knowledge produced in social research is not a view onto nature but a construction within nature that interacts with the future. We conclude, in Chapter 9, by arguing that social research should push toward knowledge that empowers people.

CHAPTER 2

Epistemology
How We Know

> Pragmatism asks its usual question. 'Grant an idea or belief to be
> true,' it says, 'what concrete difference will its being true make in
> anyone's actual life? How will the truth be realized? What experiences
> will be different from those which would obtain if the belief were
> false? What, in short, is the truth's cash-value in experiential terms?'
>
> (James, 1907, p. 97)

This chapter examines epistemology, namely, the often-implicit theories
of how knowledge is made that guide our research and methodological
choices. One of the reasons why epistemological assumptions are central
to methodology is that they outline what kind of knowledge is considered
truthful or valid and false or coincidental. Scientific research is mainly concerned with distinguishing truth from error and, as such, necessarily makes
commitments regarding the nature and acquisition of knowledge. As we
will discuss in this chapter, these commitments go beyond simply identifying criteria for what can pass as valid conclusions and reflect deeper understandings of our place in and relation to the world: Are we in a privileged
position to uncover universal Truths or are we unable to escape human
biases? Does truth emerge from human action or rational contemplation?
Is truth "objective" or "subjective" (relative to our perspective)? And, if the
latter is the case, how can we claim to be sure of anything? What kinds of
societies would we live in should there be no truth we could all agree on?

We start this chapter with a brief discussion of what it means to live in a
society where the factual basis of truth can be undermined – the post-truth
climate many are decrying today as a global phenomenon and for which
Western democracies seem to be ill-prepared. We outline several popular
conceptions and misconceptions about epistemology and then map out
the prominent epistemological positions. In the second part of the chapter, we argue for pragmatism as an epistemology that can help us deal with
the complexities of doing empirical research in a post-truth context by

transcending the old realist–relativist divide and fostering methodological pluralism. In doing so, we argue for knowledge that works and thus develop our first pragmatist proposition *that truth is in its consequences*.

2.1 The Post-truth Context

The problem of what passes for valid knowledge is debated in society today well beyond the confines of universities. For millennia, philosophers have been concerned with the issue of truth and, as we will see, came up with various criteria for what is truthful. But the "crisis of truth," particularly in public debate (e.g., Trump, Brexit, vaccine hesitancy), has prompted "lay" people to reflect on truth and seek to expose misinformation. Post-truth became more than a label; it was named "word of the year" in 2016 by *Oxford Dictionaries* after a 2000 percent spike in usage (McIntyre, 2018). It also turned into an obsession for people on both sides of the political divide who are eager to accuse each other of contributing to the current climate. And yet, for those who study epistemology, this heated societal debate does little more than place the proverbial old wine in shiny new bottles.

This chapter is concerned with how we know and validate what we know and how these issues feed into social science methodology. While the topic of post-truth is beyond our scope here (for more detail see Baggini, 2017; Kakutani, 2018), old and new debates about the nature of truth provide the background for our specific methodological focus. They are also a useful reminder of why epistemology matters. To set up this background, we examine conspiracy theories, a key term within the post-truth vocabulary, to demonstrate how specific conceptions about gaining (valid) knowledge guide research.

2.1.1 The Trouble with Conspiracies

Conspiracy theories present us with an interesting paradox when it comes to uncovering the truth. They propose a worldview in which hidden but powerful actors influence events without us ever noticing them (Douglas et al., 2019). To hold a conspiracy theory, then, is to make sense of something that is either unexplained or explained in different terms. In some ways, it is to doubt and question given knowledge, to deconstruct what is usually taken for granted, and to criticize power structures – which is often considered a valuable practice, including in research. The problem with conspiracy theories is that many of them are demonstrably untrue (but not all; some emerge when we do not have any definitive answers, and others are impossible to prove wrong) and, even more, they prompt those who hold them to construct explanations that serve their worldview and resist reasonable evidence. So, what exactly can we study about them?

Overall, researchers have been concerned with three main aspects of conspiracy theories: what triggers them, what they correlate with, and what their consequences might be. To take a concrete example, Swami and colleagues (2014) reported various studies showing that analytic thinking reduces belief in conspiracy theories. They investigated this relationship in both correlational and causal terms, finding that there are statistically significant associations between specific thinking dispositions (e.g., lower analytical thinking, lower open-mindedness, and higher intuitive thinking). But there is more than co-occurrence at play: Stimulating analytical thinking, for instance, through a verbal fluency task, led to less belief in conspiracy theories. These findings have been replicated on general population samples focused on conspiracies around the July 7, 2005, bombings in London. The practical consequence of these studies is plain: If we can stimulate analytical thinking, then we might be able to fight conspiracist ideation. However, this intervention is based on the assumption that one specific mental process underpins a variety of conspiracies, ignoring differences between beliefs and the groups or communities who uphold them. Research done in this individual differences tradition, therefore, focuses on the person and their psychological attributes rather than the beliefs themselves and the societal contexts in which they are formed.

In contrast, Moscovici (1987) discussed conspiracies in intergroup terms, arguing that when social and economic conditions toughen, specific minorities start being accused of conspiring against the majority, usually with the help of foreign enemies. This approach goes beyond the particular psychological profile of those who believe in conspiracies (although dogmatic and ethnocentric thinking are possible precursors) and focuses on the conspiracy mentality as a whole, as a form of collective thought. Conspiracies grow out of an often-irrational fear of minorities and "strangers" and the challenge of accepting minorities as different. This view might strike one as rooted in a psychodynamic frame of group relations, and in many ways, it does reflect a concern for emotional and social dynamics. But it also presents us with a different research question: What do conspiracy theories tell us about groups that create, espouse, and propagate them?

2.1.2   The Role of Epistemology

On the surface, one might say that Moscovici (1987) and, more recently, Swami and colleagues (2014) are simply guided by different questions.

We can even relate these questions back to the different theories they use, social for the former, cognitive for the latter. What we will argue in this chapter is that the differences run deeper and are, in fact, epistemological. They showcase two broad assumptions about what shapes conspiracist knowledge – that is, psychological attributes versus collective forms of thought – and, in turn, about how we can produce (valid) knowledge about conspiracies – that is, through a study of cognitive processes versus one of minority–majority relations. At a deeper level, Swami and colleagues (2014) assume that there "exist" such things as thinking dispositions, that they are relatively stable at an individual level, and that they can be effectively measured (and elicited when needed). On the other hand, Moscovici assumes knowledge is distributed between people and groups in society and growing out of interactions and power imbalances rather than (isolated) thinking processes. These explanations can be complementary but, taken separately, they also reflect different understandings about the acquisition of knowledge in the social arena, realist versus constructionist, understandings that unavoidably shape its empirical study.

2.2 (Mis)conceptions about Epistemology

2.2.1 Epistemology Guides Research

Epistemology guides the research, but often in "invisible" ways (Roots, 2007). On the one hand, epistemological concerns are often left implicit, particularly in studies that use standard methodologies where collective habit means there is no need to justify methodological choices. On the other hand, methodological training often suffers from a dearth of epistemological discussions seen either as too philosophical or too complex for empirically minded researchers. This is a missed opportunity given that every aspect of a research project – starting from the question and choice of topic to what is considered data and ending with how these data are analyzed – reflects epistemological choices. As epistemology concerns the researcher's theory of knowledge and the criteria used to validate knowledge, it always remains an integral part of a study, even when left unexamined.

To take a classic example from research on conspiracy theories, Goertzel (1994) surveyed 348 New Jersey residents about ten different conspiracies and found that most believed that at least some of them were probably true. Even more interesting, he discovered that those who believed in one conspiracy were more likely to believe in other conspiracies. Based on a correlational design, he also showed that beliefs in conspiracies are associated with a series of other personal and psychological characteristics like lack of interpersonal trust and insecurity about employment. Ethnicity and age also played a role with black and Hispanic participants, and, to some extent, young people, being more likely to believe in conspiracies. No significant findings were reported for gender, education, and occupation.

This study draws on a social psychological approach in which the basic assumption is that specific psychological characteristics (primarily related to cognition and personality), as well as specific social variables (group memberships captured by basic demographic categories), will impact a person's beliefs and behavior (in this case, beliefs in conspiracy theories). In other words, to get to know why some people are sensitive to conspiracies, we need to collect information about their other beliefs, preferences, and identities. Second, we can collect knowledge about any of these by using self-report measures, assuming both that the respondents understand and report on the variables used in the study and that they, on the whole, are not motivated to deceive the researcher. Third, the statistical methods used to process the data – primarily correlational analysis – are based on the supposition that beliefs and preferences can be translated into a numerical form. It rests on the assumption that beliefs can be measured, that there are meaningful units of belief, and that two units of belief are more than one unit. These are realist assumptions. They are based on the view that valid knowledge about beliefs can be gained from empirical research in which psychological and social variables (in all their diversity) can "really" be captured using categories and scales. Moreover, the role of the researcher and his or her beliefs is not reflected upon (e.g., deciding which theories are conspiracy theories), the sociocultural and normative context in which conspiracies develop and circulate remains unquestioned, and there is little interest in the subjective experience of the participants (from the lived experience of a conspiracist mindset to that of taking part in a study on this topic) or the practical aims conspiracy theories might serve (e.g., they may function to create communities, to channel dissatisfaction, or to make the inexplicable explicable). Of course, these issues could be addressed in additional research, but our point is that the epistemological lenses used limits what can be asked and studied. If a psychological trait "exists" within the person, then it cannot be, at the same time, stable and constantly reconstructed within the ongoing flow of experience. The former view allowed Goertzel to run correlations, the latter might have pushed him toward new, phenomenological questions and concerns; both these approaches contribute something different and potentially useful.

2.2.2 Epistemological Purism versus Pluralism

A common misconception about epistemology is that researchers necessarily embrace a single theory of knowledge. Continuing the earlier example, this would mean that studies of conspiracy beliefs would necessarily adopt either a realist epistemology, which claims that beliefs exist within the individual mind and can be objectively measured, or a constructionist epistemology, which claims that beliefs are constituted through language (discourse) and cannot be studied outside of their particular context (e.g., Bjerg & Presskorn-Thygesen, 2017). In other words, the realist epistemological approach focuses our attention primarily on the individual and asks what exactly makes them adopt a conspiracist mindset. It thus leads to explanations that have to do with particular cognitive styles, personality structures, and even forms of psychopathology (e.g., paranoia; Imhoff & Lamberty, 2018). In contrast, the constructionist epistemology makes sense of conspiracies in sociocultural and discursive rather than purely psychological terms. It does not, as such, pathologize conspiracies but tries to understand them as forms of meaning-making by individuals who are part of communities that foster such forms of knowing; conspiracies become efforts "to explain some event or practice by reference to the machinations of powerful people" (Vermeule & Sunstein, 2009, p. 205). Can a study bridge both epistemological approaches?

Most research, even when grounded primarily in one epistemological position, does engage with or at least acknowledge other approaches. In an influential paper about misinformation and how it can be corrected, Lewandowsky and colleagues (2012) start from the premise that misinformation and conspiracies originate from a variety of social, cultural, and ideological sources such as rumors, works of fiction, and the vested interests of specific groups in society. The use of new media is also considered, especially regarding the transmission of misinformation. This contextual approach is complemented by a review of individual-based cognitive factors that make people resistant to efforts to correct false beliefs. Typical psychological processes are discussed in this regard, from the memory for misinformation to personal worldviews. It is the latter rather than the former that offers the basis for final recommendations as to how to fight misinformation, online and offline, including through public information campaigns. On the surface, Lewandowsky and colleagues consider, side by side, knowledge as socially constructed as well as knowledge as cognitively situated. We could say that their work draws, as such, on multiple frameworks that span cognitive and social psychology with potential interdisciplinary connections, from neuroscience to sociology. Is this also an issue of epistemology? Yes, on two levels. From the standpoint of misinformation and conspiracies as forms of knowing, we are presented with different assumptions about the origin, processes, and consequences of such beliefs. How these assumptions are prioritized, and, at times, integrated, is reflected in particular in the correctional measures proposed. At the level of producing scientific knowledge about misinformation and conspiracies through research, epistemology is markedly pragmatist. The researchers are concerned by not only how knowledge can lead to changes in the world but also how knowledge coming out of different traditions, each with its own epistemological underpinnings, can serve this purpose.

2.2.3   The Limits of Epistemology

Finally, each epistemological stand has its limits and serves some human interests better than others (see also Chapters 4 and 8). If we want to educate individuals separately about misinformation and conspiracy theories, then we are best served by understanding their system of beliefs and the relatively stable traits and processes that might support a general conspiracist mindset. For instance, research by Lewandowsky and colleagues (2013) pointed to several predictors of people denying climate change and being skeptical of science, all situated at an individual level. In this case, endorsement of free-market economics and belief in other conspiracy theories predict the rejection of climate science. This is certainly useful to know for two reasons: It can help construct a more detailed (psychological) profile of those who are likely to uphold and even spread misinformation and can guide those who built programs for fighting misinformation. But this kind of realist positioning regarding the existence, stability, and measurability of psychological traits can easily obscure how people's conceptions and misconceptions are forged through action and interaction. For the latter, the problem is less how people are, or how they think, and more what kinds of interactional contexts and dialogues they are part of (and there is a growing literature on modeling behavioral trajectories online; Cresci et al., 2020). In each case, however, the basic assumption is that behind either the person or world there is a simple structure that can be revealed in patterns and associations (see also Chapter 3). This structure just becomes more complex as we study or understand it further. The effort to still reduce it to its essential components is a trademark of positivist science. More radical epistemological positions would challenge these assumptions and point to a world in flux in which individual or social patterns, if they exist, are continuously being reconstructed. Hence, the human interest best served here would be to capture evolving complexity. It might lead to less tools for practical action, but it is well equipped to help us understand phenomena holistically.

In the end, we cannot explain everything with a single epistemology, and there is no absolute epistemological standpoint to adopt: They each have value when measured against specific human interests and concerns. This is not to say that they are all equally useful in practical terms. In fact, the pragmatist approach, which we adopt, advocates for pluralism in methodological terms, matched by sustained critical reflection.

However, just as epistemologies emerge as tools (see also Chapter 3) that can be used to highlight various aspects of a phenomenon – shedding light on patterns or their transformation, on individual properties or types of dynamic, on similarities or differences – we cannot ignore their consequences, some of which are intended, some of which are not. Positivist science can be reductionist and exclude marginal positions from its understanding of reality. In contrast, constructionism points to the coconstruction of psychological and social phenomena in the course of action. The postmodern embracing of the latter takes us further and can be used to question whether a stable single reality exists. And it is precisely this last, radically relativist, epistemology that is often blamed for the current post-truth climate. As such, in order to grasp the limits of different epistemological standpoints, we need to take yet another detour through the context that made "post-truth" the word of the year in 2016 and a major nuisance since.

2.3   The "Death" of Truth?

It was Aristotle who offered us one of the most straightforward definitions of truth, when he wrote: "To say of what is that it is not, or of what is not that it is, is false, while to say of what is that it is, and of what is not that it is not, is true" (Baggini, 2017, p. 4). The correspondence between the meaning of a statement and the events in the world that correspond to this meaning has been used through the centuries to distinguish valid knowledge from lies and misinformation. But, as with all things related to knowing, its power is derived from adopting a particular epistemological standpoint, in this case, a realist one that satisfies three basic preconditions: (1) Language as a medium for expressing thought carries meanings that can be decoded unambiguously; (2) we can perceive "correctly" events in the world and construct mental images that we then compare with the (unambiguous) meaning of statements about the world; and (3) our statements are separate from the world and can more or less mirror the world (see also Chapter 3). The devil, for some, is hidden within these claims.

2.3.1   Definitions of Truth

The post-truth era entails attacks on these assumptions. On the one hand, we have many examples of denying the veracity of people's senses, for example, in Donald Trump's (in)famous assertion that he had one of the largest audiences at his inauguration. The very notion of "alternative facts," uttered in this context, delivers a mighty blow to old correspondence theories of truth – if everyone can choose what facts they prefer, and if "alternative facts" are as socially consequential as "traditional facts," then the need for a match between statements and the world becomes obsolete. This crisis of truth is exacerbated by an avalanche of misinformation and outright lies presented on social media that, even when not fully trusted, still raise the question of what is the case and whether we would ever be able to know it. And then, there are attacks addressed to language and its capacity to convey clear and unambiguous messages. Trump, again, was a rather skilled participant on Twitter who used this platform to make incendiary comments (e.g., saying there were "very fine people on both sides" when it came to neo-Nazi demonstrators in Charlottesville), often misspelled (e.g., the viral "covfefe"). Without ever backtracking or apologizing for his views, when pressed about his intended meaning, he would claim that his statements were being misinterpreted, especially by the "fake news media." This tendency to question whether saying something does count as what has been said came to a head during the Ukraine inquiry in which the meaning of quid pro quo started to be problematized to the extent to which conditioning help on the offer of "a favor" was no longer irrefutable proof of it. These, and many similar processes in our contemporary public sphere, put into question the capacity of language to unambiguously mean something about the world and people's intentions.

Academics and journalists have identified many culprits responsible for the crisis of truth. On the one hand, we can point to societal-level phenomena such as the decline of reason, the rise in science denial, and the new culture wars (Kakutani, 2018), and, added to this, the quasi-collapse of traditional media outlets paired with the low entry costs for unreliable "journalism." On the other hand, we are directed toward psychological phenomena assumed to be universal in human beings, like the cognitive biases that make us sensitive to information confirming our initial beliefs (McIntyre, 2018). But most commentators agree that a big part of the "blame" is to be attributed to social media and their use to create silos and tribes, as well as spread fake news and propaganda (Ball, 2017) – although some consider the role of social media overestimated (Guess et al., 2018). A new and exciting medium that was supposed to democratize our access to information and, more importantly, to other people and their view of the world has been turned by conspiracists, internet trolls, and malicious bots into a war zone in which those who spread misinformation are better equipped and more agile than those who want to correct or censor them. As D'Ancona (2017, p. 52) aptly noted regarding social media, "never has the old adage that a lie can travel halfway around the world while the truth is putting on its shoes seemed so timely." However, one more rather unexpected actor contributes to the post-truth climate: academics. Not all academics, to be sure, but those in the social sciences and humanities who, inspired by thinkers like Derrida and Foucault, have embraced postmodernism and proclaimed it as a new era of radical doubt and of dismantling all sorts of hegemonies – among them, the hegemonic and seductive power of the single unquestionable truth.

2.3.2   Blaming Postmodernism

The debates about epistemology, which used to inhabit mainly philosophy classes, have spilled into society in post-truth debates and attempts to distinguish between accurate and damaging understandings. The debates are acute for postmodern readings of truth that relativize it and turn it into a matter of discourse and opinion. There are undoubtedly many versions of postmodernism, and not all of them embrace an extreme form of relativism, but on the whole, "postmodernist arguments deny an objective reality existing independently from human perception, contending that knowledge is filtered through the prisms of class, race, gender, and other variables" (Kakutani, 2018, p. 47). The simple Aristotelian formula is found to be lacking, and any "God's eye view" that claims objectivity is deconstructed. While this sounds like a practice with devastating consequences in our current political climate, it is worth remembering that postmodernist thinkers aimed at recognizing multiple forms of knowing and at empowering the oppressed against those who wanted to impose singular views of the world and, through them, to control their life and experience (e.g., scientists, clergy, governments). Coming from art, literature, architecture, philosophy, sociology, and psychology, the promoters of this position often embraced the epistemology of social constructionism (e.g., Berger & Luckmann, 1967). This allowed them to advocate for more pluralist societies in which the working of power is exposed and its bases in predetermined ideas of goodness, beauty, and truth constantly questioned.

The academics who contributed to postmodernism in the 1980s and 1990s, mostly left-wing intellectuals who had hoped to build more egalitarian and diverse communities, could hardly have imagined that their epistemological arguments would be used in the early twenty-first century by far-right commentators and conservative politicians to destabilize consensus, radicalize individuals and groups and brand anything that does not conform to their worldview as "fake news." Beyond the act of lying, which still needs the acknowledgment of truth to subvert it, post-truth social actors question the very existence of truth and turn it into a matter of perspective. What counts as truthful depends, as the postmodernists argued, on who makes the truth claim, and in polarized societies, this means that disregarding truths that make one uncomfortable becomes as easy as promoting one's own truth, even if devoid of evidence. This formula was used to, paradoxically, ensure that the oppressors remain in power. As McIntyre (2018, p. 145) laments, "what a complete misfire of the original politics that motivated postmodernism, which was to protect the poor and vulnerable from being exploited by those in authority."

What is the way forward? Fortunately, we have entered a period of sustained reflection, in academia and society at large, about what counts as truth and how we build common ground based on evidence. The current challenge is to understand the radical critique posed by postmodernism and recover the positive aspects of its practices of deconstruction – for example, the ability to criticize the operation of power – without falling back on simple (and often simplistic) positivist criteria for what counts as valid knowledge. We need, as Caputo (2016, p. 9) proposes, to "defend the plurivocality, ambiguity and non-programmability of truth while also defending the right to say that some things are not just different, they're wrong." To reach this desired state, however, we need to come back to epistemology and understand the positions in more depth with their advantages, limitations, and possibilities for research.

2.4 Mapping Epistemological Positions

We started by noting that epistemology concerns the theory of knowledge and, as such, has significant consequences for empirical research, first and foremost, by addressing the possibility of gaining valid knowledge and, second, by offering criteria for it. But "what constitutes valid knowledge" is not the only focus of epistemology. In fact, while the issue of ontology, or the theory of the world as is, tends to be kept separate from the episte-mological – in that one can make epistemological claims without making ontological claims, and vice versa – the two commonly build on each other (Al-Ababneh, 2020). After all, how can we claim the world is "knowable" if we do not have a theory of what the world is and of our place within it?

In this section, we will review some key epistemological positions (see Figure 2.1) above and beyond realism and positivism, as markers of moder-nity, and constructionism and relativism, as markers of postmodernism (our definition of these positions is based on Blackburn, 2005). When we think about epistemology in its relation to ontology and, as we shall see later in the book, to ethics, we notice various questions that are fundamen-tal for research. Key among them are:

1. What is the nature of reality? And in what sense does it exist?
2. What governs the world and nature? Are there universal laws behind them?
3. What types of truths are we looking for?
4. How do we reach valid or truthful knowledge?

While the great bulk of empirical research does not set out to directly answer these questions, all research is premised on a specific understand-ing of each of them. Returning to the case of studies of misinformation and conspiracy theories, most of the research mentioned earlier starts from the assumption that there is indeed a reality "out there" against which truth claims can be judged. How could we otherwise distinguish informa-tion from misinformation? It also assumes that there are patterns behind the generation or spread of (mis)information and, in fact, this is often what empirical studies aim to explain (e.g., how personality traits or sets of beliefs, social interactions, and wider ideologies give the phenomenon a certain regularity). The truth looked for is often that of "objective" fact – pitted against the assumed lack of objectivity of conspiracist beliefs – and this truth can be discovered only empirically.

Before discussing the details of each epistemological concern, the posi-tions associated with it, and their implications for research, it is important to note that the "map" included in the figure does not aim to be exhaustive (for a more in-depth discussion of the metaphor of maps, see Chapter 3). Each epistemological standpoint tends to have a great degree of complex-ity and also a long history of debate in philosophy and in science, a kind of richness that is necessarily simplified in this section. Not only is it the

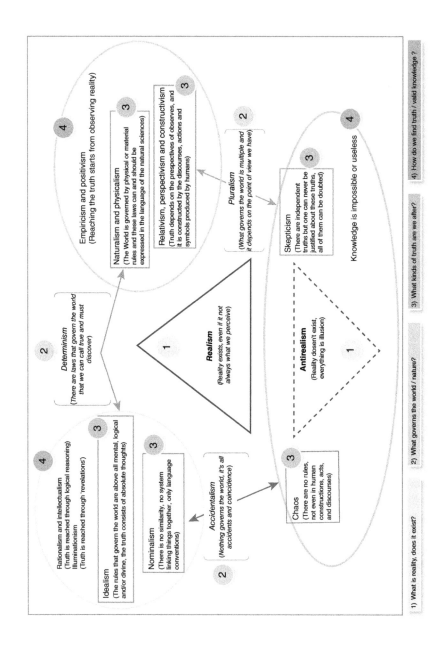

Figure 2.1 Mapping epistemological positions and the relations between them

Realism
(Reality exists, even if it not always what we perceive)

Antirealism
(Reality doesn't exist, everything is illusion)

Empiricism and positivism
(Reaching the truth starts from observing reality)

Determinism
(There are laws that govern the world that we can call true and must discover)

Naturalism and physicalism
(The World is governed by physical or material rules and these laws can and should be expressed in the language of the natural sciences)

Relativism, perspectivism and constructivism
(Truth depends on the perspectives of observers, and it is constructed by the discourses, actions and symbols produced by humans)

Pluralism
(What governs the world is multiple and it depends on the point of view we have)

Skepticism
(There are independent truths but one can never be justified about these truths, all of them can be doubted)

Knowledge is impossible or useless

Rationalism and intellectualism
(Truth is reached through logical reasoning)
Illuminationism
(Truth is reached through 'revelations')

Idealism
(The rules that govern the world are above all mental, logical and/or divine, the truth consists of absolute thoughts)

Nominalism
(There is no similarity, no system linking things together, only language conventions)

Accidentalism
(Nothing governs the world, it's all accidents and coincidence)

Chaos
(There are no rules, not even in human constructions, acts, and discourses)

1) What is reality, does it exist?   2) What governs the world / nature?   3) What kinds of truth are we after?   4) How do we find truth / valid knowledge ?

case that new positions could be added to it but the schema could potentially be reorganized when considered from new angles (e.g., through the lenses of other questions). This particular representation does, however, have a few advantages. First of all, it covers considerable epistemological ground, highlighting what is usually depicted as a "fight" between realists and idealists or relativists, between modernity and postmodernity. Second, it specifies a set of relations between various positions, showing that even those orientations that might look like opposites could have some shared assumptions or be brought together by a similar view. Finally, this map can be used by researchers to reflect on the epistemological (and ontological) assumptions embedded in their own studies, helping them find their place while, at the same time, considering this place vis-à-vis a broader picture.

2.4.1 The Question of Reality

Regarding the question of reality – a key theme in today's post-truth debates – we find two opposing views in the center of Figure 2.1: realism and antirealism. As the name suggests, the former recognizes the existence of reality, often independent of any perceiver, while the latter makes the rather provocative claim that there is no underlying reality to the world, often assuming that everything is constructed by the senses and minds of individual perceivers. This is, according to Bhaskar (1975), an "epistemological fallacy": Just because we cannot know the world as it is, it does not logically follow that there is not a world independent of us. While it might seem, on the surface, that antirealists would have a hard time arguing their case, the "reality" of the matter is much more complex than the usual accusation that imagining the world differently will not actually change it (e.g., believing the incoming train is not real will not save anyone from the consequences of the impact). A famous thought experiment, sometimes attributed to George Berkeley (Campbell & Cassam, 2014), is captured by the following question: "If a tree falls in a forest and no one is around to hear it, does it make a sound?" A widely accepted answer is that, in fact no, it would not make a sound if there is no (human) ear to hear it *as* a sound. It will produce, however, air vibrations because these do not depend on the presence of an observer endowed with the biological and psychological mechanisms needed to turn vibrations into sound. From a research perspective, this basic epistemological positioning can easily become problematic, with some researchers studying social phenomena in a realist tradition when they could be better served by a deeper consideration of perceiver-dependency, while others are doing the reverse (see Parker, 1998). In the concrete field of misinformation research, this epistemological dilemma is particularly poignant as it makes the difference between, for instance, considering conspiracies as outright dangerous lies and as meaning-making mechanisms with some value for the person (as misguided as they are).

2.4.2   *The Question of Universal Laws*

If we can indeed agree that some form of reality does exist, even if it is, in the extreme, the psychological reality of the perceiver or thinker (Descartes, 1637), then the next epistemological question becomes whether it is orderly enough to derive valid knowledge about it. In other words, we need to know if the world follows knowable norms and principles. The big dichotomy here is that between determinism and accidentalism. The former claims that the functioning of the world is determined by a variety of factors, at least to some extent. In the example of research on misinformation and conspiracies, these can be psychological traits and mindsets but can also be societal norms and patterns of social interaction (and, indeed, both these categories are widely studied; D'Ancona, 2017; Lewandowsky et al., 2017; McIntyre, 2018). Nonetheless, perhaps it is not universal laws that govern the universe but chance, accident, and coincidence. This is not an epistemological position often found in scientific research simply because science is grounded, to a great extent, in prediction and there is no prediction without determinism (Cleland, 2011). And yet, concerns specific for accidentalism do come up in scientific research, especially concerning accidents and serendipity, quantum mechanics, and complexity theory (especially the idea of sensitivity to initial conditions; Byrne & Callaghan, 2013; Guastello et al., 2008). Interestingly, the debate does not have to fall back on extreme positions. We can also identify a pluralistic epistemological stance according to which reality is rules-based, but these rules are multiple (or probabilistic) and knowing them (also) depends on the position, in the world, of the perceiver. This is not a stance specific to constructionism as much as it is for pragmatism, as we shall see later on.

2.4.3   *The Question of Types of Truth*

A third epistemological question that gets us close to what we would normally consider core epistemological issues is what types of truths we are looking for. For example, Truth with a capital "T" is timeless, independent of humans, while truth with a lowercase "t" is related to direct observations and experiences of the world, dependent thus on humans (and often referred to in plural, as truths). Interestingly, as depicted in Figure 2.1, the answers to this question cut across the determinism–accidentalism–pluralism and even the realism–antirealism divide (leading to the associated risk of not realizing that there are still fundamental differences between these approaches). Starting from a position similar to antirealism, for which true knowledge is either impossible to achieve or illusory, we have traditional skepticism on the one hand and pure chaos on the other. The first doubts the possibility of ever fully knowing reality while the second challenges the existence of any deep-level regularity in the world (an assumption that brings it close to accidentalism). It is interesting to note, in this context, that conspiracist mentalities are often grounded in skepticism rather than chaos in the sense that those who share them do believe that things happen for a reason, even when this reason is concealed (hence the connection between paranoia and belief in conspiracies; Imhoff & Lamberty, 2018). Idealism and nominalism are the other two epistemological positions that point us toward where we can find Truth about the world: not as much in what we perceive and do, as in what we imagine, think, and talk about. For idealists, the rules that govern reality are primarily psychological and symbolic. For nominalists, language conventions give substance to our world as human beings (and not a set of internal or external rules). These orientations have a lot in common with but are different from constructionism, perspectivism, and relativism as epistemologies that make truth relative to the context of the observer and their perspective (and are commonly seen as the main postmodern culprits in the war against Truth; D'Ancona, 2017). In reality, however, not all constructionist arguments need to be relativist or antirealist, just as not all perspectival philosophies follow an "anything goes" philosophy. What these orientations are not, however, is naturalist or physicalist. They are, thus, far from the assumption that only materiality really matters and that everything that is thought or language can, at best, express what is real and, at worst, mislead us about it, but cannot shape or change it (in the way a range of other epistemologies, from idealism to constructionism, would claim). And these "best" and "worst" scenarios bring us to the final question: If we can build knowledge, is this knowledge valid?

2.4.4 *The Question of How We Reach Valid Knowledge*

This last question builds on the previous three and, as can be seen in Figure 2.1, it connects to three main epistemological clusters: the antirealism pole, on the one hand, and the dichotomy between rationalism/intellectualism/ illuminationism and empiricism/positivism, on the other. The first pole denies the possibility of knowledge, and as such, it can substantiate conspiracist and post-truth views of the world but not scientific research. The old-age debate between rationalism and empiricism (see Markie, 2004), however, is intrinsically relevant for any discussion of methodology. In essence, rationalism and intellectualism postulate the predominant role of reason or the intellect when it comes to accumulating knowledge about reality while empiricism, as the name suggests, focuses our attention on the empirical world and the knowledge we obtain about it from the senses; with positivism, there is also the assumption that we can do this with a high degree of objectivity. Most research in psychology and the social sciences – including misinformation research – builds on empiricist and positivist assumptions, above and beyond their naturalist or constructionist inclinations (although this has not been the case historically, see Jovanović, 2010). It is, after all, for good reasons that most scientific studies are said to conduct "empirical" research. This means that, if procedures are presented in a systematic and transparent manner, then researchers are allowed to claim not only valid but objective knowledge (which means, among others, knowledge that could be generalized to multiple contexts, independent of the scientists or participants). Rationalism shares, in fact, the same drive toward universal claims but places the origin of true knowledge elsewhere, in the workings of rationality. As a consequence, theory-building takes priority over empirical studies, which can support or refute the theory but cannot, in and of themselves, produce knowledge without the involvement of reason. At the other end of the spectrum, empiricists would aim to take the minds of researchers out of the equation because of their intrinsic biases and general fallibility and, instead, let the data or evidence "talk." Is there a different path available – not a middle but a third one?

2.5   Epistemological Pragmatism and Methodological Pluralism

2.5.1   Weaponizing Doubt

In a landmark book, Conway and Oreskes (2012) describe how a handful of scientists obscured the truth on issues from tobacco smoke to global warming. They documented the successful campaign by tobacco companies in the 1950s to plant the seeds of doubt regarding otherwise overwhelming scientific evidence that smoking causes lung diseases. And they also showed how the same strategy seems to be helping big polluters today to promote climate science skepticism. This strategy, interestingly for our discussion of epistemology, has to do with cultivating distrust in the scientific consensus. Concretely, in 1954 the Tobacco Industry Research Committee was set up as a corporate-sponsored organization aimed not at denying scientific research about smoking causing cancer but at contesting the idea of a unified scientific view. It did so by foregrounding the voices of a few fringe scientists who questioned the mounting evidence. In other words, their aim was to foster doubt about consensual scientific facts and create a false equivalence between scientists who linked tobacco use with lung cancer and those who did not. In the words of D'Anconda (2017, p. 42), "the objective was not academic victory but popular confusion" – and it worked for many years, until in 1998 the Tobacco Institute and the Council for Tobacco Research were closed as part of the master settlement between tobacco giants and the attorneys general of forty-six US states who raised legal charges against this practice.

The intellectual legacy of this initiative to sow doubt continues, and it remains potent within today's post-truth climate. A big part of this potency comes from the fact that doubt has a vital role to play in the construction of knowledge according to multiple epistemological positions. It is not only the foundation of skepticism but a core principle of positivist science, based on the Popperian theory of falsification or the idea that all knowledge is provisional and in need of further testing. Doubt is also a central value within constructionism and postmodern critique, interested first and foremost in empowering "marginal" voices and questioning hegemonic ones; after all, how else would we question taken-for-granted scientific knowledge and the invisible relations of power embedded within it? Its power is reduced only when we start asking what is the pragmatic consequence of specifically doubting the scientific consensus about tobacco use or, more recently, climate change? By focusing on what this practice achieves, and whom it benefits, we can start questioning doubt itself.

2.5.2 The Pragmatist Position

This focus on consequences is specific to pragmatism, an epistemological position that cuts across many of the dichotomies mapped in Figure 2.1. One important conclusion from that illustration was that epistemological positions cannot be reduced to a simple antinomy between realism/naturalism/positivism, on the one hand, and constructionism/relativism/

postmodernism, on the other. Not only is it the case that these "poles" are less unitary than usually thought (e.g., realism is not the same as naturalism, and constructionists are not all extreme relativists), but their specific suborientations might answer different epistemological questions or answer the same question differently. What sets pragmatism apart when it comes to both realism and constructionism is its nonfundamentalist approach to ontology and epistemology. Instead of coming up with preconceived assumptions about how the world is or trying to build knowledge based on "first principles" (e.g., all derived from reason or the senses), pragmatists start from the here and now of the problem at hand and are ready to work with whatever can solve or shed light on it. Instead of universal principles that guide exploration, we are left with practical action. Instead of abstractions, what is foregrounded is experience. This position has, thus, some interesting implications for epistemology and especially epistemological purism. Rather than attempting to always be consistent in terms of one's predetermined principles, blinded to what is going on by our commitments, we are welcome to draw on whatever we can – including any helpful epistemological resources – in order to deal with the issue at hand (in our example, misinformation and conspiracy theories). In many ways, pragmatism gives researchers "permission" to be less epistemologically consistent and, instead, utilize any methods that contribute to the issue at hand (see also Seale, 1999).

Pragmatism engages with all the four questions outlined earlier (the start of Section 2.4) and, at the same time, offers answers that show some variability across pragmatists. Charles Sanders Peirce's (1955) work, for instance, engaged with the issue of determinism by reacting against it and claiming, in particular, that instead of reinforcing deterministic laws science brings evidence against them. In the pragmatist tradition, his focus was on the actual practices of scientists rather than convenient post hoc accounts. As he noted, the more we refine our methodological tools, the more we notice differences and variations rather than uniformity in nature. William James (1912) complemented this view with his emphasis on pluralism, or the idea that we can never build knowledge that can account for everything in the world, and that there will always be room for new perspectives and new forms of understanding (Goodman, 2012). This is yet another challenge to deterministic accounts of reality that tend to describe it in absolute or universal terms. By focusing on human action and experience, pragmatists are well equipped to question the easy assumptions that reality exists "out there" or is created "inside" by the individual mind. Or that our knowledge of the world is either objective or subjective. In fact, a fundamental tenet of pragmatism is the effort to overcome all sorts of dualisms, a theme especially evident in John Dewey's (1917) writing.

2.5.3 Beyond Realism and Relativism

One of the most problematic dualisms to transcend is between positivist and postmodern approaches to science, truth, and knowledge. This tension, exploited by different actors within the current social and political context, is generated by the difficulty in bringing together a realist and a perspectival account – in other words, the idea that reality "exists" and can be known through the "right" perspective and the notion that everything we know is a perspective, nothing else, and that perspectives are all equally valid. Finding a way out of this particular dualism would go a long way when it comes to the current post-truth debate, in which one side claims that their "truth" is as good as anyone else's while another insists that every issue can be solved by applying Aristotle's old correspondence theory – if knowledge does not correspond to what is the case, then it is false. Unfortunately, as the current crisis demonstrates, things are more complicated than this. Not every perspective is correct, that is certain, but neither can we easily dismiss the power of perspectives to "create" reality. Pragmatism makes a valuable contribution to this debate given its deep connections to realism and perspectivism and its emphasis on the consequences of developing specific perspectives in and on the world. In fact, this epistemological position has been described in the past as embracing "perspectival realism" (e.g., in relation to the work of George Herbert Mead; Martin, 2006), a view according to which perspectives are not solipsistic mental constructions but real action-based relations (Gillespie, 2004, 2005a). This makes them neither subjective nor objective but intersubjective and, as such, is a way of recognizing the contribution of external reality to the construction of the person, and vice versa. Moreover, there is a recognition of the fact that perspectives not only grow out of a shared world but they also adapt us to it. In other words, far from an "anything goes" approach, which perspectival and postmodernist accounts are accused of, a pragmatist standpoint invites us to consider what perspectives *do,* namely, what consequences they have for self and others. The truth value of a specific body of knowledge can be established not by considering the person, the knowledge, or external reality in isolation but by analyzing how they shape each other.

Pragmatism can help us avoid the pitfalls of both positivism and relativism and, in fact, gain from their strengths. Pragmatist researchers are concerned with reality, first, as the background against which positions and perspectives are formed and transformed and, second, as the world in which those positions and perspectives exist. Pragmatism is also interested in the power of particular perspectives to change how we understand our reality. This process of transformation, especially its consequences, is fundamental. Pragmatist perspectives are part of nature, and they can change nature; changing perspectives are part of reality itself evolving. They involve a commitment to understanding the phenomena under study in a developmental and systemic manner, and the knowledge we derive about them as reflecting intersubjective perspectives forged at the person–world encounter.

To capture this dynamic reality, we need methodological pluralism, as no single method or body of data could account for differences in perspective and the study of human action. The rather monological focus of positivism on using the experimental method is certainly reductive, and so is the discursive nature of the method of postmodern deconstruction. The first assumes our ability to step outside our experience and develop "objective" perspectives on the world that come from no particular position within it (God's point of view). The second, on the contrary, denies the possibility of even approximating a "true" perspective and, instead, embraces a fragmented and multiple understanding of knowledge. This epistemological and methodological gap can be bridged only by acknowledging the fact that research itself is a form of human activity that contributes to constructing new perspectives on (and in) the world and that this process is both creative and emergent, and one that is constrained by material and social demands, including by the perspectives of others. What comes to be recognized as a "true" perspective depends on the interplay between all these factors – including the resistance of reality to our attempts to construct it according to our intention – and is best evaluated – epistemologically and ethically – in terms of the actions in the world it engenders.

2.6 The Consequences of Pragmatism

We started this chapter by examining the post-truth climate that has marked the social and political landscape of several nations, including the United States, the United Kingdom, Brazil, Myanmar, and the Philippines. This societal context is relevant for a discussion of epistemology for several reasons. First, epistemological attacks on the Aristotelian notion of truth, amounted primarily by constructionists, relativists, and postmodernists, are claimed to have laid some of the ground for the current crisis (see Baggini, 2017; McIntyre, 2018). Second, the fact that belief in misinformation and conspiracy theories tends to correlate with anti-science sentiment (Prasad, 2022) has led to a backlash against these epistemological standpoints and an attempt to reinstate naïvely positivist notions of Truth. Third, and related to the points above, these tensions have direct consequences for methodology and research as a constructionist account of conspiracy theories, for instance, will be different than a positivist one. The latter is much more common in the existing literature, at least in psychology, than the former. This begs the question of how we can consider, in both research and in society, the issue of truth and valid knowledge in more complex terms, moving away from the simplistic opposition between "anything goes" and "nobody can argue against facts."

What we advance in this chapter is the proposal that adopting a pragmatist epistemological standpoint might take us a long way, in science and public debates, toward a nuanced view of knowledge and truth. For pragmatists like James, Peirce, Dewey, and Mead, the value of knowledge is established in action on the world and coordinating our actions with those of others. By trying to build a bridge between realism and perspectivism and promoting antideterministic and pluralist views that allow for human agency, pragmatist thinkers help us address the post-truth debate in new ways. Instead of looking to legitimize specific perspectives (e.g., scientific, political, conspiracist) as universally valid, it invites us to reflect on their practical and ethical values in the way they are used in practice and in terms of their consequences. It can be assumed, in this regard, that perspectives associated with misinformation fail the pragmatist test by failing to explain the patterns in the data, benefiting some groups but disadvantaging many others, including creating a divided and polarized society that is to the detriment of everyone (Chambers, 2021). Also noteworthy, from a pragmatist standpoint, to research misinformation and conspiracies, is to study the variety of perspectives associated with them and try to understand their origin, function, and relation to other perspectives. It is a common misconception, especially in public debates, to assume that understanding a perspective means either accepting it or agreeing with it – in fact, it means only to understand it in its proper context and across time, in a developmental manner.

These key markers of a pragmatist epistemology – contextualization, developmentalism, perspectival realism – guide us in writing the present book on methodology. Arguably, the most consequential implication of pragmatism for methodology is to avoid analytical reductionism and methodological fixedness. The first refers to an attempt to reduce complex phenomena to simple processes, particularly psychological ones, cut away from their social, political, and material embedding. In the case of post-truth, this is reflected in studies that focus on cognitive or clinical variables without any effort to connect these back to the fields of action and interaction that support them. And this analytical separation becomes easier to operate when one's epistemology favors methodological fixedness, which is the assumption that a given question (e.g., about cognitive processing of information) can be meaningfully answered with the help of a given type of data (e.g., psychometric tests) and the use of a narrow range of methods (surveys, experiments, or interviews). Pragmatism breaks away from these common practices by welcoming plurality regarding theoretical perspectives, datasets, data collection tools, analytical methods, and human interests. The subsequent chapters will explore each of these in turn.

CHAPTER 3

Theory
What We Know

We carve out groups of stars in the heavens, and call them constellations, and the stars patiently suffer us to do so – tho if they knew what we were doing, some of them might feel much surprised at the partners we had given them ... What shall we call a thing anyhow? It seems quite arbitrary, for we carve out everything, just as we carve out constellations, to suit our human purposes.

(James, 1907, p. 106)

This chapter develops our second pragmatist proposal that *theories are tools for action*. These tools, instead of mirroring the world, are part of the world. This idea is an alternative to realism on the one hand and relativism on the other. For realists, theories pertain to timeless objective Truths that are independent of human observers and exist behind the buzzing confusion of experience. For relativists, theories are inescapably subjective, bound to human experience and culture. The pragmatist alternative bypasses the subjective–objective dualism and instead focuses on human activity: What does the theory enable us to do?

The term "theory'" is used in various senses (Abend, 2008). Sometimes it is used loosely to refer to the work of great thinkers, to fundamental debates, or to have an observational stance; these are not our focus. We aim to conceptualize narrower theories, that is, theories about a specific phenomenon. People with realist tendencies tend to define such theory in terms of propositions about relationships, often causal, between variables that mirror Reality. People with relativist tendencies tend to define these theories in terms of interpretations, discourses, and ways of seeing. Pragmatism, in contrast, defines theories as semiotic tools crafted (e.g., using common sense, trial and error, or scientific methods) to identify regularities in our interaction with the world that reduce surprise and enable future action.

Pragmatists criticize realism for associating theory entirely with the object, arguing that a theory completely independent of humans would be incomprehensible and useless. Pragmatists criticize relativism for associating theory entirely with the subject, arguing that this leads to impotent skepticism that fails to take a critical stance on the consequences of knowledge. The pragmatist alternative aims to overcome Descartes' dualism (see Chapter 1) by focusing on the relation between the subject (person) and object (world). From this standpoint, theories are simultaneously consequential and historical; they capture regularities in our relation to the world, but they are also shaped by human interests.

This chapter reviews realist, relativist, and pragmatist approaches to theory. Our focus is on the pragmatist idea that theories are not "mirrors" of the world but tools in the world that empower (or disempower) human activity. We illustrate this pragmatist approach to theory in creativity research to show how various theories open different lines of action (e.g., for individual agency, environmental support, and social evaluation). Overall, we argue that pragmatism focuses on making theories that are useful, constructed through disruptive experiences, and evaluated in terms of their practical and social consequences.

3.1   A Realist Approach to Theory

Plato's allegory of the cave vividly captures the idea that "behind" our infinitely particular, fractal, and continually changing experience of the world are simple, timeless, and absolute Truths (Reeve, 2004). Plato argued that the phenomena we perceive (e.g., horses, tables, and triangles) are akin to mere shadows projected onto a cave wall by a fire. Knowledge, he argued, entails going beyond these shimmering two-dimensional shadows to understand the stable three-dimensional sources. Behind the diversity of horses that one perceives, Plato argued, there is a single Ideal Form of a horse, the essence of a horse, which is valid for all horses and which is the source of all manifest horses. This idea was appealing because it reduced the blooming buzzing confusion of empirical experience to a smaller set of Ideal Forms that were True and timeless and, thus, a seductively solid foundation for knowledge.

> Archimedes, that he might transport the entire globe from the place it occupied to another, demanded only a point that was firm and immovable; so, also, I shall be entitled to entertain the highest expectations, if I am fortunate enough to discover only one thing that is certain and indubitable. (Descartes, 1641, p. 85)

Descartes (1641) found unshakable truth in rationality, logic, and mathematics; geometry was akin to operating with Ideal Forms directly. Descartes speculated that all perceptual experiences are potentially illusionary, such as when dreaming or hallucinating (Gillespie, 2006a). Imagining an all-powerful daemon manipulating his perceptions, Descartes retreated into thought and famously realized that the only thing he could not doubt was his doubting. This Truth, contained within thought itself, became his immovable point. Rebuilding his knowledge on this foundation led him to privilege rational thought, especially mathematics. For example, the mathematical structure of a triangle (e.g., that all angle sum to 180 degrees) is true independent of any empirical manifestation of a triangle. Indeed, perfect triangles do not exist empirically (each actualization is only an approximation), yet the rational truth is timeless.

In contrast to Descartes' rationalism, empiricism (see Chapter 2) argues that experience is the only reliable source of knowledge and that rational ideas are merely derivative of sensory experience (e.g., the rational idea of a perfect triangle is a generalization of the experience of triangles). In its most extreme variations, empiricism implies that humans are born *tabula rasa*, as "white paper, void of all characters, without any ideas" (Locke, 1847, p. 104). The human mind, reason, and logic develop through experience; thus, rather than being secondary, experience is the sole pathway to Truth. The problem, however, is that experiences can be deceptive (refraction, optical illusions, and hallucinations). Accordingly, the scientific method is a collection of techniques (e.g., for gathering data, testing hypotheses, and making inferences) that aims to separate objective and subjective elements of experience. To this end, Popper (1934) argued, theories need to be falsifiable, that is, stated in ways that observations can contradict. Theories that observations cannot refute, Popper argued, were unfalsifiable and thus not scientific theories.

Limiting theories to falsifiable statements about the world limits the scope of science and potentially fails to take account of underlying mechanisms. Critical realism (Bhaskar, 1975) presents a broader vision of science: It distinguishes between "observations" and the "Real" world beyond observations. The Real exists independently of observations and theories. The problem is that our observations are shaped not only by the Real but also by our expectations. That is to say, only observations, not Reality, are tainted by humanity. Relativism, Bhaskar (1975) argues, makes an epistemic fallacy: Limitations of our epistemology (uncertain observation) are overextended into a limitation of ontology (uncertain Reality). According to critical realism, epistemology is limited, but it does not follow that there is no Real ontology to the world; it just means that we have limited access to it. Critical realism aims to reconstruct the world beyond observations that is independent of humans from the traces it leaves in our observations.

However, critical realism is not just about "realism" but also about being "critical." The problem is that social critique is normative (i.e., cultural, historical). Hammersley (2002) doubts that critical realism can derive what should be based on what is (i.e., deriving "ought" from "is"). There is nothing in Reality that implies social critique; it just is. In contrast, pragmatism can more easily introduce the critical and normative aspect of "ought" because it incorporates human interests from the outset. That is to say, by starting with the impact of knowledge on people and guided by human interests of fairness and liberty, critical judgment follows easily.

Contemporary realists are rarely naïve, in the sense of failing to distinguish their theories from Reality. Few openly state, with complete confidence, that their theories capture timeless and universal Truths. The cautious scientist knows that measures are "constructs" in researchers' minds. The subtle statistician understands that averages, standard deviations, and latent variables are not "behind" the diversity of datapoints but are strategies for researchers to simplify the complexity of empirical observations.

However, in practice, the language of research often slides into naïve realism. Theories are routinely defined in terms of things-in-themselves, not observations. For example, Corley and Gioia (2011, p. 12) define a theory as "a statement of concepts and their interrelationships that shows how and/or why a phenomenon occurs." Thus the "constructs" slide from being relational (between researchers and the world) to being independent of the research process (about the phenomena itself). The researchers, who are sensemaking about their observations and experiments, are effectively erased from the theories they produce. At a statistical level, the averages and latent variables that simplify complex data may not describe anyone in particular, yet they substitute for the phenomenon itself (Fisher et al., 2018). Seduced by the certainty of infallibility and and the completeness of formal unity, cautious claims grounded in contextual observations give way to an imperialistic attitude that overextends itself, is found wanting, and thus weakens science and, ironically, opens the door to relativism (Midgley, 2003).

3.2   A Relativist Approach to Theory

The relativist approach to theory is a radicalization of the skeptical argument against realism. Ancient Greek skeptics argued that all knowledge is inescapably a human product. Pyrrho, probably influenced by Buddhism (Beckwith, 2017), argued that certainty was self-evidently impossible because people disagree about things, things change over time, and all observations depend upon assumptions shaped by custom. There are six refinements of these classical skeptical arguments.

First, Darwin's (1859) publication of *Origin of Species* bolstered the critique against timeless Truths. While Darwin's contribution is primarily to biology, Dewey (1910b) argues that he also made a fundamental contribution to philosophy. Species were prototypical Ideal Forms, especially humans (e.g., made in the image of God). Darwin demonstrated that species change and evolve. This undermined the idea that each species was "of a type" that was clear and distinct (i.e., if horses were evolving, there could not be an Ideal Form of a horse). Darwin, as read by Dewey, inverted the realist hierarchy. The blooming variability is not noise secondary to Truth, to be stripped out; variability and noise are the truths of evolution.

Second, studies of the history of science also undermine the idea of timeless Truths. Science does not progress uniformly; there are moments of revolution when there is a paradigm shift, and what was once taken for granted becomes questioned (Kuhn, 1962). Gravity was conceptualized by Aristotle as the tendency for objects to return to their origin, Newton as the gravitational force, and Einstein as a bending of spacetime. This historicity is even more evident in the social sciences. Theories about mental illness and criminality have changed hugely, shaped by shifting power relations (Foucault, 1973, 1975). Scientific racism, widespread in the early twentieth century, used ideas from physical anthropology, psychometrics, and genetics to create a hierarchy of discrete races that justified colonialism (Said, 1978). These theories, now debunked (Gould, 1981), reveal the historicity of truths and also the role of human interests and politics in shaping any so-called Truth.

Third, surveys of scientific progress challenge the reductionists' dream of simplicity "behind" complexity. In contrast, the evidence points to a reductionist's nightmare. Behind ostensibly simple observations is irreducible, fractal, and spiraling complexity (Stewart & Cohen, 1997). Although there have been some remarkable successes in finding patterns behind complexity (e.g., Darwin's theory of evolution by natural selection, Einstein's general theory of relativity, and Crick and Watson's description of the double helix), there have also been many domains of escalating complexity. With telescopes and microscopes, the more we zoom in and out, the more complexity we discover. The microscope finds a universe within a drop of pond water. Consider the growth of knowledge in encyclopedias. The *Urra=hubullu*, created in Babylonia in the late first millennium BC, comprised twenty-four clay tablets. Pliny the Elder's *Natural History*, created in Italy in AD 79, synthesized 2,000 works and 20,000 facts into 400,000 pages. The *Encyclopedia Britannica* has about forty million words, and Wikipedia has about four billion words in English. Philosophy spawned moral philosophy and natural philosophy, which spawned a growing list of disciplines with countless subdisciplines (Abbott, 2000). Encyclopedias are not shrinking. Disciplines are not concluding. In short, knowledge is not getting simpler; it is getting ever more complex, subtle, and intricate – especially in the human sciences.

Fourth, theories are necessarily incomplete. There is always a gap between our theories and the world. Imagine the innumerable interactions of a rock rolling down a hill, tumbling on scree, bumping into larger rocks, and brushing tufts of grass. What simplicity could lie behind it? One could try to model the interactions mathematically, but the number of variables and complexity of the interactions would rapidly spiral out of control. While the first few milliseconds of the tumbling rock could be modeled, the rock and the model will diverge over time. Sensitivity to initial conditions makes precise prediction impossible; thus, we rely upon incomplete probabilistic models (Yao & Tong, 1994). Quite likely, the rock rolling down the hill is the most accurate representation of itself; arguably, no simpler but equally accurate version can be made. Extrapolating, it is likely that the most simple and accurate model of the world is the world itself.

Fifth, theories are not the phenomena they describe. Imagine that one did create a perfect model of the rock rolling down the hill – a quantum computer simulation, instantiated in millions of lines of code, with an unmanageable number of unfeasibly precise measurements setting up the initial conditions. This algorithm, however, is quite different from the rock. It would be absurd to suggest that the rock is doing mathematics while rolling down the hill. The rock is just doing its thing; the mathematicians, modeling the rock, are just doing their thing. The description is not the thing (Deacon, 2011). Equally, the description of a distribution (e.g., a mean or standard deviation) is not the population, and to reify the numeric mean above the distribution itself is an unhelpful inversion. The seductive temptation is to view statistical descriptions as akin to Plato's Ideal Forms – the underlying Truth that generate the messy data. But these statistical techniques reduce diversity and risk creating nonexistent phenomena. On average, people drive near the middle of the road, raise 1.25 children, and have one testicle. While these maybe useful simplifications, they are not Reality. The actual mean often does not exist; only context-bound ideographic cases exist (Hayes et al., 2019; Valsiner, 1998). Nevertheless, it is common for researchers to build their models using means and latent variables, created at the level of groups, and assume these apply to individuals (Fisher et al., 2018). This can lead to theories that work statistically but are disconnected from what is actually going on.

Finally, theories are additions to the world. Not only are theories, or any descriptions, not the phenomena that they describe but they are also new phenomena in the world (that need new descriptions). Instead of describing the world, a new theory is a growth in the world that makes the world more complex. New theories are not mere descriptions; they have consequences and interact with other aspects of the world. Sometimes these consequences are limited to academia (e.g., getting articles published, securing tenure), and other times these consequences impact society (e.g., ideas about feminism, persuasion, nudging). These consequences are independent of the veracity of theories. For example, classifying mental illnesses has proved challenging due to the paucity of pure cases and the bewildering diversity of presentations (Hayes & Hofmann, 2020), leading to ongoing debates about criteria. However, despite the manifest failure to uncover the simplicity behind the symptoms, these criteria have been consequential. These criteria organize who receives what treatments (Rose, 1998). Based on criteria that now seem historically peculiar, people were medicated, incarcerated, and subjected to harmful procedures (Foucault, 1973). Thus, these criteria do not pull back the veil on Reality; rather, they expand upon reality, adding another layer of meanings through which actions are guided.

These six skeptical arguments, among others, have led some researchers toward a relativist stance. This stance focuses on how knowledge is created through social interactions, how knowledge changes over time, the effects of knowledge, and how knowledge can benefit some groups to the detriment of others. These approaches encompass a wide variety of ways of thinking about reality (the everyday truths of practice) and Reality (timeless truths), but they are broadly described as "constructionist" (Hacking, 1999). These approaches do not necessarily reject Reality, but they do bracket it aside as unhelpful when analyzing how knowledge is actually constructed. A degree of relativism, they argue, is useful for critical projects that aim to uncover ideology within what is taken for granted as Real (see the discussion of postmodernism in Chapter 2).

The problem with relativism in general, and postmodernism in particular, is the tendency to go from the epistemological limitation (we encounter the world only through our experience) to the ontological limitation (the epistemic fallacy; Bhaskar, 1975) or even to an epistemological helplessness and skepticism (we cannot know anything about the world). Being unable to know the world as it is does not mean that all knowledge is equally subjective;

it just means that all knowledge is limited. Ignoring this subtlety and adopting an extreme relativist position has two problematic consequences.

First, extreme relativism implies that evaluating the quality of knowledge is impossible. Knowledge only ever expresses something about its producer and can only be valued as such. On the one hand, this renders methodology meaningless. Why attempt to systematize and improve knowledge production if there are no criteria for quality? On the other hand, assessing the quality of research becomes impossible. Without asserting the quality of some research over others, the entire operation of science dissolves; any discomforting finding can be dismissed as mere interpretation. In contrast, from a pragmatist standpoint, the historical record provides data, or facts, that cannot be dismissed and that any theory needs to account for.

Second, extreme relativism can neuter the critique. While it is often ethical and valuable to give voice to marginalized perspectives (e.g., minorities, patients, children), it does not follow that all marginalized voices are equally valid. Should we be tolerant of intolerant views (Verkuyten, 2022)? Sometimes marginal voices want to impose upon others, spread ideology, or rewrite history. Are conspiracy theories (see Chapter 2) about stolen elections, climate change, and the Holocaust as valid as evidence-based views? Relativism not only has trouble countering such views but can even contribute to them (Wight, 2018). In contrast, from a pragmatist standpoint, such conspiracy theories are dangerous and can verifiably lead to undesirable consequences.

Relativism causes problems both within the academy and beyond. Although relativism is often the paradigm of choice for critical researchers, ironically, it can undermine the potential of critique by making it difficult for good research to gain traction and easy for it to be dismissed. Beyond the academy, relativism can be used to undermine coordination on collective issues, such as health, inequality, and climate change (Conway & Oreskes, 2012). It enables dismissing disruptive facts as "fake news" countered with "alternative facts" (Cooke, 2017; Gillespie, 2020b). Even without refuting rigorous knowledge, merely sowing doubt and confusion undermines our capacity to address problems of common concern (Conway & Oreskes, 2012). However, naïvely asserting realism risks exacerbating skepticism because science is fallible and filled with human interests. Theories will fail and be revised, they will become historical, and they may eventually be seen as ideological and thus fodder for post-truth arguments. We need to acknowledge the historicity of science while also retaining the ability to distinguish between the quality of evidence and theories. To this end, pragmatism provides a way forward.

3.3 A Pragmatist Approach to Theory

Descartes (1641; see Chapter 1) created a dualism between the subjective (mind) and the objective (things). This dualism has shaped both realism (i.e., objectivism) and relativism (i.e., subjectivism). Realism focuses on the object, and tries to exclude anything that is subjective. Relativism focuses on the subject, highlighting how it is impossible to escape the human element. In contrast to both these approaches, pragmatism focuses on human activity as the relation between the subject and the object. Realism locates theory "behind" experience, as an explanation for experience. Relativism locates theory entirely in the subjective side of experience. Pragmatism locates theory in the subject–object relationship: Theory is the means through which the subject interacts with the object. For pragmatism, a good theory enables action vis-à-vis the object by reducing unexpected consequences.

James (1907) criticizes the realist position for taking words, which are tools for socially coordinating in relation to objects, and then imputing them behind the object as an explanation of the object. Realism, he writes, entails

> taking the mere name and nature of a fact and clapping it behind the fact as a duplicate entity to make it possible … But this is like saying that cyanide of potassium kills because it is a 'poison,' or that it is so cold to-night because it is 'winter,' or that we have five fingers because we are 'pentadactyls.' These are but names for the facts, taken from the facts, and then treated as previous and explanatory. (James, 1907, p. 263)

The words "poison," "pentadactyl," and "winter" describe observations; thus, they cannot be explanations for those observations. However, this is not to say that these words are all "in the mind." These terms are useful; they enable action, coordinate interaction, and can reduce surprise. For example, the term "winter" is useful in Europe to describe the recurring pattern of cold weather each year. Although this pattern has held in the past, there is no guarantee it will hold in the future (especially with global warming) or that a specific date in winter next year will be cold – it might not. Nonetheless, the term guides us into the future with sensible expectations. It is not cold because it is winter; we put away our sunglasses and take out our thermals because it is winter.

Our theories, just like our words, are saturated in humanity. "The trail of the human serpent," James (1907, p. 64) writes, is "over everything." In this sense, pragmatism agrees with relativism but disagrees with the conclusion of epistemological despair. Some theories are more effective than others. Some theories advantage certain groups more than others. And, some theories, such as pure relativism, can actively undermine the possibility of group coordination to address issues of common concern. Accordingly, despite the challenges, social researchers have a responsibility to advance theories that have desirable consequences.

The pragmatist critique of naïve realism does not undermine science; it protects science. Calling out the overextension of science, along with challenging fundamentalist ideas about timeless Truths, is scientific; it is removing nonempirical dogma from science. It redirects science away from grand metaphysical dramas and toward what it does best: practical empirically grounded investigations that incrementally extend humans' capacity to act effectively in an unknown future. The world is messy, and science is necessarily complex. Midgley (2003, p. 21) writes that this "complexity is not a scandal." There is no grand unifying theory that unveils simplicity behind complexity. Our theories are context-specific guides to action – proliferating in proportion to the increasing number of contexts we encounter.

From a pragmatist standpoint, theories are "for humans" and anchored in the practical consequences for humans. Theories synthesize previous experiences into guides for future action. When pragmatists talk of "facts," they are referring to what has happened (which cannot change despite potentially diverse interpretations), not what will happen (which is always an expectation). Thus, pragmatism makes a sharp distinction between what is in the past (what has happened, independent of current debates) and what is in the future (fundamentally uncertain and in the process of being created, in part, by humans). The aim of science, and most knowledge creation, is to equip us better to navigate and shape an undetermined future.

> Observations of fact have, therefore, to be accepted as they occur. But observed facts relate exclusively to particular circumstances that happened to exist when they were observed. They do not relate to any future occasions upon which we may be in doubt how we ought to act. They, therefore, do not, in themselves, contain any practical knowledge. Such knowledge must involve additions to the facts observed. (Peirce, 1955, p. 150)

Theories are a type of practical knowledge that are derivative of the facts of prior experience. But, as Peirce writes, these aspects of prior experience do not in themselves provide a guide for action; prior experiences need to be integrated, synthesized, and packaged into usable knowledge. Theories, from a pragmatist standpoint, are this repackaging of past experiences into useful guides for the future.

3.3.1 Theory: A Mirror of Nature?

Metaphors are ubiquitous in scientific theories (Lakoff & Johnson, 1980, 1999). Key metaphors in the natural sciences include the big bang, superstring theory, cells, DNA blueprints, and dark matter. Indeed, many scientific debates entail a clash between metaphors (Holton, 1975), such as whether quanta are "waves" or "particles." In psychology, metaphors are widespread, such as the idea that the mind is like a computer with modularity (e.g., long- and short-term memory systems), limited capacity processing, and culture being semantic software run on biological hardware (Leary, 1990). At a deeper level, even basic psychological terms are grounded in metaphors. Skinner (1989) analyzed the etymology of eighty cognitive terms, and in each case, he argued, the terms originated in everyday human activity. For example, the etymological root of "comprehend" is grasp, "agony" is struggle, and "understand" is to stand under. It seems impossible to create theories entirely independent of "the trail of the human serpent" – even mathematics is grounded in embodied metaphors (Lakoff & Núñez, 2000). This ubiquity of metaphors throughout science reveals that all our theories are peculiarly human creations.

Why do metaphors pervade our theories? Just as a tool must be molded for human hands (e.g., a hammer needs a handle), so theories are molded for the human mind. The domain of the most immediate understanding has variously been called the here-and-now (Schuetz, 1945) and immediate interaction (Lakoff & Johnson, 1980). This domain of concrete interaction does not need a metaphor; it is the wellspring of metaphors. We do not use metaphors to understand opening, eating, or talking; instead, we use these everyday experiences as metaphors to understand more abstract phenomena. Arguably, understanding is anchoring an abstract phenomenon in concrete daily experiences.

To use a computational metaphor, a good metaphor is like a compressed computer file, shrinking the cognitive load but remaining on hand to be unpacked when needed. We are, as the cognitivists say, limited capacity processors (Norman, 1967). Most humans can remember only between five and nine random numbers (Miller, 1956). Yet we have managed to write books, create cities, and fly to the moon. A key question is: How have we leveraged our limited capacity? Metaphors are one method of extending memory. Because of their sensuous quality, they are easier to remember than random numbers (Luria, 1968), but more than this, metaphors can be "unpacked" (or "unzipped") using common sense, to reveal much more than is first apparent. A good metaphor can condense many viable paths of action around an object into a sensuous image. A good metaphor guides its users to insights latent within the metaphor. But metaphors can also be misleading, blinding us by their simplicity to the world's complexity.

Rorty (1981) provided a powerful critique of the naïve realist paradigm, arguing that it has been seduced and blinded by the metaphor of theory as a "mirror" of nature. He argued that theories are merely words we use to talk about the world and coordinate with one another. A sentence, Rorty argues, may afford a particular action, lead to an anticipated result, and, in hindsight, may be called true. However, none of this implies that the sentence "mirrors" the world in itself. Sentences are as much "for us" as they are "for the world." Theories enable us to coordinate our actions in relation to nature, and they may be effective or ineffective, but they are not mirrors of nature.

Rorty (1998, p. 48) vividly conveys the pragmatist argument by arguing that theories have "no more of a representational relation to an intrinsic nature of things than does the anteater's snout." The anteater's snout is an adaptation to its environment, which mediates between the anteater's desire for ants and the existence of ants in hard-to-reach places. The snout may be effective, but this does not make it a mirror of ants in hard-to-reach places. Equally, human knowledge of horticulture is not a mirror of the timeless Truth of plants; it is a purpose-driven mediator between the human desire for food and the world. Horticulture is evaluated not by whether it "mirrors" Reality but by whether it successfully enables humans to grow food.

The metaphor of theory as a mirror of nature permeates our thinking. It is latent in Plato's allegory of the cave (see Chapter 1), with the Ideal Forms casting pale shadows upon the wall. It is evident in the etymological root of "representation" in "showing" and everyday phrases such as "in the mind," and talk of beliefs "corresponding" to reality. It is also used in arguments: In contrast to one's own "objective" facts, other people have "beliefs" and "opinions" with a dubious correspondence to reality.

The mirror metaphor is useful if one wants a simple way to talk about false beliefs. However, it also creates problems, or anomalies. First, it elevates correspondence as the main criteria of evaluation, downplaying the criteria of both usefulness and ethics. In this sense, it disconnects theories from human values (Putnam, 1995). Thus, research ethics focuses on data collection but is mute on what the research is for, whom it benefits, and whom it might exploit (e.g., research on advertising to children, or microtargeted advertising). Second, it frames the researcher as a detached observer, naïvely suppressing the role of the researcher in creating theory.

It obscures the fact that theories are for humans. For example, it cannot explain why metaphors permeate all theories. Third, it separates the theory from nature, failing to conceptualize how theories are part of the social world and can have real consequences. This creates a problem for how to deal with theories that are true but of potentially unethical consequences (e.g., torture; Bohannon, 2015). So, what metaphor does pragmatism suggest?

3.3.2 *Theory: A Tool, Map, and Model*

The trail of the human serpent is throughout the social sciences, evident in the bricolage of quintessentially human metaphors used. This stubborn fact makes realists recoil and relativists give up. However, pragmatists are unfazed. Pragmatism advocates becoming critical evaluators of the metaphors we choose to use. Do they serve our purposes? Do they empower? Or do they create unethical outcomes or ineffectual surprises?

From a pragmatist standpoint, theories are tools that enable people to grow food, fly planes, and create artificial intelligence. There is a tendency to think of tools as merely serving practical purposes, but, arguably, some of the most powerful tools enable us to act on ourselves (e.g., extending memory, transmitting experience, and empowering social coordination). Our cognitive capacity is boosted by writing, typing, and searching (Gillespie et al., 2012). Our identity is transformed by mirrors, photographs, and social media (Gillespie et al., 2017). Our ability to coordinate is empowered by calendars, to-do lists, and communication devices (Aldewereld et al., 2016). Moreover, the trajectory of society is shaped by our social technologies for collectively imagining a future together (Jovchelovitch & Hawlina, 2018; Wright, 2010; Zittoun & Gillespie, 2015). But, in science, theories have a narrower function: They empower the mind, direct our attention to specific issues, and guide our actions through the many branching paths within a dataset.

> Effects are produced by the means of instruments and aids, which the understanding requires no less than the hand; and as instruments either promote or regulate the motion of the hand, so those that are applied to the mind prompt or protect the understanding. (Bacon, 1620, p. 345)

Scientific knowledge creates theories that empower human thought and action. Theories, in this sense, are simply part of the scientists' toolkit. Lewin (1943, p. 118) describes theory "as a tool for human beings." Similarly, Mead (1936, p. 351) writes: "[W]hen we speak of a scientist's apparatus we are thinking of the very ideas of which he can make use." Just like the scientist's apparatus, the scientist's theory mediates interaction with nature. In the same way that we cannot say that a scientist's apparatus "mirrors" nature, we should not think of theories as "mirrors" of nature but rather as tools for interacting with nature – like the anteaters' snout.

Tools, however, come in many varieties: What type of tool is a theory? Arguably, theories are like maps. Maps are tools for getting us from one location to another. Theories are tools for getting us from one situation to another, from the present to a desired future. Theories are like maps because they both synthesize many observations, make past experiences accessible to a broader audience, enable human activity, require training to use effectively, and are necessarily incomplete. A perfect map would be as detailed as the terrain and thus useless (see Borges' short story, "On exactitude in science"; 1999). Theories, like maps, simplify to focus attention on a given purpose (Midgley, 2003). There are geological, political, and deprivation maps of the same region, and we do not ask which is the "True" map: "[W]e know that the political world is not a different world from the climatological one, that it is the same world seen from a different angle" (Midgley, 2003, p. 27). Both theories and maps are created by human choices, with trade-offs between accuracy, parsimony, and usability (Toulmin, 1973). Equally, each theory has been created for particular purposes and thus reveals the world from a particular (potentially useful but always incomplete) angle.

Theories are also like maps because, in the face of uncertainty, it is prudent to have multiple, even contradictory, maps. Explorers lost in an unfamiliar land may have several incompatible mental maps of the area. They do not decide which map is infallible and discard the rest.

> Instead, they had better bear them all in mind, looking out for whatever may be useful in all of them. In the field, they can eventually test one suggestion against another, but it need not always turn out that either suggestion is wrong. The river that different earlier maps show in different places may actually be several different rivers. Reality is always turning out to be a great deal more complex than people expect. (Midgley, 2003, p. 27)

All maps are imperfect, made at different times (when the rivers were full or dry) and for different purposes (for navigating by land or sea), and are always deployed in a future context that is necessarily somewhat novel. Equally, theories aim to extend past experiences into partially uncertain futures. And rather than choosing the timelessly True theory and discarding the rest, it is more prudent to view theories as a collection of resources that may or may not be useful (or true with a small "t") in particular contexts, depending on the problems that arise.

One limitation of the map metaphor is that maps do not respond to our actions; but the world (especially the social world) is, in part, shaped by our actions, which, in turn, are shaped by our theories. We do not simply move through the social world; we contribute to it and, in some small way, shape it. Although theories may provide a map of the social world, the social world is changed by the existence of these maps. There is a looping effect, whereby our descriptions of social phenomena feed forward into the phenomena (Hacking, 1995). For example, the representation of autism changes the consequences of having autism (Heasman & Gillespie, 2017), and simply naming and explaining techniques of persuasion can undermine their efficacy (Gillespie, 2020a). This looping means that theories in social science usually lag behind the future they encounter, because the future encountered can, in part, be a response to the theory.

Another tool metaphor, related to maps, that better captures this looping effect is that theories are "models." Consider an architect's model of a building. Advanced digital models of buildings can simulate the flow of people through an office, the traffic over a bridge, and the effects of wind on a skyscraper. They support architects in imagining the consequences of design choices (e.g., adding a stairwell, reinforcing a span, or substituting materials). The model is not a mirror of the truth of the unbuilt building; rather, it is a dynamic exploration of what the building could be that will feed forward into what the building becomes.

Conceptualizing theory as models that support future-oriented action is consistent with a simulation approach to cognition (Gallese & Goldman, 1998). The idea is that our minds are structured not in terms of formal propositions but in terms of rich embodied simulations. For example, when we think of a bike, we activate the neural circuits for riding a bike – the muscles for balancing, peddling, and steering. This idea that concepts, even abstract concepts, entail mental simulation goes back to phenomenology (Merleau-Ponty, 1945), but now it is backed up by brain study research. For example, the same areas of the human brain are activated in response to the word "pain" as are activated in the direct perception of pain (Lamm et al., 2011). Equally, when we try to understand other people's minds, we do so by simulating, or creating a model of, how we would feel if we were in their situation (Schilbach et al., 2013; Vogeley, 2017). Thus, there is growing evidence that theories might be like simulations – mental models, or maps, for rehearsing, and speculating about, possible interactions with the world.

The idea that social science theories are simulations has some beneficial consequences. It draws attention to how theories enable us to think through if-then scenarios. These models can develop through embodied ethnographic experience or experimental interventions. But the outcome is the same: an intersubjectively shared simulation, or a shared mental model (Van den Bossche et al., 2011), of what will happen and could happen under various circumstances. These models are not timeless mirrors of the world; rather, they are dynamic simulations with multiple possible futures. They enable playing with scenarios, evaluating possible interventions, and guiding consequential actions that will change the course of events. Indeed, the purpose of such models is not to predict what will be but rather to enable people to shape what will be. The model that central banks have of inflation will shape our future inflation; the taxation model that politicians have will shape our future finances; and the model of mental illness that a therapist has will shape his or her intervention. In short, rather than "mirroring" the world (an infinite, directionless, and futile task), models guide humans in "making" the world.

Sometimes a model's main purpose is to avoid a predicted outcome. For example, models of the impact of past, present, and future human activity on global warming are both descriptions of and interventions in human behavior. One hopes, possibly naïvely, that the catastrophic consequences predicted do not materialize because the predictions motivate humans to take corrective action. If global warming is halted, it will not mean that the predictions were false; rather, it will mean that the models successfully altered our actions. In 2020, during the early stages of the Covid pandemic, models of predicted infection and mortality rates led many governments to institute lockdowns, avoiding the worst predicted outcomes. Does this mean that the predictions were wrong? No. It means that in social science, our knowledge does not mirror the future; instead, it contributes to the future (Hacking, 1995). In short, theories are tools, or supports, for human activity.

The metaphor of theory as a model to guide activity is particularly evident in statistical modeling. Driven by the increasing quantities of data available, there is a corresponding increase in the scale and ambition of statistical modeling. This ranges from modeling big datasets to agent-based simulations (Helbing, 2012). Naïve realism embraces these models as Plato's Ideal Forms, revealing the underlying Truth of which all data are a pale reflection. Relativism dismisses these models as one of many alternatives, each with associated histories and interests. In contrast, pragmatism views these models as more or less useful tools for acting, coordinating, and navigating an uncertain future. "Good" models are thus empowering, enabling us to take responsibility and ensuring that our individual and collective actions are effective and ethical with as few unintended consequences as possible.

3.3.3   *Theory Development and Disruptive Data*

Theories, from a pragmatist standpoint, develop through encountering disruptive data. Theories synthesize past experiences into expectations for the future, which are often thwarted. Theory development begins in this moment of disruption when action fails.

Consider the example of the door that won't open from Chapter 1. As one approaches, the embodied expectation is that the door will effortlessly open inward to reveal the hallway. However, although the door handle obliges, the door does not. The disruption stimulates the mind to revise the expectation; maybe the door opens outward? But pushing does not work. Double-checking, one alternates between pulling and pushing. Ineffective repetition of this sequence gives way to a deeper reflection: Can the handle go down further? Can the handle be raised? Is the door jammed? Is the door locked? Is there a key? Is there a release button? Is there a knob lock or a deadbolt? Is the latch bolt moving? Is this really a door? Is there a second door? Interspersed are tangential thoughts: What if there is a fire? Where is the bathroom? Is someone playing a practical joke? Expectation has been disrupted; the mind is alive in the reconstructive effort. The stream of thought attempts to revise the map, or schema, on how to exit the room. The initial guidance failed, and a new path of action is needed. The stream of thought alternates between multiple possibilities, but what cannot be ignored is the stubborn fact that the door will not open.

The scientific literature shapes researchers' expectations for research. When these expectations fail, when there is an anomaly, there is the opportunity for a contribution. However, unlike the example of the jammed door, scientific action is rarely definitively blocked. Disruptive results do not stop one from having lunch, and they can always be abandoned in a bottom drawer (Earp & Trafimow, 2015). In most domains, disruptive facts are not as disruptive as a door that will not open or a car that will not start. In most cases, disruptive facts can be circumvented, deferred, or glossed over. This is a problem for science. Good science, with genuine advances, embraces disruptive facts, listens to them, and learns from them.

Scientific revolutions often begin with overlooked disruptive facts. A paradigm shift, Kuhn (1962, pp. 52–53) writes, "commences with the awareness of anomaly, i.e., with the recognition that nature has somehow violated the paradigm-induced expectations." The defining feature of the anomaly is that it resists explanation in terms of existing theory; instead, it challenges existing theory. In Piaget's (1977) terminology, it requires accommodation, that is, that one's assumptions and expectations need to change in order to accommodate the disruptive fact. Or, in Bateson's (1972) terminology, it requires double-loop learning. In any case, as the new paradigm, or worldview, begins to form, it gives researchers a new conceptual standpoint from which additional anomalies become visible.

Scientific progress is facilitated by embracing anomalies, reminding oneself that all expectations are fallible, and engaging earnestly with alternative theories. This does not mean that all theories are equal; some explain the anomalies better than others. What it means is a continuously inquisitive attitude. "Scientific advance," Mead (1917, p. 178) writes, "implies a willingness to remain on terms of tolerant acceptance of the reality of what cannot be stated in the accepted doctrine of the time, but what must be stated in the form of contradiction with these accepted doctrines."

We distinguish between data in general and disruptive data (what Mead and Peirce termed "facts"). Data are an accumulation of observations in the past that are synthesized, recombined, and extrapolated into guides for the future (Peirce, 1955). Disruptive data are the subset of data that do not conform to expectations – obstinate observations that challenge accepted doctrines. Scientists should appreciate and cultivate disruptive data because they are the seeds of theoretical advances. Disruptive data arise when our interactions with the world break down, reminding us, yet again, that the world is subtler, more abundant, and more intricate than any theory (Feyerabend, 2001). Disruptive data demarcate the limits of current theory and spur future theory to be more useful and yield fewer surprises.

The distinction mirrors Bateson's (1972, p. 453) definition of information as "a difference which makes a difference." Bateson builds on Kant's observation that there are an infinite number of facts about a single piece of chalk: Each molecule within the chalk is different from every other molecule, and the position of each molecule relative to every other molecule could be calculated as differences; and when complete, one could start calculating the position of each molecule relative to every molecule in the universe. These are but a tiny subset of the infinite facts about the chalk. However, despite the veracity of each datum, the net result is not informative. In our terminology, all these measures provide much data but, we expect, little disruption. That is because genuine information, in a pragmatist sense, is not just a difference (i.e., a measure) but a difference that makes a difference (i.e., is of consequence for a theory or practice). The value of empirical data is not merely in the accumulation of measurements, it is also in the disruptive pushback against expectation. As Deacon (2011, p. 384) argues: "[I]f there is no deviation from expectation, there is no information." That is to say, valuable information, the "gold" within mere data, is disruptive data consequential for theory and practice.

Disruptive data arise within a web of taken-for-granted expectations. "No actual problem [disruptive fact] could conceivably take on the form of a conflict involving the whole world of meaning" (Mead, 1917, p. 219), because theoretical work entails integrating the disruptive fact back into the broader taken-for-granted meanings. Science is a method for world reconstruction, for patching up and repairing the ship of knowledge – while at sea. Science resolves localized problems by aligning them with the bricolage of taken-for-granted meaning. Theories created at time one are taken for granted at time two and potentially problematized at time three. Science is a nonfoundational procedure for finding, interpreting, and accommodating disruptive facts.

It is important not to separate models and disruptive facts completely. An overharsh separation would fall back to a mirror theory of nature, whether the model "mirrors" the facts. For pragmatism, all data are connected to theory (e.g., data are disruptive or not only from the standpoint of a theory) and all scientific theories are connected to data (e.g., the history of their adaptation to disruptive facts). There is a continuum from data (observations, correlations) through definitions and classifications to theory (models, propositions) that is better described in terms of degrees of conceptualization and cognitive processing (Abend, 2008; Alexander, 1982). Specifically, disruptive data, or anomalies, are not self-evident; they require interpretation for their significance to be realized. This is why anomalies often become evident only from the standpoint of a novel emerging paradigm (Kuhn, 1962). Not only do anomalies create new theories, new theories make visible overlooked anomalies.

3.4 Illustration: Theory in Creativity Research

The field of creativity research illustrates realist, relativist, and pragmatist approaches to theory. This field has seen dramatic paradigm shifts, with diverse theories of creativity proposed. It is thus a useful domain to illustrate how pragmatism shifts the question from "which theory is right?" to "what does each theory enable us to do?"

The dominant approach in creativity research is realism, which assumes that creativity is an objective quality of people, objects, or ideas that has an acontextual presence and that researchers can objectively measure this quality. This approach focuses on discovering the causes, correlates, and consequences of creative expression by measuring creativity and examining its causes and consequences (Runco, 2010). The interest here is to reach empirically based, universally valid, and generalizable theories of creativity. The researcher and the research aims are bracketed aside; the focus is on creativity in itself.

Since the 1980s, constructionism has provided an alternative approach. The constructionists argue that creativity cannot be evaluated objectively but necessarily resides "in the eye of the beholder." In the extreme, nothing binds together the artifacts labeled creative, except social agreement and cultural convention. This approach focuses on the variability of what is viewed as creative across time and place. Nothing can be called "creative" in absolute terms except with reference to some point of view, or audience. For example, Csikszentmihalyi (1990) theorized how gatekeepers (e.g., publishers, curators, and art critics) determined what was and was not creative. From a realist standpoint, this systemic approach resembles relativism, and it is challenging to operationalize rigorously.

From a pragmatist standpoint, focusing either on the pure qualities of creativity or on the cultural judgment of what is creative misses the self-evident point that creativity is always enacted (Glăveanu, 2020b). In human action the subjective (interests, motives, belief) and the objective (materiality, situation, context) interact. More than most actions, creative actions are consequential, are future-making, and can leave a long-lasting mark on individuals, groups, and society. Thus, the pragmatist approach directs researchers' attention to the creative act and its consequences: How is creativity done? What are the heuristics? What are the consequences? How can it be supported?

At the level of research, pragmatism directs attention toward what theories and metaphors of creativity have enabled. Glăveanu (2010) has identified three cross-cutting paradigms in the field, each anchored in a different root metaphor: the He-paradigm, the I-paradigm, and the We-paradigm.

The He-paradigm labels highly visible creators and creations as revolutionary and seeks to understand them. This can inspire some people to develop their potential to the fullest, but it can also disempower the majority – if geniuses are the only "real" creators, then most people's actions are generic reflections of authentic creative power. The I-paradigm democratizes creativity by emphasizing that everyone and everyday activities can be creative. This paradigm encourages everyone to cultivate their creative potential. Yet this potential remains rooted within the person; this means that, should someone fail to achieve creative success, they have only themselves to blame. Finally, the We-paradigm radically reconceptualizes agency and change. These are no longer underpinned solely by personal abilities; they are embedded within society and shaped through joint action. The We-paradigm makes us aware that society is malleable and can be transformed only through coordinated creative action.

How should we evaluate these three paradigms? For the realists the sequence of paradigms is the march of progress. For the constructionists the shifting paradigms is further evidence of the absence of a timeless Truth. For the pragmatist the truth of the paradigms is in their consequences. Each paradigm has generated different paths of action. The He-paradigm is useful if one wants to train geniuses. The I-paradigm is useful for bolstering individual creativity. The We-paradigm is useful for fostering society-wide creativity. There is not one infallible true paradigm lurking within these three options; rather, they provide different maps for getting to different destinations.

Creativity research also illustrates disruptive data. One long-standing debate has been whether people are more creative alone or in groups. Many experiments have been conducted showing that people produce more ideas when alone than when in groups (DeRosa et al., 2007; Mullen et al., 1991). However, there is a disruptive fact: There are countless naturalistic observations of people being creative together (e.g., famous bands, scientist teams, comedy groups, and art collectives). One attempt to reconcile these disruptive observations is the idea that ideas produced alone and in groups have a different quality. Specifically, Glăveanu and colleagues (2019) showed that ideas produced in groups are more communicable and practical, while ideas produced by individuals are more idiosyncratic. In this case, the disruptive observation, the anomaly, creates tension that can easily be overlooked (i.e., experimentalists ignoring creativity practitioners and vice versa). But exploring the tension prompts the abductive insight that creativity is not simply "more" or "less" but also different in type (i.e., peculiar vs. communicable). Thus, the question shifts toward how different social configurations shape not the quantity but the content of creative outputs.

3.5 The Consequences of a Pragmatist Approach to Theory

Pragmatism evaluates theories in terms of their consequences. Accordingly, what are the consequences of conceptualizing theory as a tool or a map? Does this pragmatist approach to theory add any value?

First, a pragmatist approach to theory enables critical evaluation of the interests served by a theory without becoming relativist. Theories, as sociohistorical tools, are always born of a context and always answer to some human interests (see Chapter 8). No theory is completely neutral or detached, and some theories clearly privilege some groups over others. This does not, however, mean that all theory is equally and irreducibly biased. Some theories are useful for obtaining publications, grants, and tenure. Other theories are used by corporations to increase engagement, market share, and sales. Yet other theories are distributed freely, for example, to empower people in daily life (e.g., principles for decision-making, cooking heuristics), to enable parents to raise their children (e.g., techniques to help babies sleep, to encourage exploration), to help people to cope with illness (e.g., support groups, assistive technologies), and to improve social coordination (e.g., wikis, *Roberts Rules of Order*). A critical analysis of the interests being served by theory does not imply relativism. Indeed, it is precisely because theories are consequential for daily living that critique is necessary. Moreover, these same consequences are the nonrelativist fact that enables a pragmatist critique to analyze who benefits from a given theory.

Second, a pragmatist approach to theory sensitizes researchers to the emergence of new problems and anomalies. Theories, despite being potentially useful, are grounded in peculiar social and historical contexts. Contexts change, old problems cease to be relevant, and new problems arise. Each year brings new social problems for social science to address (e.g., the Covid pandemic, the cost-of-living crisis, generative artificial intelligence, and remote working). A pragmatist approach to theory expects these shifting contexts and problems to lead to revisions and replacements of theory. Pragmatism never complacently assumes that Reality has been unveiled; instead, it keeps researchers alert to the need to adapt theory to emerging problems and contexts. Moreover, it sensitizes researchers to anomalies. By not reifying theory (i.e., confusing our theories with the phenomena they describe), it keeps our critical faculties alive to the potential for anomalies. A pragmatist approach to theory is not threatened by anomalies, edge cases, and disruptive data; it tolerates them and sees in them the seed of scientific progress.

Third, a pragmatist approach focuses attention on the usability of theory. Concealing the role of humans in constructing theories, trying to pass theories off as mirrors of nature, overlooks the importance of making theories communicable and accessible to a wide range of potential users (Cornish, 2020). Theory-building in social research is usually object-facing: sampling, measurement design, validity tests, and so on. Conceptualizing theory as a tool reminds us that there is also a subject-facing side to theory. A hammer has both a head (orienting to the object, or nail) and a handle (orienting to the subject, or user). The user-facing side of theory, the handle of the hammer, pushes toward theories that are parsimonious, memorable, and accessible to a wide range of people. Communicable and accessible theories benefit social science because they enable researchers to integrate theories from diverse domains. But, more significantly, it reconnects social science with laypeople. As discussed earlier, Kant's bit of chalk has an infinite number of truths, but most of them are not worth studying. "Truth" and "rigor" cannot be the only criteria for social science – there are an infinite set of useless truths that can be rigorously studied. If social science wants to have an impact and be part of social life, it needs to enshrine usefulness as a criterion for selecting and pursuing research questions.

Fourth, a pragmatist approach argues against null hypothesis testing and favors model-building. The metaphor of the mirror of nature dovetails with null hypothesis testing. One creates a falsifiable hypothesis to do a one-shot test about the correspondence between the theory and observations. The focus is on the probability that the observations could have occurred if the hypothesis was incorrect. Null hypothesis testing has been the subject of much recent critique because it puts too much emphasis on a true/false binary decision, which is open to many distortions (Masson, 2011; Trafimow, 2022). The alternative is to shift toward model-building. Instead of testing hypotheses about the world, one tries to build a model to describe the cumulating data on a phenomenon. This approach usually results in the construction of several models of the data, models that may even be logically incompatible. These models are evaluated not in terms of being true/false but in terms of the degree of fit with existing data, new data, and their overall utility.

Fifth, a pragmatist approach to theory reveals there can be no end to theorizing. With the advent of big data, it has been argued that the end of theory is near (Anderson, 2008). The idea is that with enough data, computers will create models based on incomprehensible volumes of data, making our attempts to theorize with limited data obsolete. Theory, it is argued, will be replaced by brute prediction based on ever-growing datasets. There is little doubt that these models will be powerful. Humans, at a group level and over time, are quite predictable. But in what sense will these models contribute to human understanding? Or might they just empower some at the expense of others? Big data models will challenge our definitions of theory and understanding (Boyd & Crawford, 2012). Does a prediction, created by an algorithm, constitute understanding? No. Theory is not just for prediction – that is only a narrow technocratic interest. Theories are also for providing insight and empowering human activity (see Chapter 9). Understanding must be "for humans." Human understanding requires vivid metaphors and mental simulations anchored in the taken-for-granted activities of daily life.

Finally, because social theories do not merely describe the world but are also part of the world (having social consequences), research is necessarily entwined in ethics (see Chapter 8). From a pragmatist standpoint, it is artificial to separate knowledge from values (Brinkmann, 2010, 2013; Putnam, 1995). Theory enables acting on the world, on others, and on one oneself (e.g., predicting, nudging, influencing, rewarding, judging). To create a social science theory that is ethical, Cornish (2020) advocates the acid test of being able to present the theory to the people on the receiving end of it and to ensure that they do not feel undermined, objectified, or otherwise disempowered by the theory. One way to ensure that theories orient to a broad range of interests is to ensure broad participation in the creation and/or evaluation of the theory. Indeed, because theories of social behavior do not "mirror" the world and instead are enabling/disabling tools in the world, they are more likely to be successful if they have buy-in from those impacted by them.

3.6 Impoverishing versus Enriching Theory

All theories are incomplete. Theorizing any phenomenon necessarily entails simplification. The world is infinitely rich; from the macroscopic to the microscopic, from the natural world to the human domain, there is fractal complexity (Abbott, 2000; Kauffman, 1996). Theory entails a "conquest of abundance" (Feyerabend, 2001), namely, pressing the infinite richness of the world through the procrustean bed of human understanding. Chairs are talked about in general terms, but there is no such chair; each chair is particular. Eggs are interchangeable and come in boxes of six, but each egg is unique. Each falling rock and gathering crowd is unique. Theories, from gravity to crowd psychology, are conceptualized in ideal terms, but the ideal is a nonexistent simplification. Privileging abstract simplifications over the social world's blooming complexity is impoverishing. Pragmatism is enriching because it embraces particularity, contextualism, and open-endedness.

From a realist standpoint, the incompleteness and impoverishment of theories vis-à-vis the abundance of human experience is a disheartening anomaly. However, from a pragmatist standpoint, this is unproblematic because theories (like words and numbers) are not meant to "mirror" nature; rather, they are tools for human action. Perfect correspondence between our models and the world would entail models as rich, abundant, and complex as the world itself, providing no aid to human action. Models enable human action precisely because they simplify. Words, numbers, and theories abstract regularities in our interactions with the world, providing a necessarily imperfect but an increasingly good enough model for guiding humans by taming, to some extent, the uncertainties of the future.

Although theories simplify the world in terms of description, they enrich it in terms of practice. Rejecting the separation between description (words, numbers, theories) and the world, between the map and the terrain, pragmatism conceptualizes the theory as a new growth within the terrain. Good theories genuinely create new possibilities within the world. "May not our descriptions," James (1907, p. 256) writes, "be themselves important additions to reality?" The key insight is that theories "loop" back into the world, are part of the world, and change the world (Hacking, 1995). Theories in natural science rarely change the phenomena they describe, but they do change the world by enabling, for example, nuclear reactions. Theories in the social sciences have the added potential to interact with the phenomena they describe, such as when people are made aware of a particular bias and thus alter their behavior (Nasie et al., 2014).

To conceptualize social research as the mere pursuit of Truth is impoverishing because it fails to appreciate the role of social research in contributing to the truths of tomorrow (Gergen, 1973, 2015). Stimulus–response theories created institutions based on reward and punishment. Utility maximizing theories appeal to and cultivate self-interest. Theories that emphasize our limited capacity processing support the techniques of nudging. Theories that focus on collaborative creativity yield new techniques for working together. Each of these theories have been used to create institutions and practices within which lives are lived. Do these theories make the most of human potential? Are we making theories that enable people to help each other, show gratitude, build social connections, and find meaning in life? A pragmatist approach requires taking responsibility for the theories we create (see Chapters 8 and 9). "The world," James (1907, p. 257) writes, "stands really malleable, waiting to receive its final touches at our hands." Thus, a pragmatist approach to social research shifts the question away from what people and society *are* and toward what they could become.

CHAPTER 4

Creating Questions

"Alright," said Deep Thought. "The Answer to the Great Question..."
"Yes...!"
"Of Life, the Universe and Everything..." said Deep Thought.
"Yes...!"
"Is..." said Deep Thought, and paused.
"Yes...!"
"Is..."
"Yes...!!!...?"
"Forty-two," said Deep Thought, with infinite majesty and calm.

Adams (2017, p. 180)

All human knowledge is anchored in human activity, and, without it, knowledge becomes meaningless. In *The Hitchhiker's Guide to the Galaxy* (Adams, 2017), a science fiction novel, the supercomputer Deep Thought is asked the ultimate question: What is the meaning of life, the universe, and everything? After computing for over seven million years, Deep Thought produces the answer: forty-two. An absurd answer to a fundamentally flawed question. The question is too ambitious. The question and answer are meaningless because they are not anchored in any frame of reference, such as a human interest (see Chapter 9). Thus, there is no criteria for assessing the answer.

In Chapter 3, we conceptualized theory as a tool (i.e., map or model) that enables human activity. Theories can thus be evaluated in terms of the activity enabled (or disabled). The question is not "what is the best map in absolute terms?" but rather "what is the best map for getting from A to B?" Without knowing what we are trying to do, or where we are trying to go, building a model is meaningless. What does the theory-as-tool enable us to do? What do we want the theory to enable us to do? And how can we find a theory that can enable us to do something new and exciting? More fundamentally, what is our interest in the world, and how should we convert this into guiding research questions?

The guiding proposal for this chapter is that *research is as much about creating questions as answering questions*. Most research methodology is focused on answering questions, yet, often, the most significant scientific breakthroughs (especially in social science) are characterized by asking new questions. The routine operation of science, what Kuhn (1962) characterized as "normal science," entails routine work on unsurprising questions that refine understanding within a paradigm. However, scientific breakthroughs, which Kuhn (1962) characterized as "revolutionary science," entail asking new questions, which launch science in a new direction. But where do these exciting new questions come from?

In this chapter, we examine the types of questions that guide research, distinguishing qualitative and quantitative questions. We differentiate between inductive, deductive, and abductive questions. Then, we consider how new questions arise: the role of data, logic, and human creativity. We conclude the chapter with pragmatist heuristics for creating insightful and useful research questions.

4.1 Qualitative versus Quantitative Research

Human interests are operationalized in research through questions. The research question expresses the will to know and do. Methodologies, both qualitative and quantitative, are tools for addressing questions. So what is the relationship between questions and methods? What is the range of possible questions? And which methods are best suited for which type of questions?

4.1.1 Incommensurable Paradigms?

It has been argued that qualitative and quantitative methods are incommensurable. Qualitative research focuses on contextualized meanings and interpretation, whereas quantitative research focuses on decontextualized variables and statistics (Coxon, 2005; Flick, 2002; Morgan, 2007; Power et al., 2018). Each makes a different assumption about what should be studied: measurable quanta for quantitative methods and interpretable qualia for qualitative methods (Shweder, 1996). One benefit of this incommensurability argument is that it has enabled the development of qualitative methods with tailored quality criteria (Bauer & Gaskell, 2000). As a result, the field of qualitative research has burgeoned to address questions that are beyond the scope of quantitative methods. To ignore these differences, to try and reduce one approach to the other, would be to ignore the added value of each method (Denzin, 2012).

The strong incommensurability argument maintains that qualitative and quantitative methods stem from fundamentally different paradigms. Quantitative methods stem from realist and postpositivist paradigms, while qualitative methods stem from more constructionist paradigms (Guba & Lincoln, 1994). Building on this epistemological alignment, some authors have argued that mixed methods stem from a pragmatist paradigm (Feilzer, 2010; Morgan, 2007).

However, the incommensurability argument should not be overstated. Epistemology does not determine method; one can conduct realist qualitative research and constructionist quantitative research (Onwuegbuzie & Leech, 2005). Furthermore, focusing on what is actually done reveals that qualitative data are often analyzed quantitatively and quantitative results often require qualitative interpretation. Exceptions to any claimed essential differences abound. Qualitative research often makes frequency claims (e.g., "most participants," "some interviewees," "rarely observed"). Equally, quantitative research often hinges on qualitative assessments of validity (e.g., face validity, expert raters, human-labeled gold standard data). Accordingly, the qualitative/quantitative distinction has been described as incoherent and misleading (Krippendorff, 2019; Sinclair & Rockwell, 2016). At best, the terms "qualitative" and "quantitative" refer to family resemblances, and at worst, they are intergroup affiliations (Coxon, 2005). In either case, the idea of incommensurability is a barrier to mixed methods research (Morgan, 2007) that undermines the credibility of social science research (Onwuegbuzie & Leech, 2005). Mixed methods research argues that qualitative and quantitative methods are not incommensurable despite providing different insights. Indeed, they can be combined in nonduplicative and genuinely synergistic ways precisely because they serve distinct purposes.

A pragmatist approach contributes to differentiating qualitative and quantitative research by recognizing that each method addresses different questions. In one sense, the methods are incommensurable because they do different things and address different questions. A quantitative question about whether there is a between-group difference on a measure cannot, or at least should not, be tackled using qualitative methods. Equally, a qualitative question about how people pragmatically close conversations does not afford a quantitative approach. Nonetheless, despite this incommensurability of purpose, qualitative and quantitative methods are commensurable in other ways. Precisely because they do different things, they are chained together to ask sequences of questions (see Chapter 6). For example, the question "what is it?" and "how frequent is it?" are qualitative and quantitative questions that are nonduplicative and that synergize together.

4.1.2 The Integration Challenge

The core challenge of mixed methods theory is to conceptualize how qualitative and quantitative methods can be combined to produce insights that are not reducible to either method (Fetters & Freshwater, 2015a). This "integration challenge" goes beyond the idea that one has to choose either a qualitative-constructionist or quantitative-realist paradigm (Brown & Dueñas, 2020). Instead, it shifts the focus onto how methods can be productively combined. Addressing the integration challenge is essential for legitimating mixed methods research as adding value beyond what qualitative and quantitative research can do alone (Johnson et al., 2007) and creating guidance for mixed methods researchers to maximize synergies.

A foundational concept for theorizing integration is the metaphor of triangulation (Denzin, 1970). In navigation and geographic survey work, triangulation refers to calculating an unknown point by drawing a triangle with two known points and then using trigonometry to calculate the unknown location. When applied to qualitative and quantitative methods, the idea is that the findings from each method are compared for either validation or enrichment (Hussein, 2009; Moran-Ellis et al., 2006). Triangulation for validation assumes that the results common to both methods have high validity. Triangulation for enrichment assumes that the results found with only one method are not necessarily low in validity but, rather, may reflect a different aspect of (or perspective on) the phenomenon. Validation is duplicative (both methods converge), while enrichment is additive (each method contributes something different).

However, the concept of triangulation has received criticism for being a relatively static geometric metaphor (Fetters & Molina-Azorin, 2017a). The idea of triangulation fails to capture the generative and dynamic aspects of mixing methods. For example, in a review of mixed methods research Boeije and colleagues (2013) found that in addition to validation (e.g., for instrument development) and enrichment (e.g., by providing illustrations and nuance), mixed methods studies often enabled speculating about underlying mechanisms and generating plausible theories. That is to say, integrating (rather than triangulating) methods can reveal contradictions (Greene et al., 1989) and puzzling discrepancies (Bryman, 2006) that spur theory-building.

The core rationale for mixing methods is that it should add value beyond what either method can contribute alone (Fetters & Freshwater, 2015a). The challenge is to specify the relationships between the methods, data, and findings so that the synergy is more than accidental (Moran-Ellis et al., 2006). To this end, Fetters and Molina-Azorin (2017b) identified fifteen dimensions of possible integration, including philosophical, theoretical, researcher, team, literature, sampling, design, research aims, data collection, analysis, and interpretation (see also Schoonenboom & Johnson, 2017). These insights direct attention toward the nodal points at which integration occurs, thus potentially isolating how integration can yield more than the sum of the parts (Åkerblad et al., 2021).

4.1.3   A Pragmatist Approach

A pragmatist approach can conceptualize not only how qualitative and quantitative methods are different but also why integrating them can be synergistic. While other paradigms bring into focus social justice (the transformative paradigm; Mertens, 2007) and compatibility (critical realism; Shannon-Baker, 2016), the pragmatist paradigm emphasizes the research purpose (i.e., what they actually achieve via research questions, hypotheses, aims, goals, and objectives).

At its core, pragmatism is a method for making ideas clear and distinct by focusing on their consequences (Peirce, 1878). Since the birth of philosophy, there have been debates about the meaning of truth, beauty, God, and so on. The tendency has been to rely on axioms and first principles. Pragmatism eschews this approach, instead grounding meaning, and by extension philosophy and science, in human activity. According to James (1907, p. 22), it entails "looking away from first things, principles, 'categories', supposed necessities; and of looking towards last things, fruits, consequences." For pragmatism, all beliefs, theories, and ideas are guides for action (Cornish & Gillespie, 2009). Simply put, meaning lies in consequences. The meaning of a bike is cycling; the meaning of food is eating; and, by extension, the meaning of a research method is in what it does.

Pragmatism is particularly suited to mixed methods research because it values each method for its contribution (Morgan, 2007). Thus, it offers an alternative to postpositivism and constructionism (Feilzer, 2010). Pragmatism is inclusive because, in the words of James (1907, p. 31), it has "no obstructive dogmas, no rigid cannons of what shall count as proof" and "will consider any evidence." Instead of asking whether methods are epistemologically commensurable, pragmatism asks what each method contributes to the problem at hand. "Pragmatists," Feilzer (2010, p. 14) writes, "do not 'care' which methods they use as long as the methods chosen have the potential of answering what it is one wants to know."

A pragmatist approach can contribute to the integration challenge. Instead of focusing on the rationales for mixed methods research in general (i.e., validating, enriching, developing, explaining), the pragmatist approach directs attention to the underlying qualitative and quantitative purposes, specifically to how these are combined. Thus, in contrast to the many typologies that differentiate qualitative and quantitative methods (Coxon, 2005; Sale et al., 2002), we focus on what these methods are used for within the broader logic of the research (see also Denscombe, 2021). Our aim is not to characterize qualitative and quantitative methods according to essential criteria or even identify family resemblances (Morgan, 2018). We aim to differentiate qualitative and quantitative methods in terms of what they are used for.

4.2 Differentiating Qualitative and Quantitative Research Questions

Charles Saunders Peirce (1955) identified three types of inference: induction, deduction, and abduction. Induction is based on learning from empirical observation, deduction is based on using prior experience and theories, and abduction entails speculating about possible theories. Induction seeks unbiased observation, deduction seeks logical consistency, and abduction seeks explanation. Peirce (1955) argued that all reasoning, whether in daily life or science, comprises an interplay of these three elementary forms of inference. For example, to address a problem, one usually needs to attend to particularities (induction), utilize prior experience (deduction), and make creative leaps (abduction).

Peirce's (1955) three inference types provide a framework for conceptualizing the breadth of possible research questions. Table 4.1 uses induction, deduction, and abduction to conceptualize qualitative and quantitative research purposes. There are three purposes for both qualitative (describing phenomena, theoretical framing, generating explanations) and quantitative (measuring phenomena, testing hypotheses, exploring associations) methods, and each has distinguishable questions, contributions, and indicative analyses. This typology is meant to be prescriptive rather than descriptive; it identifies what each method should be used for. Researchers can conceivably address any question with any method, but good research entails matching the method to the question (Bauer & Gaskell, 2000). This typology attempts to match recommended purposes, questions, and indicative analyses. The following subsections describe each inference type and the associated qualitative and quantitative purposes.

Table 4.1 *Typology of qualitative and quantitative research purposes*

		Induction Observing with limited theory	**Deduction** Expecting based on a theory	**Abduction** Creating new theory
Qualitative	Purpose	Describing phenomena	Theoretical framing	Generating explanations
	Questions	What is X? How do they do X? What happened? What is the experience of X? What are the marginalized views?	Does idea X provide insight? Does X occur as expected in context Y? Is X different because of Y? Does typology X fit the data? Do cases differ as expected?	Why is X? What might cause X? Why was X not present? How might X change if Y? What process might underlie X?
	Contributions	Detailed descriptions, categories, summaries, particulars, actors' accounts, subjective experiences	A lens for viewing the data, linkages between observation and the literature, categorizations based on the literature	Explanations, research questions, novel theory, new hypotheses, synthesizing insights
	Analyses	Thematic analysis, grounded theory, interpretive phenomenological analysis, thick description	Conversation analysis, dialogical analysis, theoretically motivated observation, comparative case studies	Abductive analysis, root-cause analysis, investigating outliers, problematizing, explanatory case studies
Quantitative	Purpose	Measuring phenomena	Testing theory	Exploring explanations
	Questions	Is measure X reliable and valid? How frequent is X? Does X change over time? What are the attitudes toward X? What statistical model of X emerges?	Is X associated with Y? Does Z mediate the association? Does Y predict X? Does manipulation Y increase X? Do the data fit model X?	What is associated with X? Does anything predict X? Might Y cause these clusters? Are there any possible mediators? Is a confounding variable missing?
	Contributions	Frequencies, descriptive statistics, differences, changes over time, clustered data, data-driven models	Associations, predictors, probabilities, causal evidence, statistical evidence for/against a theory	Plausible relationships, new hypotheses, multivariate visualizations, research questions, predictions, potential causes
	Analyses	Quantification, descriptive exploratory data analysis, content analysis, attitude measurement, exploratory factor analysis, unsupervised modeling	Null hypothesis testing, one-tailed tests, Bayesian inference, experiments, confirmatory factor analysis, simulations, tests on out-of-sample data	Correlation tables, heatmaps, speculative data analysis, within sample statistical modeling

4.2.1   *Inductive Questions*

Induction entails moving from the observation of regularities to a general statement. For example, if one observes a class in session every Monday at noon in room 1A, one infers the rule that there is always a class on Mondays at noon in room 1A. Induction is quintessentially empirical. The prototypical case is that, given previous observations, one infers that the sun always rises in the east. Induction starts with observation and builds theory bottom-up, remaining as close as possible to the data. Inductive research can be either qualitative or quantitative.

Describing Phenomena. Qualitative inductive research contributes thick description, using words to richly document a phenomenon, including its variants and relation to context. It often entails understanding the subjective world of others. Qualitative inductive questions include: What is X? How do they do X? What is the experience of X? Contributions to these questions are evaluated in terms of the subtlety of the description, reflexivity in observation, and participation of the researched. Ideally, the observations form an interlocking web that richly conveys what happened, people's beliefs and practices, and subjective experiences.

Measuring Phenomena. Quantitative inductive research focuses on measuring observables and abstract constructs using counts, ranks, and scaled scores. Measurement necessarily makes theoretical assumptions about the phenomenon (e.g., identifying valid observable indicators of a phenomenon, determining the most appropriate type of measurement), but it aims to foreground the phenomenon rather than the theory. Measuring questions include: Is measure X reliable and valid? How frequent is X? What statistical model of X emerges? Contributions to these questions are usually evaluated in terms of operationalization, sampling, reliability, and validity. Ideally, a measure captures what it claims to measure and can be generalized to a population.

Inductive research is often devalued as merely descriptive (Gerring, 2012). But detailed observation is the basis of science (Rozin, 2009). When we encounter a strange object, we look at it from different angles, pick it up, and squeeze it to ground our emerging understanding in empirical experiences (Blumer, 1969). Preconception is a liability for induction, potentially suppressing peculiarity (Feyerabend, 2001). The aim is to be "open" to the data, to be sensitive to peculiarity, and to be willing to be surprised. Science without induction would produce concepts disconnected from experience. But science based only on induction would cease to have bold and ambitious theories.

4.2.2   *Deductive Questions*

Deduction entails moving from a general statement, or assumption, to a logically implied conclusion. For example, knowing the finding that classes have been observed in room 1A on Mondays at noon, one expects this to be the case next Monday at noon. The quintessential deduction is a syllogism. All men are mortal (first premise), Socrates is a man (second premise), and therefore, Socrates is mortal (conclusion). Given the theory (first premise) and the observation (second premise), one can deduce the empirically verifiable hypothesis that Socrates will eventually die. Deduction is rationalist; it is what Descartes used to argue that his own doubting was indubitable. Deductive research starts with expectations based on the literature (given X and Y we expect Z) and logic (theory A predicts X, but theory B predicts Y; which is right?). Again, it has both qualitative and quantitative variants.

Theoretical Framing. Qualitative deductive research entails using theory to frame or guide inquiry. Framing uses theory as a conceptual lens, sensitizing the researcher to observable, but conceptual, phenomena. It includes, for example, using theories of conversation, impression management, or nonverbal behavior to analyze a face-to-face interaction. Typical framing questions include: Does idea X provide insight? Does typology X fit the data? Do cases differ as expected? Contributions to these questions are evaluated in terms of how suited the theory is to the phenomenon, whether the framing produces insight, and whether the theory is being overextended, oversimplified, or overly imposed.

Testing Hypotheses. Quantitative deductive research focuses on testing, namely, using theory (i.e., the literature) to specify an expectation that can be compared to observations. The classic case is null hypothesis testing, where a falsifiable statement about the relationship between variables is stated before the research is conducted and then statistics are used to calculate the likelihood of the observed results. Typical testing questions include: Is X associated with Y? Does Z mediate the association? Do the data fit model X? Contributions to these questions are evaluated in terms of the logic that leads to the expectation, priors, operationalization, and potentially confounding variables.

Deductive research is a mainstay of qualitative and quantitative research (Scheel et al., 2020; Tavory & Timmermans, 2014). Deduction is powerful because it leverages the literature (previous studies and theories) so that the research does not start anew but builds on prior insights. We see farther than our predecessors not because we have better vision but because we stand upon their shoulders (John of Salisbury, 1159). Science without deduction would cease to be cumulative. But science based only on deduction would yield deductions entirely disconnected from practical experience.

4.2.3   Abductive Questions

Abduction entails reasoning from observation and prior expectations to forge a new theory beyond both. For example, observing a class in room 1A on Mondays at noon but finding that there is no class on a particular Monday at noon, one generates the plausible explanation that there might be something called a "timetabling department" that has changed the rules or a thing called "term time" that suspends the rule. In either case, abduction explains the anomaly by introducing an idea outside the data (i.e., the timetabling department, term time). Abduction often begins with a disruptive fact or contradiction (Tavory & Timmermans, 2014); the outcome is an explanation that, although not in the data, explains the data. Einstein's theory of general relativity explained observables with nonobservables (i.e., spacetime). Darwin's theory of evolution postulated a mechanism he did not observe (i.e., natural selection). What makes abduction inferential (rather than unconstrained imagination) is that a "hypothesis cannot be admitted, even as a hypothesis, unless it be supposed that it would account for the facts" (Peirce, 1955, p. 151).

> A mass of facts is before us. We go through them. We examine them. We find them a confused snarl, an impenetrable jungle. We are unable to hold them in our minds. We endeavor to set them down upon paper; but they seem so multiplex intricate that we can neither satisfy ourselves that what we have set down represents the facts, nor can we get any clear idea of what it is that we have set down. But suddenly, while we are poring over our digest of the facts and are endeavoring to set them into order, it occurs to us that if we were to assume something to be true that we do not know to be true, these facts would arrange themselves luminously. That is abduction. (Peirce, 1992, pp. 531–532)

Generating Explanations. Qualitative abductive research is widespread and aims to generate explanations and theories (Power et al., 2018). Being close to raw data, observing particularities, and being relatively free to approach the phenomenon from multiple theoretical standpoints make qualitative research fertile soil for generating plausible explanations (Tavory & Timmermans, 2014). Typical questions include: Why is X? What might cause X? What process might underlie X? Contributions to these questions are not judged by the logic of derivation (deduction) or by the rigor of the process (induction). It does not matter if the abductive leap occurs while lucid dreaming or sitting in the bath; what matters is whether it aids understanding, chimes with prior theories, explains the puzzling observations, and yields productive lines of action.

Exploring Explanations. Quantitative abductive research aims to stimulate ideas by exploring relationships within data. Although often undervalued relative to hypothesis testing, exploring the associations between measures can spur the creation of new hypotheses firmly grounded in data (Tukey, 1977). Typical exploring questions include: What is associated with X? Does anything predict X? Is a confounding variable missing? Contributions to these questions, as with qualitative abduction, are evaluated not in terms of the rigor of the observations or the logic of the deduction but in the fruitfulness of the emergent insights.

Abductive research has received little theorization, possibly because it entails a creative leap outside standardizable procedures (Tavory & Timmermans, 2014). However, induction and deduction are insufficient to explain most scientific breakthroughs in the natural (e.g., heliocentrism, theory of natural selection, dark matter, the structure of the double helix) or social (e.g., equality, feminism, power, impression management, ideology, culture) sciences. Abduction is aided by sensitivity to contradictions and anomalies, and openness to revising one's expectations. In short, abduction thrives when there is a puzzle to solve. Science without abduction would cease to have revolutions. But science built solely on abduction would perpetually introduce new ideas without any criteria for evaluating them.

4.2.4   Matching Questions to Methods

A pragmatist approach to research questions starts with the insight that methods are tools for action. Instead of trying to distinguish methods from first principles, methods are differentiated in terms of their research purposes.

The typology in Table 4.1 guides when to use qualitative, quantitative, and mixed methods. Scholars have characterized differences in epistemology (Denzin, 2012) and subject matter (Shweder, 1996) and distinguished family resemblances (Coxon, 2005; Morgan, 2018). But we propose a contingency table of when to use qualitative, quantitative, and mixed methods. Qualitative methods can describe phenomena, provide theoretical framing, and generate explanations. Quantitative methods can measure phenomena, test hypotheses, and search for explanations. Mixed methods are necessary when research benefits from multiple purposes (e.g., describing a phenomenon to measure it better, generating hypotheses about why an experiment produced surprising results). Differentiating these purposes can guide researchers in selecting suitable methods for the problem they are addressing. This can help researchers avoid the "methodological monologic" described by Bauer and Gaskell (2000, p. 338):

> The hammer is not well indicated for certain tasks – repairing a water pipe, for example. The skillful person will select the appropriate tool for the particular task. But if the person only knows how to handle the hammer, then all problems of fixing things in the household become a matter of hammer and nail. This implies that proper indication necessitates the awareness of and competence in using different methodological tools. To transform every piece of social research into a set of interviews or a discourse analysis, or for that matter an experiment, is to fall into the trap of methodological monologic.

Differentiating qualitative and quantitative methods in this way gives each method a separate domain of legitimacy. From this standpoint, asking whether qualitative methods are better than quantitative methods, or vice versa, is like asking whether a hammer is better than a saw. It depends on what you want to do. Moreover, to assume that social science can get by with only one of these methods is to dismiss an entire row of indicative questions in Table 4.1. Both qualitative and quantitative methods are legitimate because they are the best tools we currently have for specific purposes.

4.3 Heuristics for Creating Questions

Popper (1934) influentially separated the context of discovery (creating hypotheses) from the context of justification (testing hypotheses). He argued that the philosophy of science and epistemology related only to the context of justification. "The act of conceiving or inventing a theory," Popper (1934, p. 7) wrote, "seems to me neither to call for logical analysis nor to be susceptible to it." Popper's focus was on theory testing, and specifically falsifying a theory, without concern for how the theory was created. This influential view has created a huge gap in the literature. While the literature on hypothesis testing fills many library aisles, there are only a handful of publications on creating questions worth testing. However, creating questions is central to scientific progress, especially paradigm shifts.

The gap in the literature is, perhaps, as much a function of a lack of progress as of willful neglect. As Jaccard and Jacoby (2020, p. 52) write, in a book on creating theory, "there is no simple strategy for generating good ideas or explanations." Despite several academics tackling question creation, no eloquent theory or multistep procedure can guide researchers infallibly toward a profound insight.

A pragmatist approach is comfortable with this uncertainty (Rorty, 1989). Instead of any guarantees of insight, we only have tips, tricks, and heuristics – a bricolage of suggestions that have been fruitful in the past. We begin by reviewing these heuristics in terms of Peirce's (1955) distinction between induction, deduction, and abduction. We then argue that these heuristics are not mutually exclusive, and thus moving between inductive, deductive, and abductive heuristics is a potent context for discovery.

4.3.1   Creating Questions Inductively

Although high-quality inductive research, such as detailed observation, should be the bedrock of science, it is disappointingly rare in social science (Blumer, 1969; Gerring, 2012) and psychology (Rozin, 2001; Rubin & Donkin, 2022). Psychology has been overly focused on deductive development of hypotheses and subsequent confirmatory statistical testing, while devaluing nonconfirmatory or exploratory research (Krpan, 2022; Scheel et al., 2020). But confirmatory research should not be rushed into; it is the last step in a sequence of questions that begins with patient and detailed description and concept formation (Scheel et al., 2020). Without these rigorously inductive descriptions, concepts risk becoming vague, disconnected from everyday life, and low in validity despite being reliable. If the creation of new questions comes only from deduction, then it is overly determined by the literature and insufficiently attentive to our continually evolving practical problems.

Beyond psychology, detailed description is widespread (Rozin, 2009). Darwin's theory of evolution by a process of natural selection did not arise through deductive hypothesis testing; rather, it rests upon numerous patient descriptions. Similarly, Crick and Watson's breakthrough model of the double helix is, first and foremost, a description. Turning to the social sciences, conversation analysis (Schegloff, 2007) is also built on elaborate and painstakingly detailed descriptions. In sociology, Goffman's (1959) groundbreaking analysis of self-presentation in everyday life is also based on rich descriptions of human interaction. Psychology, in contrast, is rushing headlong into experimentation without extensive description (Rozin, 2009; Rubin & Donkin, 2022). Such premature enthusiasm for confirmatory research, with a disregard for descriptive research, is likely counterproductive for a young science, like psychology, that is striving for scientific legitimacy (Krpan, 2022; Scheel et al., 2020). It can, for example, lead to overextended theories that fail to replicate, and which thus foster skepticism in psychology (Baucal et al., 2020; Mede et al., 2021; Open Science Collaboration, 2015).

Blumer (1969), a neopragmatist building on the work of George Herbert Mead, used the term "inspection" to conceptualize the inductive phase of social research. Inspection aims to describe the peculiarity of a phenomenon. Consider encountering a strange, suggestive, and confusing physical object:

> [W]e may pick it up, look at it closely, turn it over as we view it, look at it from this or that angle, raise questions as to what it might be, go back and handle it again in the light of our questions, try it out, and test it in one way or another. (Blumer, 1969, p. 44)

Inspection tries to put aside assumptions and expectations. It entails attending carefully to the empirical particulars. Inspection is part of our natural everyday attitude, and it is also a hallmark of science.

Inspection can be both qualitative and quantitative. For example, inspecting people talking could include counting the number of participants or conversational turns, noting a peculiar tone of voice, or understanding the content of what was said. Qualitative inductive research is good for close-up inspection, rich description, revealing practices, identifying heuristics, and finding puzzles (Becker, 1998; Crano et al., 2014). Quantitative inductive research identifies differences between groups, changes over time, and outliers (Jaccard & Jacoby, 2020). And combining these inductive methods can produce added synergies. For example, one might start by using qualitative research to describe a feature of talk (such as conversational repairs; Schegloff, 1992) and then quantitative research to measure the frequency of the phenomenon (conversational repairs occur every 1.4 minutes; Dingemanse et al., 2015).

Inductive inspection helps generate questions because it ensures that the research is firmly anchored in what is going on. It can reveal the boundary conditions for a previously established phenomenon (Jaccard & Jacoby, 2020), a challenging or conflicting observation (Crano et al., 2014), or simply a novel event (Becker, 1998). The critical ingredient is being attuned to peculiarity (Becker, 1998; Crano et al., 2014; Jaccard & Jacoby, 2020; McGuire, 1997). In so far as inductive inspection conforms to expectation, it yields data, and in so far as it disrupts expectation, it yields disruptive data that can generate new theory (Chapter 3).

Valuable sources for inductive question generation include participant observation, deviant case analysis, biographies, diaries, news stories, historical events, introspection, role play, and even fictional stories (Jaccard & Jacoby, 2020). It can also be valuable to talk to practitioners to understand the frontline issues and the existing practical solutions (Jaccard & Jacoby, 2020). Going further in this direction, participatory action research is a useful methodology for harnessing and building on the insight of communities to generate novel questions (McIntyre, 2008).

Case studies are a particularly compelling method for generating research questions inductively. Too often, research cuts up phenomena in unnatural ways, with the actual sequence of events suppressed. In qualitative research, quotations from people unfamiliar with one another, perhaps even from different regions, are presented side by side, without regard for the sequencing of what was said. In quantitative research, the focus is on central tendencies and averages (which may not exist in any single case), with outliers discounted or even removed. Case studies, in contrast, focus on a singular event and conceptualize it holistically – as a system of people and parts. There is no statistical average or central tendency; there just is what happened. This bedrock level of "what actually happened" is fertile soil for creating new questions (Eisenhardt, 1989). Why? Because theories can become detached from actual events. And despite the sometimes-low status of descriptive research, observations of particulars (i.e., what actually happened) should always be privileged over abstract theory (i.e., what is expected to happen). Thus, juxtaposing grand theories with specifics can reveal oddities, which grow into disruptive facts, or anomalies, becoming the wellspring of a new idea.

4.3.2   Creating Questions Deductively

Deduction is often proposed to be the ideal method for creating questions. Theories are used to create research questions and hypotheses that are tested empirically (Popper, 1969). The key to generating questions deductively is conceptual analysis, especially thinking through the logical implications of theories (Jaccard & Jacoby, 2020; McGuire, 1997).

A common approach to deductive question generation is to take an established concept and identify subtypes and variants, perhaps manifesting in peculiar contexts (Crano et al., 2014). This is aided by defining concepts, refining concepts, challenging definitions, and speculating about subtypes and unaccounted-for variables, and introducing novel concepts (Jaccard & Jacoby, 2020). For example, the contact hypothesis (Allport,

1954) originally proposed that contact between outgroups could reduce prejudice under certain conditions. Initially, these conditions were concise: The contact should be between people of equal status, sharing a common goal, with the parties being interdependent in the achievement of the goal, and the contact should be supported by relevant laws, institutions, and customs. However, since this original formulation, the theory has been refined through numerous questions (Hewstone & Brown, 1986; Paluck et al., 2019). These refining questions include: What if the outcome of the joint activity ends in failure? What if the members of one group are not prototypical? And what about the frequency of contact? Or what about pressure to achieve the goal? What if member behavior is or is not seen to be prototypical of their group membership? What if the contact is face to face, technologically mediated, or even imagined? Such question generation is within-paradigm, leading to refinements of the original theory.

Although identifying subtypes and subconditions is widespread, it is often unsatisfying. In the case of the contact hypothesis it has been criticized for producing "an open-ended laundry-list of conditions" (Pettigrew, 1998, p. 69). Each additional condition, mediation, or variable does refine the theory, but it makes the theory conceptually weak, as it becomes a list of if-then propositions. Newell (1973) famously characterized this type of theorizing as trying to "play 20-questions with nature." That is to say, deduction is used to pose binary questions to nature that are tested with an experiment. This, Newell argues, necessarily produces fragmented "if-then" type theories. This mode of theorizing, and developing questions, is suited to testing big theories once they are in place, but it is not suited to generating big integrative theories.

A more exciting way to generate research questions deductively is to take an idea that seems obvious and investigate the alternative (Jaccard & Jacoby, 2020; McGuire, 1997). The world is rarely one-sided, and there are usually contexts in which the opposite holds. For example, Billig (1985) noted that most of the literature on social identity had focused on categorizing (i.e., grouping people into categories), and he made a compelling case for the counterbalancing process of particularizing (i.e., seeing people as individuals and not categories). Relatedly, Gillespie (2007a) shows how within moments of differentiation from outgroups there can also be moments of identification. Finally, Moscovici and colleagues (1994) observed that conformity (or majority influence) must have a counterbalancing mechanism that prevents everyone from becoming the same (i.e., total conformity), and they advanced the influential concept of minority influence. This kind of deductive theory generation is stimulated by taking theories to extremes (e.g., if there was only conformity) and then probing the processes that prevent the extreme.

A final approach to the deductive creation of research questions is to hold multiple theories in mind, such that tensions can be surfaced and competing accounts for observations can be generated (Crano et al., 2014; Jaccard & Jacoby, 2020). We can never have complete certainty in any theory, and thus it is prudent to entertain multiple possible theories. Like the lost explorers described by Midgley (2003; see Chapter 3), it is prudent to operate with multiple mental maps. The idea that a theory is infallible and timeless is an obstacle to this mode of deductive speculation because it blinds one to anomalies and leads to discarding alternative theories prematurely. When Darwin (2001) sailed on the HMS *Beagle*, he entertained both the biblical view of the earth being created a few thousand years ago and the challenging ideas of Lyell that the earth's geology was shaped over millions of years. Darwin's theory of evolution was not a direct contribution to the debate about the age of the earth, but the heretical idea that the earth was much older than traditionally assumed was necessary for him to formulate his theory of natural selection. The point is that, given that theories are tools (Chapter 3), more theories enable more diverse ways of thinking about and acting on observations. In short, more paths of action in and through data increase the potential to find a novel pathway, question, or theory.

4.3.3   Creating Questions Abductively

Scientific revolutions have rarely been the result of mere induction or deduction; they have usually entailed a creative leap of abduction. The idea that the planets revolve around the sun, that evolution operates by natural selection, and that space and time are relative to the observer all entailed abductive leaps. Somewhat more controversially, but nonetheless abductively, are the social science theories that conceptualize the mind as a computer, people as utility maximizers, and languages as underpinned by a universal grammar. None of these ideas were deduced from first principles. None of them were created by merely aggregating observations. In each case, there is a creative leap of abduction that goes beyond the evidence and preexisting ideas.

Abduction entails going beyond the data to posit something that explains the data. Although Sherlock Holmes (Doyle, 1892) frequently describes his own method as deduction, it is usually abduction; there is a weaving of a pattern and the positing of a story behind the events that makes sense of the events. "Abductive inference," Krippendorff (2019, p. 38) writes, "is Sherlock Holmes's logic of reasoning." When Sherlock Holmes is confronted with the ostensibly bizarre facts of a case (e.g., the stabbed murder victim in a windowless room locked from the inside), the process of abduction is to imagine possible scenarios. The first step is to attend to the stubborn facts (e.g., the locked door, the footprints, the hesitant responses). The second step is to generate plausible explanations (e.g., was it suicide, was the victim hypnotized, might the victim have been fatally wounded and sought refuge in the room). Abduction is the process of simulating possible explanations until, like a key in a lock, the explanation fits the facts.

Creating questions abductively entails imagination. Abduction is not about what *is* (either empirically or logically); it is about what *might be*. It entails leaving behind the here and now to viscerally inhabit alternative scenarios (Zittoun & Gillespie, 2015). It brackets aside assumptions and aims to generate plausible accounts that might (or might not) explain the known facts. Often, such imagination will not provide added explanatory power. But, sometimes, it provides the seed for a new line of inquiry. Abduction is facilitated by questioning assumptions, challenging taken-for-granted theories, focusing on the most irrefutable details, and being playful in generating alternatives but harsh in evaluating them. Abduction entails tolerating competing and even incompatible theories, seeking peculiarity and anomalies, and pursuing possible lines of inquiry regardless of how surprising or heretical they are.

To generate explanations abductively, the researcher should continually ask "what?" and "why?" (Becker, 1998; Jaccard & Jacoby, 2020). First, it is important to fixate on what actually happened, the sequence of events, and the step-by-step details of the case. These details are the obstinate data to be explained. Second, each datum within the tangled mess of facts should be probed: Why did X happen? Why did Y not happen? What else could have happened? To this end, one needs to be clear about the difference between the facts to be explained (the "what") and the speculations about those facts (the "why"). As Sherlock Holmes said: "It is a capital mistake to theorize before one has data. Insensibly one begins to twist facts to suit theories, instead of theories to suit facts" (Doyle, 1892, p. 163). The "what" (or data) are firm anchor points, the "why" are speculations. The "what" should be shorn of interpretation, the "why" is enhanced by imagination. The "what" can never lead one astray, but the "why" can bring false hope, and become a chimera that inhibits progress with dead ends. The "what" is in the past, and not open to revision, while the "why" should always be open to revision.

To think creatively about the "why" – that is, to generate explanations for the "what" – can be enhanced with analogies and metaphors (Haig, 2005; Jaccard & Jacoby, 2020). As discussed in Chapter 3, human understanding is grounded in the here and now of daily practice. Metaphors pervade social science. They underpin theories in psychology (e.g., the mind as a computer; Leary, 1990), communication (e.g., the conduit metaphor of message transmission; Axley, 1984), human development (e.g., organic growth; Zittoun & Gillespie, 2020), sociology (e.g., mechanism and functionalism; Swedberg, 2020), and economics (e.g., the marketplace; McCloskey, 1995). Indeed, in this book, we have relied heavily on metaphors, such as likening theories and methods to "tools" and describing abduction as "Sherlock Holmes style" of inference. Hiding metaphors is blinding; being open about them enables discussing the potentials and pitfalls of all metaphors (Swedberg, 2020), and in so doing, one can liberate the imagination to try alternative metaphors, to see what they elucidate, prompt, and enable.

Finally, thought experiments are a particularly powerful (but often neglected) method for developing research questions abductively. Thought experiments have had a significant impact on science and have been central to several breakthroughs. Einstein (1982; Norton, 1991) famously used thought experiments, such as trying to chase light and being on a train moving at the speed of light. Searle (1982) powerfully argued against strong artificial intelligence using the thought experiment of a person in a room converting inputs into outputs using an incomprehensible rulebook. Putnam (1974) argued that meanings are not just in the mind by positing a twin earth in which everything was identical except the chemical composition of water. In the veil of ignorance thought experiment, Rawls (1971) asks how one would decide upon the rules of society before knowing one's position in society (i.e., profession, ethnicity, gender, income, wealth, social status). Thought experiments do not need to be elaborate scenarios. For almost any social phenomenon, one can engage in basic thought experiments by asking: Could this have occurred a thousand years ago? Might this occur a thousand years in the future? How would this play out in a world where everyone had perfect information, nobody lied, there was no emotion, or everyone was equal? Literature is an excellent resource for thought experiments. Franz Kafka (1915) explores what it is like to wake in the morning transformed into a huge insect. Phillip K. Dick (1962) explores what life in America might have been like if it had lost World War II. Cixin Liu (2014) examines what might happen to human society if it was known that aliens were en route and would arrive in 450 years.

While some have argued that thought experiments are merely arguments dressed up as stories (Norton, 1991), this is to underplay their value for us *as humans*. As argued in Chapter 3, knowledge is "for us" and works best when anchored in everyday life. Thought experiments are invaluable because they give us more than a dry argument, mere numbers, or prediction. Instead, they provide a visceral and meaningful simulation, anchored in an intelligible first-person perspective. They enhance our embodied identification and thus ground abstract thought in everyday human activity (Ludwig, 2007). In short, thought experiments are "intuition pumps" (Dennett, 1991, p. x) that enable us to "feel" problems from the inside, take ideas to extremes, and run simulations with impossible conditions (McGuire, 1997). This playfulness stretches the space of the possible, opening a semantic space within which abductive questions arise.

4.3.4 *Mixing Induction, Deduction, and Abduction*

It is a mistake to oppose induction, deduction, and abduction. Morgan (2007; table 2), in an otherwise excellent article, claims that a pragmatist approach focuses on abduction instead of induction (which he associates with qualitative research) or deduction (which he associates with quantitative research). But Peirce (1955, 1992) valued all three modes of inference and argued that they work best in tandem. Abandoning any mode of inference would be antipragmatist, because it would be a tribal affiliation to one form of inference; it would fail to leverage the insight that each mode of inference can provide. Peirce's (1955) differentiation between induction, deduction, and abduction is conceptual. In any practical context, these modes of inference work together, yielding synergies that cannot be reduced to any one mode of inference operating in isolation.

When trying to solve a problem, we leverage insights from the past (deduction), attend to the concrete particulars of the problem (induction), and make leaps of speculation (abduction). Peirce (1974, sec. 1.72–1.74) gives the example of Kepler's discovery of the laws of planetary motion. Throughout a long investigation, Kepler weaves together previous theory, empirical observations, and abductive reasoning to arrive at his theory. Without induction, his theory would have been disconnected from empirical observation. Without deduction, he would not have been able to frame certain observations as surprising. Without abduction, he would not have been able to leap beyond both observations and existing theory to realize that planetary orbits were elliptical rather than circular.

In social science, these three modes of inference are woven into the fabric of most empirical articles. The introduction section is usually deductive, drawing inferences from the existing literature. The empirical findings should be inductive, with inferences being based on the data collected and the analyses performed. Abductive inference is sometimes evident in a surprising research question that posits a novel angle on an established problem and sometimes evident in the interpretation of surprising findings. The key point is that these three modes of inference synergize: Deduction leverages the past to generate expectations; abduction generates ideas that escape the confines of deductive expectation; and induction tames unfounded expectations and excessive speculation.

Moving between modes of inference can help to generate research questions. This moves beyond discovering tensions between observations (induction) or between theories (deduction) and opens the possibility of discovering tensions between what is expected and what is observed, between what should be and what might be, and between what is and what could be (Jaccard & Jacoby, 2020; McGuire, 1997). The point is that moving between modes of inference opens the research process up to additional and productive tensions that can spur insight and foster new research questions.

Research questions can also be generated by moving between qualitative and quantitative methods. This is an extension of moving between modes of inference. Each mode of inference (i.e., induction, deduction, and abduction) has qualitative and quantitative variants (see Table 4.1). It has long been argued that mixing methods is a powerful means of generating new theories (Greene et al., 1989). The core idea is that integrating qualitative and quantitative methods should lead to a 1 + 1 = 3 synergy, but specifying how this occurs is challenging (Fetters & Freshwater, 2015a). The theoretical literature on mixing methods tries to identify how this creativity is more than accidental and can be traced to particular integrative strategies (Åkerblad et al., 2021) and dimensions of integration (e.g., assumptions, aims, data, interpretation; Fetters & Molina-Azorin, 2017b).

Table 4.1 differentiates both modes of inference and qualitative and quantitative methods. This provides a basis for conceptualizing emergent synergies. It is precisely because each mode of inference and method does something different, and answers different questions, that they are complementary rather than competing. Thus, these methods can be chained together to produce synergistic findings. For example, describing a phenomenon qualitatively ("what is it?") often leads to measuring the phenomenon quantitatively ("how frequent is it?"); testing a theory ("does the data cluster according to typology X?") often leads to a qualitative search for an explanation ("why did the clustering not work?"); and generating an explanation ("what might cause X?") feeds forward into testing the explanation ("does Y cause X?"). These chains of investigation are examined in detail in Chapter 6.

Mixing modes of inference, and associated methods, increases the chances for disruption. Such disruptions are central to scientific progress (Kuhn, 1962). While much science is routine, entailing fitting data to theories to flesh out a given paradigm, there are key turning points in science, revolutions, that establish new paradigms. Whether engaged in normal (i.e., within-paradigm) or revolutionary (i.e., paradigm-creating) science, the key is to be sensitive to anomalies such as disruptive observations, confounded expectations, and contradictory theories. Normal and especially revolutionary science progress by addressing such anomalies. It follows that any research practices that increase the chance of anomalies arising will advance science and lead to increasingly robust knowledge. Research that is siloed within a subdiscipline, operates with a narrow range of methods, or insulates itself from real-world practices and consequences is protecting itself from disruptive surprises and, thus, the potential for scientific progress.

4.4 Being Sensitive to Surprise

From a pragmatist standpoint, the key to creating questions is being sensitive to surprise. What does it feel like to make a discovery in social science? What is the phenomenology of an emerging insight? It is, we argue, the feeling of something odd, out of place, oversimplified, difficult to empathize with, glossed over, or otherwise puzzling; in short, it is the feeling of surprise. As we argued in Chapter 3 and will develop in Chapter 9, humans are future-oriented. Knowledge crystalizes experience from the past to prevent surprises in the future (Friston, 2010; Peirce, 1955). If we create theories to reduce surprise, it follows that being sensitive to surprises will guide us toward increasingly robust theories.

There are many sources of surprise: data, contradictory theories, daily practices, logical puzzles, and emerging phenomena. But, in each case, the phenomenological experience is the same: There is a kink in the logic, effort is required to overcome it, and the path of least resistance is to skip over it. The surprise can be accompanied by emotions of discomfort, disappointment, or even defensiveness. But this feeling of resistance, this desire to bypass the uncertainty in favor of more familiar ground, is the feeling of being at the edge of knowledge. Arguably, this is the moment of science: The deciding factor is whether one pauses and probes or whether one passes by.

Pausing and probing are done by asking questions. At the heart of science, even within the phenomenology of the moment of discovery, is turning surprises into productive research questions. Research methodology is the formalization of ways to answer questions rigorously. There is a circular dynamic: Questions beget answers, and answers beget questions. A pragmatist approach to methodology aims to make this loop more effective, creative, and ethical. Within this loop, research questions form the connecting thread, linking human interests to the consequences of knowledge and providing the criteria for choosing data (Chapter 5) and methods of analysis (Chapter 6).

CHAPTER 5

Eliciting and Transforming Data

> We must be careful not to confuse data with the abstractions we use to analyze them.
>
> William James (cited in Rice, 2007, p. iii)

The word "data" comes from Latin, where *datum* means something that is given – this term is also, incidentally, the singular for data in English. This linguistic root has led to a simplified understanding of what data represent. For many researchers, especially following the positivist tradition (see Chapter 2), data are a nonproblematized category, which includes aspects of events that are recorded and ready for analysis. And yet, there are many gaps between what is given in experience (i.e., events), raw data (the records or traces of events), transformed data (raw data that are processed), and data analysis. In the earlier quote, William James reminds us that raw data should not be confused with data that are transformed into categories, concepts, and codes; moreover, raw data always have the potential to disrupt expectations that have been shaped by theory (see also Chapter 3). The data we end up working with are far from "what is given" as a separate, static, and finite outcome. Data are transformed through research and analysis – through action (and interaction) guided by theories, questions, and interests (see Chapters 3 and 4).

Data are produced in various ways – from experiments and interviews to corpus construction – and take many forms, including numeric, text, sound, and image. We define data as the traces of experiences researchers use to address a research question. Data are the cornerstone of empirical social research. This is because they can capture experiences of breakdown or stumbling in which our theories are shaken by unexpected empirical evidence and our analytical methods prove insufficient (for the distinction between data and disruptive data, see Chapter 3). However, not all data provoke a rupture in our understanding; otherwise, the term would be relatively narrow, depending on what researchers find surprising or thought-provoking. However, we maintain that all data have the *potential* for disruption and, when adopting a pragmatism stance, we are particularly interested in exploring this potential. To this end, we argue, we need to be sensitive to the gaps or differences between phenomena, data, and analysis and, particularly in the context of new forms of data available nowadays, the importance of data construction as a recurring – not given and once and for all – process. Hence the pragmatist proposition we advance in this chapter: *Data are always transformations*.

In this chapter, we first review the different roles data have in research – as reality, as construction, as disruption – and propose to conceptualize it as a process, whereby records of a phenomenon (raw data) are collected and transformed (becoming transformed data). Importantly, for the purpose of this chapter we do not distinguish between the event as it happened (the noumena) and the experience of the event (the phenomena) and designate both using the same term. For instance, if an interview is an event, raw data can be the audio recording while transformed data start from the transcription, which entails choices (e.g., the system of transcription), and continue with the extraction of excerpts for detailed analysis and include word frequencies, which transform the raw data into numeric values. Second, we develop a classification of existing data collection methods and data types. Third, we discuss how technology has profoundly impacted data production, making large naturally occurring datasets available, including big qualitative datasets. Finally, we examine the opportunities and challenges of big qualitative data and discuss how pragmatism can help achieve these potentials and avoid the pitfalls.

5.1   What Are Data?

The vocabulary of data in psychology and social research is expansive, and it includes notions such as variable, information, fact, statistic, input, sample, population, finding, theme, and meanings. But, most of all, it includes the pervasive distinction between "quantitative" and "qualitative" data (Henderson et al., 1999; Holton & Walsh, 2016). The main difference made is thus between numerical and nonnumerical data. For example, household earnings, frequencies of the use of pronouns in a political speech, or the count of how often children interact with each other are recorded as numbers and, as such, are considered quantitative. In contrast, the drawings made by an artist, the sounds produced by an orchestra, or the words uttered to convince a friend to go bowling are considered qualitative. Data taking the form of visuals (still or moving), sounds, smells, touch, and, most of all, text (oral or written) are all considered qualitative. However, we suggest that this division is primarily analytical and often does not hold upon closer scrutiny. This is because numerical data always originate in "qualitative" experience, and all nonnumerical data can be counted and thus used in statistical analysis. In our examples, political speeches and school interactions are grounded in text, sound, touch, and so on; yet various aspects of them are quantified. Conversely, musical scores are a formal language that can easily be translated into numerical terms, but the sounds made by an orchestra and, in particular, the experience of listening to the orchestra in question are not (unless it is a digital audio recording). Quantifying the qualitative and qualitizing the quantitative are common processes within research. For most researchers, these transformations are part of the treatment or preparation of data for analysis (i.e., "moving" data from one state to another). We propose that data can change "state" as part of this processing (e.g., the movement from raw to transformed data and back again, including back and forth between qualitative and quantitative forms) and always afford further transformations depending on the research purpose and question. Thus, processes of data creation and transformation take center stage instead of being mere "data collection."

To note, there is a continuum between data transformation and data analysis but there is also a qualitative difference between them. While processing data from raw to transformed still keeps the focus on the data themselves (the main outcome is the new and transformed data), analysis moves between data and findings that answer a research question (and so the main outcome is the finding). Of course, researchers can also draw findings or conclusions from the process and outcome of data transformation but this is not their primary aim when working with data in the sense used in this chapter.

Even though data are the cornerstone of empirical research, they are often undertheorized. Methodology books usually present typologies of data rather than discuss what data are for or problematize practices of collecting and working with data. This omission goes back partially to the implicit definition of data as "what is given" and a general focus on data analysis rather than data collecting and creating. When data collection is a topic, it is primarily discussed in terms of samples and sampling methods (e.g., Devers & Frankel, 2000; Faugier & Sargeant, 1997; Marshall, 1996), although there has been some questioning of what "collection" actually entails (e.g., Backett-Milburn et al., 1999; Smagorinsky, 1995). Within these critical reflections, the notion of collecting data is regarded with suspicion given that it seems to suggest that data preexist the process of research; similarly, the established article section of "findings" to report research results suggests that conclusions are found rather than created. In contrast, pragmatism leads us to consider both data collection and data analysis as constructive processes and, in essence, data as resulting from the constrained engagement of the researcher with the world. In order to situate this latter view, we review below some common understandings of data in social science that build toward a pragmatist view of data as a process.

5.1.1   Data as Reality

Collecting data with the assumption that one is collecting aspects of a transcendental and universal Reality is peculiar to the realist traditions (in a narrow sense; Daston, 1992). Within the positivist paradigm, data are judged primarily in terms of their accuracy and truthfulness. The ostensibly independent quality of "good" data implies that it reflects reality and can be used to study phenomena in a direct, unmediated, and universal manner. This view ignores the constructed nature of data and removes the role of the researcher and the broader social and cultural context in shaping the research. This is not to say that there are no such things as "facts" or that this notion has no place in the pragmatist approach. In our post-truth and postfact context (Berentson-Shaw, 2018), truth must remain an essential criterion in science and public debate. The problem, however, is that the "data as Reality" approach is static and reductionist. It focuses on a narrow correspondence between theory and world, data and events. At the extreme, this approach equates the data collected with the phenomenon under study.

5.1.2   Data as Construction

The idea that data are constructed through research is widespread within the social sciences, especially among qualitative researchers operating within more constructionist paradigms (see Chapters 1 to 3). This approach places the researcher back into the relationship between data and world and focuses on the researcher's role in data elicitation and transformation (Carolan, 2003; Hagues, 2021). This goes beyond discussions of prompted or unprompted data, covered later in this chapter, and starts from the very decision to call specific information "data" and consider it relevant for a given research question. All the choices made following this (e.g., sampling, collection, transcription, codification, and analysis) reveal that data do not simply exist "out there," like a carving waiting to be extracted from the marble, but are produced as part of a human activity – the activity of research. Like all activity, research is guided by human interests (see Chapter 4) and mediated by culture (Wertsch, 1998); as a consequence, its tools and products are necessarily cocreations in the triangular relationship between the researcher, the phenomenon, and culture (including theories, the literature, and commonsense). Holding the view that research constructs data might sound relativist but it does not have to be – it is not "everything goes" (e.g., everything is data, all data are equal); rather, it foregrounds the mediated relation between data and events in the world.

5.1.3 Data as Disruption

Pragmatism acknowledges the constructed nature of data and the facticity of data (not in a transcendental or Real sense but as a truth of human activity). It emphasizes the potential of data to disrupt our expectations. This disruption entails both object (data) and subject (expectation). This understanding draws on the view that reflective thinking, or executive function, begins when we encounter obstacles or problems (see Dewey, 1903, 1997). In George Herbert Mead's words, "analytical thought commences with the presence of problems and the conflict between different lines of activity" (1964b, p. 7). Data that trigger analytical – and creative – thought typically originate in a conflict between our theories/assumptions and the new data encountered. Data as disruption are the unsettling of old views and thus the seed of new interpretations, which is the basis of scientific progress. However, one problem with adopting this position is that it downplays "nondisruptive" data. Nondisruptive data are essential for research because there could be no exceptions, surprises, or disruptions without established patterns, theories, and assumptions. No data are intrinsically disruptive or nondisruptive; it all depends on the research question, the theory, and the broader research assumptions. Thus, from a pragmatist standpoint, research should be clear about its guiding theories and questions and remain attentive to the disruptive potential of data.

5.1.4 Data as a Process

The guiding pragmatist insight we develop in this chapter is conceptualizing data as a process. This is the idea that data are dynamic rather than static, as something crafted rather than given. The path from data to analysis entails transformations. It is not only the case that data emerge from an initial transformation of raw data (traces or recordings of human activity) into "something" that can be analyzed (excerpts, categories, numbers) – but our relationship with data also changes in the process of research. This process should not be understood exclusively in terms of preparing data for either quantitative or qualitative analysis (Manikandan, 2010; Rubin & Rubin, 2005). It should not be confused with conducting more than one analysis on the same piece of data (for instance, using two types of statistics or employing both thematic and discursive analyses). Data as a process involves a continuous reflection on the kinds of transformations available – to consider the same data through different lenses, especially lenses that cut across the quantitative and qualitative divide. This potential for transformation rests in the fact that all raw data are *perspectival* (i.e., they can always be approached, understood, and acted upon differently, including within the same study). An online comment or an internet meme, for example, can be part of a much larger sample and coded numerically to identify patterns while, at the same time, being used for in-depth semiotic analysis. The raw data remain the same yet their "collection" and treatment are no longer static; the raw data are "processed" in various ways to afford various analyses.

In order to unpack data as a process, we need to distinguish between four distinct levels of data: (1) *the events* – the object of interest in the world, in all its complexity and tangled with other events; (2) *the record or raw data* – the traces of the events, such as archives, memories, survey scores, audio recordings, and digital footprints; (3) *processed or transformed data* – transforming the raw data to enable certain types of analyses, such as selecting excerpts, wrangling numbers, categorizing types, and quantifying qualities; and (4) *the analysis* – finding patterns or explanations by examining the transformed data using various analytic procedures, such as content analysis, correlations, discursive analysis, and linear regression. The events are facts that exist in the past. The raw data are the traces of events in the present. While the raw data are unchangeable (any change would result in transformed data), data transformation can move freely back and forth between transformations (e.g., quantification, categorization, sampling, or aggregating) and the raw data.

There are specific processes connecting, on the one hand, the event with raw data and, on the other hand, transformed data with analysis. These transformations define what data "are," and these processes are often multiple and even open-ended. For example, several steps can be taken to move from the event (e.g., the experience of going through a war) to analysis (e.g., the themes that describe this experience). For instance, memories need to be expressed orally or in writing, and voices need to be recorded and transcribed leading to numerous selections, choices, and transformations (e.g., placing the data in a table, using time stamps, level of transcription detail, number of variables). The idea of data as a process foregrounds that there are many forking paths between events in the world and data used in analyses.

For most of the twentieth century, a key challenge for research was getting records of events of interest. In quantitative research, obtaining survey data or conducting experiments was generally more time-consuming than running the analyses on the resultant data. While the challenge of finding the right participants or alternative sources remains in place (Macnab et al., 2007), the processes of recording, transcribing, and doing descriptive analysis have been simplified nowadays by a series of technological developments, not least the invention of computers and the general availability of research software. Today we are likely to record or hold too much raw data (entering the infamous "data dungeons"; Bauer & Gaskell, 2000) while the range of analytical methods have expanded and started to include highly technical procedures (e.g., natural language processing). This reversal – the relative accessibility of data, including rise of big qualitative data, and the difficulty of analyzing it – is accentuated by another type of gap, that between data collection and data analysis.

Traditional methods like experiments and surveys and, to some extent, interviews imply (or are particularly suited to) specific analytic strategies, such as comparisons of means, correlations, and thematic analyses. These traditional methods tend to collect data that are prestructured for a specific type of analysis. What is recorded in experiments and surveys typically takes a numerical form. For example, complex actions and interactions are reduced to categorical outcomes. Interviews allow for broader analyses, but they are challenging to scale up given the resource demands of interviewing and detailed transcription. This immediate connection between record and analysis, both quantitative and qualitative, obscures the processual nature of data because the time spent between data collection and analysis is reduced. However, digitalization has changed this dynamic. There are few "ready-made" methods for analyzing naturally occurring big qualitative data and the often-rich associated data. For example, a social media post has metadata (e.g., time, location, user details) and response data (e.g., replies, upvotes, circulation). Digitization means that the "space" between records and analysis widened, records are increasingly abundant, but they are also messy. Naturally occurring traces have high ecological validity; however, they often require extra processing to become suited for research (e.g., sampling, cleaning, joining, enumerating, and wrangling). This new context lends itself to pragmatist approaches (Chapters 1 and 2), systemic theories (Chapter 3), abductive questions (Chapter 4), and, as we shall see next, more complex and creative forms of analysis (Chapters 6 and 7). Most of all, they demand a deeper reflection on data elicitation and data types, the two topics we move to next.

5.2   Data Elicitation and Data Types

Traditionally, social sciences research has understood data as something to be "collected," either in the field or in the lab. Beyond the fact that this distinction has lost a lot of its meaning with the advent of research done online – with experiments moving into people's homes and interviews taking place with researchers still in their lab – it raises more fundamental questions about what constitutes a realistic or artificial context. Indeed, while the lab is often presented as a place of increased control, where researchers can test hypotheses in a quasi-vacuum, it is also decried as an artificial situation, where events might fundamentally differ from what happens "in real life" – because no human behavior is ever in a vacuum. However, while experimental procedures in a lab might be an extreme case, most traditional data collection methods involve some degree of artificiality, in the sense that the situation in which the data are gathered is at least partially created by researchers to produce said data. In other words, researchers using traditional methods do not simply "collect" data; instead, they elicit or create data (Hood et al., 2012).

A common distinction is between *naturally occurring data* (Reader & Gillespie, 2022) – termed "unobtrusive" or "nonreactive" (Reader et al., 2020; Webb et al., 1966) – and *constructed data*. Naturally occurring data are produced outside the research process (i.e., exist independently of any instructions from the researcher). They are also part of ongoing chains of events that make up the world; they are consequential outside the research process and shape the world of tomorrow (e.g., people making plans, flying planes, contesting identities, giving feedback, making friendships, and debating points of view). For example, online posts are naturally occurring data that can become data for research even if they were not created for research (something that raises particular ethical concerns; see the final section of this chapter and Chapter 8).

Using naturally occurring data for research typically entails either corpus construction or observation. In corpus construction, researchers search for preexisting naturally occurring data that can address their research question. This could include personal diaries (Gillespie et al., 2007), formal complaints and incidents (Van Dael et al., 2021), social media posts (Whittaker & Gillespie, 2013), cockpit voice recordings (Noort et al., 2021a), and even FBI records (Gillespie, 2005b). In observational research, researchers choose a context, situation, or event and collect the data as it happens, such as during a protest (Power, 2018) or in the aftermath of a disaster (Cornish, 2021). In both cases, however, the route from data to analysis is complex. While "traces of events" might be "naturally occurring," what ends up being analyzed is necessarily a constructed subset of the actual events. The corpus construction method entails numerous choices about what is and what is not in the corpus. It requires a delicate crafting of the corpus to suit one or more research questions. Equally, the observation method filters what ends up being analyzed through the experience, questions, and concerns of the researcher (Mulhall, 2003). In both cases, events themselves are too abundant for direct analysis. Researchers have to select, simplify, or describe. To this end, research questions (i.e., researcher interests) are critical because they provide criteria for isolating, extracting, and even abstracting data.

When researchers talk about constructed data, they often distinguish "prompted data" (e.g., interviews) and "controlled data" (e.g., experiments). In interviews, the aim is to prompt answers that are guided to varying degrees by the researcher (i.e., structured, semistructured, and unstructured interviewing; Kvale & Brinkmann, 2008; Qu & Dumay, 2011). While for most interviews, there is an assumption that respondents can freely produce their views, the opinions generated necessarily bear the mark of the interactional context of the interview itself (it is an inter-view; Farr, 1984). Experiments entail controlled data since the researcher tries to standardize the setting and collect structured reactions quantitatively. It is no surprise that control and standardization are defining characteristics of the experimental method (Wolfle et al., 1949). Surveys are somewhere between prompted and controlled data, depending on how they are constructed. For example, surveys on misinformation tend to be quite controlled (e.g., controlling the stimuli, the sample, how accuracy is assessed), whereas surveys of opinions entail less control (they can be very narrow inventories of opinions, but they do not necessarily control much beyond the response format) – methodological differences that raise the problem of expressive responding or the deliberate production of insincere responses in misinformation surveys (see Schaffner & Luks, 2018).

One of the main limitations of the distinction between naturally occurring and constructed data is that it suggests that some data exist "out there"

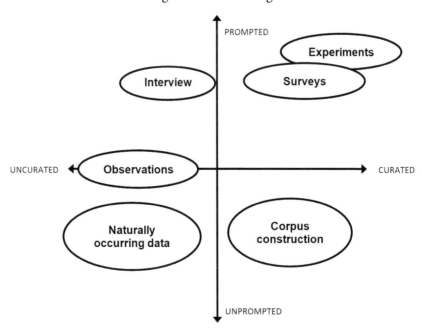

Figure 5.1   A typology of data elicitation

and researchers do little to influence them, while others are fabricated for research. However, we can think about these two categories in more subtle terms. For example, one of the most relevant criteria is related to the degree of control of the researcher. This can refer to control over the situation of data collection or control over the content of the data itself. Following this new distinction, we can talk about prompted or unprompted and curated or uncurated methods of data elicitation (see Figure 5.1 for details).

In Figure 5.1, *prompted or unprompted* refers to how much the situation is controlled and created by the researcher. Experiments offer the most control and construct more "artificial" situations for participants, followed by surveys and interviews. Observations are on the midline because, in traditional observation techniques, the researcher contributes to a certain extent to the situation. But, especially in covert observations, one could argue that the influence of the researcher is minimal. *Curated or uncurated* refers to the extent to which data are selected for inclusion into the dataset (e.g., how strict the criteria are about what constitutes data). Experiments and surveys are the most curated, as they collect only limited and pre-defined information. Constructed corpora are also heavily curated, as the data are collected based on clear criteria for inclusion/exclusion. On the other hand, interviews and video observations are the least curated, as they offer little control over what ends up in the transcript or video record.

One general observation when considering this typology is that most methodological attention tends to be focused on the opposing quadrants of *uncurated and unprompted* and *prompted and curated*. These correspond, largely, to the naturally occurring and constructed data categories mentioned earlier. And yet naturally occurring data does not necessarily have to be uncurated, as is the case for instance in corpus construction, where much effort is put in selecting relevant data to answer a research question. Some of the biggest expansions in data sources, discussed in more detail in the following section, concern what we call here (uncurated) "naturally occurring data." This is any source of naturally occurring data that is either taken as a self-contained dataset (e.g., analyzing a whole archive) or selected on arbitrary terms (e.g., analyzing the last three months of conversation on a forum). These can be closed-circuit television (CCTV) footage, interactions on social media, entire diaries available to the public, black box recordings, or public speeches. Because these data are both unprompted and uncurated, they land themselves particularly well to zooming in and out through multi-resolution research (see Chapter 7) without being the only data that can afford such analytical movements (as we shall see in Chapter 6).

In the end, when it comes to typologies, we need to move past simple dichotomies like qualitative and quantitative data and, in many ways, the field of methodology is doing so by operating increasingly with new concepts such as *structured and unstructured data* (Bolla & Anandan, 2018; Fong et al., 2015; Gillespie & Reader, 2022; Shabou et al., 2020). While structured data are generally quantitative and unstructured data are generally qualitative, these new notions shift the emphasis away from a binary toward the idea that there can be degrees of structure. They also shift focus from the implicit (and misleading) assumption that a specific type of data necessarily calls for a specific method of analysis. Instead, the focus is on "datafication" as the process of structuring records. In practical terms, structured means anything that can be neatly organized in a table or database, and unstructured is anything that cannot be put in a table without losing essential information. Of course, there is always a grey area because there are many degrees of structuring (arguably, all digital data, even when qualitative, are structured in 1s and 0s). For example, tweets can be put in a table along with related information (e.g., time sent, number of likes, retweets, responses), but their textual content remains unstructured (except in so far as it is digital). Our proposal is that the movement between structured and unstructured (what we call data transformation or data as a process) has enormous research potential. Often this move is from unstructured data to at least partially structured data through automatic or manual coding (quantitizing; Chapter 7). However, it can also be in the reverse direction, to recover the rich qualitative particulars underlying previously structured data (qualitizing; Chapter 7).

In summary, we need to rethink old terminology regarding data. In particular, we need a deeper reflection on the role of researchers in eliciting data and how much control they have over the content and context of data collection. Distinctions between prompted or unprompted and curated or uncurated add nuance and help us navigate where the abundance of new data, especially big qualitative data, is "coming from." The structured–unstructured terminology points us to processes of working with data, which is a significant advance. It is increasingly important to move beyond types of data and toward understanding how data are selected, reshaped, and used. Texts analyzed only for word frequencies are structured data. Images classified by humans or an algorithm are also structured data. But both texts and images are also unstructured qualitative data.

What is essential for our argument is that, in both cases, the unstructured (raw) form remains, *enabling the researcher to move between unstructured and structured* in the process of working with data. Both unstructured and structured data can be subjected to pluralistic forms of analysis, and this process is helped by the fact that unstructured data can always be structured and, in many cases, structured data can be unstructured. We need, however, more opportunities for the latter. For example, text can be analyzed systematically to reveal a high-level pattern while retaining the ability to zoom into individual quotes. But structured data such as survey ratings do not typically enable zooming down into the thoughts/utterances underlying the given rating except if the research is set up in such a way as to allow this (Rosenbaum & Valsiner, 2011). Luckily, as we shall discuss next, new types of data are extremely rich and can be structured in more than one manner, allowing for both quantification and exemplification and, as such, enabling us to gain both quantitative rigor and qualitative subtlety.

5.3 Big Qualitative Data

Quantities of data are increasing exponentially. Things, people, and organizations increasingly produce traces (potential raw data) as a byproduct of their activities. Digitization has made these data easy to store, search, and (security and privacy issues aside) share. This increase in data creates opportunities but also pitfalls (Salganik, 2019). From the use of smartphones to social media participation, most of us – but not everyone (Van Dijk, 2020) – leave numerous digital traces, and these records can easily be collected as data and analyzed with or without our consent. The ascendancy of big data (Yaqoob et al., 2016) and big data techniques (Foster et al., 2016), and their spread in the corporate domain, testifies to the digital data boom. These data and techniques will revolutionize traditional research methods (e.g., surveys, experiments, and interviews). Previously, numerical data collected on a piece of paper or typed in a computer were the only record available for analysis from an experiment (bar the existence of fieldnotes from the experimenter). Nowadays, there may be high-quality audio and video footage of participants during the experiment (Ross & Vallée-Tourangeau, 2021). This abundance of new data means that the gap between raw data and analysis is increasing because we increasingly need to decide how to select and structure the data for analysis. The traditional record, meant for a particular analysis, is becoming rare. We increasingly face a multitude of choices, both in terms of what we consider raw data and in terms of how we transform this into analyzable data, which is both exciting and challenging.

In practical terms, increasing digitization has three consequences for social research: new types of data, more behavioral data, and increasing quantities of data.

5.3.1 Increased Access to More Types of Data

The new types of data include social media data, video footage, live interactional data, and digital archives. While some of these have been around for decades, they have become increasingly important for researchers, and there is an upsurge in digital data and digital research (Brynjolfsson & McAfee, 2011; González-Bailón, 2013; Mayer-Schönberger & Ramge, 2022).

Social media data, including text and images (e.g., memes and emojis), conversations or posts, and a wide range of online behaviors (e.g., liking, linking, forwarding, following), are a rapidly growing data type. Whereas today we are taking for granted the diversity of social media platforms, we need to keep in mind how recent many of these platforms are and how they are transforming both individual lives and society. For instance, Facebook was founded on February 4, 2004, the first tweet dates from March 21, 2006, the first Instagram post was released on July 16, 2010, and TikTok was launched in China in September 2016. At the time of writing, the new social media apps include Supernova, Locket, Sunroom, and PearPop. No doubt, many of these new platforms will fail, and new platforms will arise – which goes to show how rapidly these technologies and social spaces are developing. Our point is that researchers are increasingly presented not only with social data but new social phenomena that did not exist before the early 2000s (e.g., de Saint Laurent et al., 2020; Stahl & Literat, 2022).

Video footage is a type of data coming from people sharing videos online and from organizations (e.g., broadcasts, CCTV, training, teaching, and news). With video footage, we can gain insight into the mundane aspects of life (whereas in the past, only special events were filmed) and gain a broader range of perspectives on a single event (e.g., videos of key events like the US Capitol Hill riot; Tynes, 2021). Since people are increasingly used to being filmed, they react less to it (e.g., CCTV), and thus it is increasingly likely that there will be video footage of critical events. Natural disasters, social uprisings, unethical behavior, and whistleblowing increasingly produce digital traces. Thus, retrospective verbal accounts will increasingly give way to rich audio-visual data that provide insight into events as they happened.

Live data come out of people answering requests to record reactions or fill up surveys while events are taking place or at specific moments during the day, but they can also include a direct record of activity (e.g., collecting browser data, real-time messaging, tweeting, recording movement on the GPS). This "live" aspect of the data, when combined with computing, can lead to real-time analysis of behavior in ways that feed back into the phenomenon itself (e.g., monitoring hate speech online; Paschalides et al., 2020). This is in stark contrast with traditional research practice, which takes months or years to get from data collection to results. In the case of live data, the research participant does the observation/data collection more or less willingly (e.g., participants install an app for recording their web activity, online interactions, or personal experiences; Christensen et al., 2003).

Digital archives are not new. From the invention of the first computer in the 1940s to the creation of the Internet in the 1980s, we have been accumulating digital archives. What differs today is the ease of access and the analytical possibilities opened by natural language processing and object recognition techniques. This has enabled archives to continue growing while remaining almost instantly searchable. Archival data are also becoming richer and more multifaceted with extra data such as time stamps, document history, and email communications and messages about documents (Beer & Burrows, 2013; Falk, 2003). Thus, digital archives are not only becoming bigger but they are also increasingly combining and stitching together multiple types of data (both structured and unstructured).

5.3.2 Increased Access to Behavioral Data

Another opportunity for researchers dealing with new data, particularly in its digital forms, is that it allows them more direct access to behavioral information. While traditional methods such as surveys and interviews are usually based on self-report (people reporting behavior), and experiments construct behavior in somewhat artificial environments, online spaces offer easy access to behavioral data. This is not limited to online behavior. The video footage, live data, and digital archives increasingly include data on offline behavior (e.g., purchases, video footage of daily life, images of important events, and reports of medical error). Although there is a debate about the relationship between online and offline behaviors (Kim et al., 2017), it is increasingly recognized that there is no relation. The digital realm increasingly contains traces of our nondigital behavior. And, although it is imperfect behavioral data, it must be compared to the alternatives, such as recollections of behavior and declarations of behavioral intent.

5.3.3 Increased Large Quantities of Unstructured Data

Big qualitative data also challenge the old assumption that quantitative (structured) data are relatively easy to accumulate in larger quantities and thus offer breadth, while qualitative (unstructured) data take more time to gather and thus offer depth. Contemporary researchers often have vast amounts of unstructured and unanalyzed data, creating new opportunities and challenges. Key questions include: How does one preserve some depth when the data are too vast to analyze manually? How does one best simplify one's data by structuring and quantifying them? How does one select what information to keep and disregard? Big data, especially of the unstructured type, make new methods possible (e.g., natural language processing; Hirschberg & Manning, 2015) while, at the same time, rendering other methods dated (e.g., the statistics taught traditionally to psychologists are not suited to big data).

The aforementioned three questions, taken together, force us to rethink our research practices. And yet most methods, books, and courses trail behind these challenges and generally stay at the level of generic tools like observations, experiments, surveys, and interviews that are presented as the methodological canon. Moreover, these books and courses also implicitly, if not explicitly, work on the assumption that some methods are better than others. For example, in the social science domains that try to emulate the natural sciences, experiments are considered the gold standard for obtaining causal information and making predictions (two key attributes of positivism; see Chapter 2). Besides the fact that the value of a method always depends on the goal we are trying to achieve with it, the reality that we now can access large amounts of data about actual behaviors should make us rethink our hierarchies, preferences, and assumptions.

From a pragmatist standpoint, the abundance of new data, especially naturally occurring big qualitative data, provides a valuable opportunity. This is because these big qualitative datasets are more likely to lead to useful knowledge. Not only are these data "big" and high-powered but they are also high in validity. These big qualitative datasets will have a huge impact on social science research because they are unprecedented in their quantitative scale, rich in their qualitative details, and have high validity due to their proximity to human behavior. These data are part of human life (i.e., naturally occurring rather than induced or artificial); thus, by analyzing them, researchers can get close to (and contribute to) what actually happens. The pragmatist point is this: To create useful knowledge for humans, it is recommended to start with what humans are actually doing.

5.4   Accessing Data and Ethical Challenges

The opportunities of abundant new data, particularly of the unstructured and digital kind, need to be understood in the context of several constraints, especially access and ethics. In this subsection, we take a closer look at the main ethical challenges surrounding big qualitative data and, connected to this, the question of how data are accessed and by whom.

5.4.1   Accessing Data

To understand issues surrounding access, we should first review some key types of data sources. *Repositories*, for example, are existing datasets that have been curated by other researchers and are made available for secondary research (Pinfield et al., 2014). Online *archives* are websites where data, usually naturally occurring and not gathered for research, are shared (e.g., parliamentary debate transcripts on government websites; de Saint Laurent, 2014). In both cases, existing data are made available. *Websites and platforms* offer ways of collecting data online where the medium is the data (e.g., social media, collaborative platforms; Kordzadeh & Warren, 2013). Finally, moving toward explicitly constructed data, we have *apps and programs* aimed at collecting data with the participants' consent (Zydney & Warner, 2016). For these, the data are actively collected by the researchers. While information from many of these sources can be freely and relatively easily accessible, this is not always the case. The optimism surrounding big data and the enthusiasm for big data research are tempered by the fact that most social media platforms restrict researchers' access to downloading and processing their content. Some of these restrictions are a response to past unethical practices (see, for instance, Facebook's reaction to the Cambridge Analytica scandal; Brown, 2020). But access is also restricted for corporate reasons. Under the banner of protecting users' privacy, companies have effectively been given private control over the conversations that make up the public sphere – and researchers who want to examine what is occurring in these online public spheres risk being locked out.

There are two main dimensions when it comes to accessing data in general and online data in particular: *extraction* and *authorization*. For online data, extraction can take several forms (see also Edwards et al., 2020). First, manual extraction can be done by downloading files manually or copying text and images from a social media platform into open documents. Second, Application Programming Interfaces (APIs) can be used to query databases directly, enabling downloading data at high speed and in a structured form. Third, web scraping can be used to automatically collect data from websites where there is no API access. This entails computer algorithms that simulate being a user of the website, opening pages, and then programmatically extracting data. Many platforms try to prevent web scraping, but it is widely used (e.g., it is how search engines construct their databases of the Internet).

Another issue for data access is authorization (Asghar et al., 2017). Sometimes the data themselves are open access, which means that everyone can have access to them (e.g., Reddit, Wikipedia). Most of the time, however, some form of authentication is needed (i.e., the researcher must register or apply for access). Some platforms use a mixture of both (e.g., the download is slower without authentication). Other times, researchers are asked to pay to access data, especially if downloading at scale. However, charging researchers for noncommercial access is a questionable practice because researchers can claim fair use (i.e., analyzing the data is in the public interest and not for commercial purposes).

As a result of these constraints, data access is often limited in practice to those researchers who have the technical skills and/or financial means to access it. A lot of studies are done using manual data collection, which limits the amount of data collected and, in addition, many platforms are deliberately difficult to copy and paste from. Consequently, less representative platforms get overstudied and third parties' profit from selling data to those who can afford to buy it (e.g., one can pay to have a dataset curated for you from social media platforms). For the latter, the main clients are companies who want to analyze markets or reputations, so the tools are oriented toward market research and the prices are often prohibitive for researchers.

5.4.2   Ethical Issues

Social scientists have an ethical responsibility to study big qualitative datasets. First, it is important to study these data because online interactions are increasingly central to people's lives. Online interactions can have significant consequences for individuals (e.g., support groups, conspiracy theories) and society (e.g., misinformation and politics; Kyza et al., 2020). At the same time, we should refrain from blindly assuming that studies about what happens offline apply to online behaviors and vice versa. Second, we should access this kind of data in order to propose a critical and pluralistic approach to it. Most digital data are currently analyzed by data scientists/computer scientists and/or for commercial purposes. Their focus is also primarily on structured data. Psychologists and social scientists have a lot to offer this field of research in terms of theoretical, methodological, and ethical reflections. Most of all, social scientists can contextualize the data themselves and the research practice they are part of in social, political, and historical terms, which is too often missing in big data investigations. For instance, social scientists have questioned the use of algorithms assumed to be neutral when, in reality, they are trained on data that are never "neutral" (Martin, 2019; O'Neil, 2016; Stinson, 2022). Third, we should access this kind of data to hold large social media platforms accountable. For example, there is considerable research interest in misinformation on social media but, because Facebook's algorithms are not accessible, researchers cannot independently verify Facebook's claims about the success of their practices in this area.

However, there is a myriad of ethical challenges for social scientists using big qualitative data. The specific issues vary depending on the details of the study. Nevertheless, key questions include: How private are the data (e.g., do people share their innermost thoughts or rate washing machines)?

Who else has access to the data? Are the data to be shared? If they are "stolen" data, have they been made widely accessible by others? How relevant are the data (e.g., are they private but about a pressing issue)? How much personal information do they contain (e.g., can people be identified, even indirectly)? What will be done with the data? Will quotes and extracts be shared in publications? Will the data be made available?

Admittedly, many of these questions do not have clear-cut answers and, as such, require considerable moral deliberation (see Chapter 8). But they should be asked by researchers before they engage in collecting and analyzing online data. As with any other type of data, safeguarding practices include *consent*, *privacy*, and rules around *data sharing* (Smith et al., 2016). Yet online data add extra concerns to each category. First, researchers often cannot ask for consent from the participants but can be asked to make the existence of the project public so that participants can opt out (which is quite difficult in practice). Good practice in this regard is to ask oneself how reasonable it is for the participants to expect their data to be publicly accessed and analyzed (e.g., is it an open platform that people know to be "watched," like Twitter, or a small forum that is assumed to be private?). When it comes to privacy, removing identifying characteristics is often not enough. If the researcher publishes quotes and extracts, he or she should consider whether it may be advisable to modify the quotes sufficiently so that they cannot be searched for online. Finally, on data sharing, if the data collected were originally public, it makes sense to share the curated dataset (which also enhances replicability). But one should ask: How "curated" is the dataset? For example, even if the data are public, if your dataset looked at the behavior of a few isolated platform users over ten years, it might be questionable to share it. Also, one should ask: What are the legal requirements? For example, in Switzerland (in 2022), data obtained by scraping open websites cannot legally be shared; only the code used to obtain them may be made public.

For these reasons, ethics committees often struggle when researchers work on "new," big, and/or digital data (Ferretti et al., 2021) because there are few specific policies in place or they are country-specific. In general, informed consent does not readily apply, underaged participants cannot be reliably screened out, data may be stolen, and public platforms have different types of users and create different expectations of privacy not easily known by nonspecialist ethics committees (e.g., users of Twitter and Reddit usually know that their data are public, Facebook users may be less aware of the extent to which their data are public).

5.5   The Potentials of Data

In this chapter, we argued that data entail a record of real-world phenomena collected, stored, and transformed to enable analysis. Instead of static instances of one "kind" or another, a pragmatist conceptualization focuses on data as a process of construction taking place between researcher and world, a process that can disrupt established theoretical views or empirical patterns. Instead of the traditional dichotomy between quantitative and qualitative research, there is a new focus on the role of the researcher (captured by whether data are prompted or unprompted, curated or uncurated) and the "movements" between structured and unstructured data. This idea of not just transforming data but retransforming them (moving back and forth between quantities and qualities) is particularly suitable for dealing with the abundance of "new" forms of data and, in particular, the digital big data boom that is currently shaping psychology and the social sciences. While these data come with ethical and access challenges, they represent great opportunities for zooming in and out of datasets that are rich, multidimensional, and often surprising. This is not meant to say that multiple forms of analysis are applicable only to online or big data. As we will see in Chapter 6, what the current data context mainly brings to the fore is the widening gap between data and analysis. Instead of predetermined and linear relationships between the kind of data being collected and their processing, we are left, due to current advances, more aware of our methodological choices in transforming data. Key among them is the possibility of *combining* structured and unstructured data (Chapter 6) and, finally, of considering in research *the same piece of data* as (potentially) structured *and* (potentially) unstructured (Chapter 7). These practices call, naturally, for mixing methods of analysis, a call that is highly congruent with a pragmatist approach.

Mixing Qualitative and Quantitative Methods

When the practice of knowledge ... became experimental, knowing became preoccupied with changes and the test of knowledge became the ability to bring about certain changes. Knowing, for the experimental sciences, means a certain kind of intelligently conducted doing; it ceases to be contemplative and becomes in a true sense practical.

Dewey (1920, p. 149)

In Chapter 5, we examined how data are elicited and transformed. These transformations foregrounded the potential of moving between unstructured and structured states of the same data. Such recursive data restructuring challenges oversimplistic distinctions between data collection and data analysis. While traditional research reporting draws a clear distinction between the two, conceptualizing data as a process prompts a deeper understanding of all the analytical tools available to us in order to make the most of the unstructured–structured continuum. The gap between data and analysis is widening due to a series of technical and societal developments, particularly the rise in qualitative big data (Adnan et al., 2020). This means that these new datasets challenge the coupling of data and analysis (e.g., between experiments and between group statistics, or between interviews and thematic analysis). Large unstructured data, especially if unprompted and uncurated (see Chapter 5), require us to reconceptualize the purposes of qualitative and quantitative research and their mixing (Lieber, 2009).

The guiding proposal for this chapter is that q*ualitative and quantitative methods are synergistic.* Qualitative and quantitative methods can be integrated to produce insights that are not reducible to either method. But exactly how this mixing produces outcomes that are more than the sum of the parts remains elusive. This "integration challenge" addresses the core promise of mixed methods research, namely, that mixing methods produces added value (Fetters & Freshwater, 2015a, p. 115; Guetterman et al., 2020). This challenge is evident whenever qualitative and quantitative findings are presented side by side, with little more than a shared topic (Feilzer, 2010; Seawright, 2016), thus failing to leverage any integrative synergy.

Addressing this integration challenge is complex because of the bewildering variety of research projects, each with multiple dimensions of possible integration (Fetters & Molina-Azorin, 2017b). Ideally, there should be a clear rationale for mixing methods and explicitly formulated "integration strategies" that specify how synergies will be produced (Åkerblad et al., 2021, p. 152). To address this challenge, we first conceptualize how qualitative and quantitative research purposes can be *differentiated* and then theorize how these purposes can be *integrated* to yield insights that are more than the sum of the parts.

Our approach is to focus on mixing qualitative and quantitative research purposes (see Chapter 4) within a pragmatist epistemology (see Chapter 2). Pragmatism considers research to be a human activity and, as any activity, it is goal-oriented, culturally mediated, and embedded within wider societal networks of norms and values. This makes research both meaningful and purposeful. The notion of purpose is thus wider than that of research questions or hypotheses and even research aims or objectives (Shehzad, 2011). The purpose of using qualitative and quantitative methods is to generate new knowledge, and this knowledge generation can be achieved in multiple ways. We use Charles Sanders Peirce's (1955) distinction between induction, deduction, and abduction to differentiate three qualitative purposes (describing phenomena, theoretical framing, generating theory) and three quantitative purposes (measuring phenomena, testing hypotheses, exploring explanations), thereby enabling an analysis of how these purposes can be productively integrated. This typology was introduced in Chapter 4 (see Table 4.1), on research questions, to outline the differences between inductive, deductive, and abductive research. In the spirit of pragmatism, our approach is not prescriptive; it does not aim to promote specific combinations of methods as superior. Pragmatism eschews such absolutist claims and instead focuses on each method's contribution to the problem at hand (Morgan, 2007).

Our guiding metaphor is tool use during carpentry. One does not ask whether the mallet is better than the saw in absolute terms; instead, the focus is on what each instrument does and specifically how these purposes can be combined synergistically (e.g., first sawing, then hammering joins to make a chair). In a similar vein, research methods are multifaceted. Some of them are designed to address specific purposes. For example, experiments are ideal for hypothesis testing, while interviews are typically used to explore experiences. And yet the same method can be used for multiple purposes (e.g., surveys can be used to explore associations and test hypotheses), and when used in combination, purposes can be integrated to produce outcomes irreducible to either method. For example, the carpenter's chair cannot be produced by either the saw or the mallet in isolation.

This chapter is structured in four parts. First, we review current approaches to the integration challenge and make a case for a pragmatist approach. This is intended not as a comprehensive review, especially since the field of mixed methods is rapidly expanding, but as an overview guided by the quest for methodological synergies. Second, we use pragmatism to differentiate qualitative and quantitative research purposes (see also Chapter 4) and show how these purposes can be integrated to produce a more granular conceptualization of the synergies within simultaneous, sequential, and recursive designs. Third, we consider the question of creativity in mixed methods designs as a consequence of adopting a pragmatist standpoint; if there is no one-to-one relationship between research purpose, method, and the problem at hand, but a one-to-multiple relation, then we have the scope and necessity to remix methods and, in doing so, foster new synergies. We end with implications for mixed methods research and prepare the ground for our own proposal in this area, discussed in Chapter 7.

6.1 The Integration Challenge: A Pragmatist Approach

The integration challenge refers to the problem of conceptualizing how quantitative and qualitative methods can be integrated to produce insights that are not reducible to either method (Fetters & Freshwater, 2015a). Addressing this challenge is essential for legitimizing mixed methods research as a third type of research (Johnson et al., 2007) and aiding researchers to leverage potential synergies. Following the pragmatist proposition of creative synergies, this challenge can be translated in terms of discovering the multiplicity of purposes research methods can serve, particularly when mixed.

One of the earliest attempts to theorize method integration was the metaphor of triangulation. In navigation and geographic survey work, triangulation refers to identifying an unknown point by drawing a triangle with two known points and then using trigonometry to calculate the unknown location. The term was originally used in the social sciences to conceptualize measurement validation (Johnson et al., 2007). Subsequently, it was appropriated within qualitative research to theorize analysis enrichment (Denzin, 2012) and it remains a key criterion for assessing quality in qualitative studies (Bauer & Gaskell, 2000). While triangulation for validation stays close to the original metaphor (achieving validity through overlapping measurements), triangulation for enrichment departs from the metaphor (nonoverlapping findings reveal different aspects of the phenomena and are equally valid). Given this confusion, we use the less metaphorically loaded term "integration," which is increasingly preferred (Fetters & Molina-Azorin, 2017a).

Reviews of research practice have revealed various rationales for mixing methods (Greene et al., 1989). In a review of 232 mixed methods articles, Bryman (2006) identified 17 rationales, with the most common being validating, obtaining completeness, explaining, developing a measure, identifying a sample, illustrating, enhancing the analysis, and including a diversity of views. These not only reflect the strength of qualitative or quantitative methods taken separately (e.g., developing a measure for quantitative and illustrating for qualitative) but, most of all, point to the benefits of integration (e.g., obtaining completeness, enhancing the analysis). Using mixed methods to ensure that a diversity of voices are represented, in particular, points to a rationale far beyond validation and enrichment (i.e., social justice; Mertens, 2007), one that is in line with the pragmatist ethos of empowering action through research (see Chapter 9 for an analysis of the relationship between human interests, research, and possibility).

These studies of mixed methods research practice have also emphasized theory creation as a valuable rationale. For example, Boeije and colleagues (2013) found that, in addition to validation (e.g., for instrument development) and enrichment (e.g., providing illustrations and nuance), mixed methods studies often enabled speculating about underlying mechanisms and generating plausible theories. In other words, mixed methods research often facilitates abduction (see Chapter 4) to complement and leverage the insights gained from deduction and induction. Specifically, it has been argued that discovering contradictions (Greene et al., 1989) and puzzling discrepancies (Bryman, 2006) can spur interpretation, reflecting the pragmatist insight that thought itself originates in confronting obstacles (Mead, 1964a).

Across the diverse rationales for mixed methods research, there is the underlying idea that integration should add value beyond what either method can contribute alone (Fetters & Freshwater, 2015a). The challenge is to specify the relationships between the methods, data, and findings so that the synergy is more than accidental (Moran-Ellis et al., 2006) and can be deliberately enhanced in research. To this end, Fetters and Molina-Azorin (2017b) identified fifteen dimensions of possible integration, including philosophical, theoretical, researcher, team, literature, sampling, design, research aims, data collection, analysis, and interpretation (see also Schoonenboom & Johnson, 2017). These insights direct attention toward the nodal points at which integration occurs, thus potentially isolating how integration is more than the sum of the parts (Åkerblad et al., 2021).

A pragmatist approach to mixing methods focuses on the nodal point of purposes to advance the integration challenge. While other paradigms bring into focus social justice (the transformative paradigm; Mertens, 2007) and compatibility (critical realism; Shannon-Baker, 2016), the pragmatist paradigm emphasizes the purpose of methods (i.e., what they actually achieve; Chapter 4) and thus helps us consider multiple methods holistically in terms of what they individually and collectively contribute to the problem at hand. The term "research purpose" subsumes research questions, hypotheses, aims, goals, and objectives and also points our attention to the articulation between what methods are intended to do, what they do, and how they do what they do. Differentiating qualitative and quantitative research purposes, we argue, provides a basis for revealing synergistic combinations of research purposes. This is because integrative synergies require a solid understanding of differences in order to under-stand grasp how methodological combinations come about and how dif-ferences in purpose can lead to creative novelty (for a broader argument about differences and creativity see Glăveanu & Gillespie, 2014).

Pragmatism reconceptualizes abstract concepts by focusing on their consequences (Peirce, 1878). It recasts debates about the meaning of truth, beauty, God, and so on in terms of what these concepts "do". Instead of relying upon axioms, first principles, or exhaustive logically consistent definitions, pragmatism grounds the meaning of concepts in human activ-ity. From a pragmatist standpoint, all theories, beliefs, and ideas are tools for action (Cornish & Gillespie, 2009). Simply put, meaning lies in con-sequences (see Chapter 1).

Pragmatism is particularly suited to mixed methods research because it values each method for its contribution (Morgan, 2007). Thus, it offers an alternative to postpositivism or constructionism (Feilzer, 2010). It rejects the purist assumption that some methods are "better" than others in abso-lute terms. Pragmatism is inclusive because, in the words of James (1907, p. 31), it has "no obstructive dogmas, no rigid canons of what shall count as proof" and "will consider any evidence." This does not imply "anything goes" relativism (see Chapter 2), in which the differences between methods are ignored. On the contrary, the differences between methods are leveraged to increase synergy. And these differences are reflected upon, from the epistemological basis of methods to their analytical steps. However, instead of asking whether methods are epistemologically commensurable or analytically compatible, pragmatism asks what each method contributes to the problem at hand. "Pragmatists," Feilzer (2010, p. 14) writes, "do not 'care' which methods they use as long as the methods chosen have the potential of answering what it is one wants to know."

The pragmatist approach addresses the integration challenge by specifying how qualitative and quantitative research purposes can be combined to achieve particular chains of inquiry. Instead of general and high-level rationales for mixed methods research (i.e., validating, enriching, developing, explaining), the pragmatist approach directs attention to the underlying qualitative and quantitative purposes and, specifically, to how these are being combined and what they help us achieve. Thus, in contrast to the many typologies that differentiate qualitative and quantitative methods based on predetermined characteristics (Coxon, 2005; Sale et al., 2002), we focus on what these methods are used for (see also Denscombe, 2021). Our aim is not to characterize qualitative and quantitative methods, in general, or delineate family resemblances (Morgan, 2018) but rather to advance a rigorously pragmatist approach grounded in research purposes.

Synergy entails both differentiation and integration; each component must remain distinct enough to add value, while contributing to an outcome that it could not achieve alone (Moran-Ellis et al., 2006). We have already differentiated the purposes of qualitative and quantitative research methods in Chapter 4. Accordingly, we now focus on how these purposes can be integrated synergistically.

6.2   Integrating Qualitative and Quantitative Research Purposes

In Chapter 4 (Table 4.1) we distinguished six research purposes. Qualitative research is suited to describing phenomena (induction), theoretical framing (deduction), and generating explanations (abduction). Quantitative research is suited to measuring phenomena (induction), testing hypotheses (deduction), and exploring explanations (abduction). Now we will use this pragmatist typology to specify more precisely how the six purposes can be synergistically combined by considering how they are "chained" together into logical sequences of investigation.

In the following subsections, we review pairings of purposes in simultaneous, qualitative first, quantitative first, and recursive designs (Creswell & Creswell, 2018). Our focus is only on mixed methods pairings (i.e., we are excluding within-method pairings). For concision, we abbreviate the six purposes and adapt the notation introduced by Morse (1991) and refined by others (Nastasi et al., 2007; Schoonenboom & Johnson, 2017) such that "+" denotes simultaneous purposes, "→" denotes sequential purposes, "→←" denotes recursive purposes, and "[]" is used to group purposes within a larger design.

6.2.1   Simultaneous Designs

In simultaneous designs, qualitative and quantitative methods are used independently. Each purpose could be pursued in isolation, but when used together they converge on a phenomenon to either validate findings or enrich each other.

Measuring + describing is a common simultaneous design for both validation and enrichment. For example, to evaluate automated techniques for modeling topics within texts, Leeson and colleagues (2019) validated automated topic modeling (measuring) of interview transcripts by comparing it with qualitative thematic analysis (describing) and found good convergence. Hagan and colleagues (2017) surveyed cancer survivors and used open-ended questions to enrich and add nuance to the survey findings. If the qualitative study is guided by theory, it becomes *measuring + framing*, as in Emadian and colleagues' (2017) validation of a diabetes questionnaire. They administered the questionnaire to a novel population and then, guided by knowledge about diet and diabetes, used interviews to evaluate suitability.

Testing + framing is another simultaneous design used for validation and enrichment. An example is Glăveanu's (2014) study of the "art bias" in lay conceptions of creativity. This bias involves favoring artistic understandings of creativity to the point at which everything art-related is automatically considered creative, and nothing is viewed as truly creative if it is not artistic. This research was survey-based, conducted online, and included two parts. The first was qualitative and required participants to think of questions they would ask to determine whether an object was creative. This helped make explicit the criteria people use to evaluate creativity and provided qualitative data. The quantitative part entailed participants evaluating sixteen professions as to whether creativity was necessary for success (with reaction times recorded). The findings showed mild support for the art bias. Art-related professions scored highly (and fast), but some other professions also showed the same pattern (particularly in everyday domains). The thematic analysis of the qualitative data showed, on the contrary, that while art-based criteria are important, they can be overshadowed by utility concerns (i.e., is it practical to use?). Methodologically, this study illustrates the simultaneous application of qualitative and quantitative methods to test an expectation derived from the literature.

The defining feature of simultaneous designs, when conceptualized in terms of qualitative and quantitative purposes, is that neither purpose grows out of the findings of the other method. Both purposes originate outside of the research process and neither finding feeds into the other method. Each analysis is conducted separately, and then the findings are compared. Furthermore, although the purposes cannot be identical, they should be similar enough to enable either validation or enrichment.

6.2.2   Qualitative First Designs

Qualitative first sequences include exploratory sequence designs (Creswell & Creswell, 2018). These sequences begin with describing phenomena, theoretical framing, or generating explanations that feed forward into measurement and testing.

Describing → *measuring* occurs when creating a measure based on a qualitative description. A typical scenario is creating a survey in an unknown domain. For example, Senteio and colleagues (2019) used exploratory interviews to create survey items to measure how physicians incorporated psychosocial information into treatments. Another scenario is when a description leads to questions about prevalence. For example, Feltham-King and Macleod (2016) began by describing the discourses used to talk about women in South African newspapers, and then they used quantitative content analysis to measure the changing frequency of these discourses.

Another illustration of this scenario is Glăveanu's (2011) study of social representations of creativity in the United States and the United Kingdom. The focus was on how ideas about creativity are anchored in symbols. A survey was used to assess how participants would rate common symbols of creativity (quantitative) and explain their rating (qualitative). This survey, combining open and closed questions, illustrates a simultaneous design. The "qualitative first" aspect was in the creation of the symbols to be rated. An initial qualitative analysis of the first 500 images in a Google search for creativity identified the key symbols (e.g., lightbulb, brain, paintbrush and colors, computer, toy, musical note, children's drawings, and jigsaw puzzle). The subsequent survey, built around these findings, showed that the symbol most indicative of creativity was a paintbrush and colors, closely followed by children's drawings. The point, however, is that these quantitative findings were based on an initial open-ended qualitative analysis of symbols of creativity.

Framing → *measuring* is like describing + measuring, except it has greater theoretical motivation. This arises when creating a measurement tool for a predefined concept. In such a case, qualitative research is often used to provide theoretically framed illustrative data that inform the creation of survey items (e.g., Mearns et al., 2013). A similar approach is used when creating textual measures. For example, Graham and colleagues (2009) used moral foundations theory to identify candidate words in context, qualitatively assessing whether each indicated the desired concept. They subsequently added selected words to their dictionary measure, which they then used to score moral foundations in liberal and conservative speeches.

Framing → *testing* implies a theoretically motivated qualitative study that feeds forward into a quantitative test. For example, Obradović and Sheehy-Skeffington (2020) used this sequential design to examine EU integration in Serbia. First, a qualitative analysis of interview transcripts, guided by theory, identified perceived power imbalances as a barrier to integration. Second, a survey provided a quantitative test, showing that participants who perceived Serbia to be powerless identified less with the European Union.

Generating → *testing* begins with a qualitative study motivated by something that requires explanation. For example, Festinger's (1956) qualitative case study of a cult that did not dissolve after their end-of-the-world prophecy failed led to the idea of cognitive dissonance, which was subsequently tested experimentally (Festinger, 1957). A more recent example is Haugestad and colleagues (2021), who investigated climate activism in Norway, guided by the paradox that Norwegians have benefited hugely from oil. Interviews were used to generate an explanation that was subsequently tested using surveys.

Qualitative first designs are distinguished by the second quantitative purpose arising out of the findings from the first qualitative purpose. Uncovering the underlying purposes reveals an otherwise opaque heterogeneity. For example, the differences between describing → measuring (e.g., creating a measure) and generating → testing (e.g., creating and testing a theory) are lost within the more general qualitative → quantitative conceptualization. Specifying the underlying purposes reveals how these purposes synergistically combine into superordinate purposes (e.g., creating a measure, establishing a new theory, or putting existing findings to the test).

6.2.3   Quantitative First Designs

Quantitative first sequences include explanatory sequence designs. In such designs, the findings for any quantitative purpose (e.g., measuring, testing, exploring) feed forward into a qualitative purpose.

Measuring → *describing* refers to a second qualitative study that provides descriptions and illustrations for initial quantitative measurements. This sequence of purposes occurs in natural language processing when quantitative topic modeling techniques are used (e.g., to cluster Tweets or other texts) and then the qualitative analysis describes the themes within each cluster, usually with illustrative quotes (Hamad et al., 2016). In another example, Van Huizen and colleagues (2019) quantitatively counted the number of multidisciplinary meetings that led to recommendations and then conducted interviews to document the benefits and limitations of the multidisciplinary meetings. If they had sought to explain the observed frequency, it would have been a measuring → generating sequence.

Measuring → *generating* entails a quantitative measure yielding a finding that feeds forward into qualitative speculation about possible explanations. For example, studies have begun with measures revealing physician overprescribing (Voigt et al., 2016) and low female participation in a swim safety program (Gupta et al., 2020); then, qualitative methods were introduced to address the question of "Why?" These studies typically conclude with proposed explanations. However, if these explanations are tested in subsequent research, then the chain of investigation would become measuring → generating → testing.

Testing → *generating* is similar to measuring → generating, except it starts with a deductive test and then qualitative research is used to explain the findings. For example, Mannell and colleagues (2021) began with a randomized controlled trial of an intervention and then used a visual participatory method to aid the interpretation of the trial findings. Generating explanations often follows testing that yields surprising results. For example, Wee and colleagues (2016) tested their assumption that distance to a primary care clinic was a barrier to cancer screening in Singapore. However, inconclusive findings fed forward into interviews that revealed distrust and embarrassment as additional barriers to screening.

Another example of testing → generating is Glăveanu and colleagues' (2019) study of divergent thinking of individuals and dyads. This research was conceived as an experiment with individuals and dyads brainstorming. The aim was to understand the differences in originality, practicality, surprise, and overall creativity between the two conditions (individual and social). However, these outcome-based quantitative analyses were inconclusive. Accordingly, the authors conducted a qualitative study of the video recordings of dyads working together in order to generate ideas about what was occurring during the task. This analysis related the nature of the proposed idea (e.g., original or not, practical or not) with the response it received (positive, negative, indifference). The finding was that in the social condition, more practical ideas are better received. This "practicality effect," as named by the authors, was supported by a temporal quantitative analysis that found originality being high for initial ideas and then gradually reduced while practicality remained valued throughout. This study then suggests that working together does not reduce the creativity of ideas as much as it steers creative ideas toward the practical rather than wildly original. The design was *testing → generating* in which what initially seemed like an experimental nonfinding was reinterpreted in light of qualitative results.

Testing → framing entails testing a model quantitatively and then using the model as a frame for a qualitative analysis. This sequence has been refined by Seawright (2016), who advocates quantitative testing of causal pathways followed by qualitative assessment of the extent to which these causal pathways are evident in particular cases. For example, Kreuzer (2010) investigated the social conditions conducive to the emergence of proportional representation. He used a regression analysis to develop a model and then proceeded with a case-by-case examination to assess whether each country evidenced the model.

Exploring → generating arises when quantitative exploratory data analysis yields findings that require an explanation (Tukey, 1977). For example, Moore and Gillespie (2014) explored misunderstandings between people with brain injury and their caregivers using a survey. They found that people with brain injury tended to overestimate their abilities relative to the views of their caregivers. Qualitative analysis of verbal comments while filling out the survey indicated that caregivers actively encouraged their partners with brain injury to feel more capable and thus less of a burden than they were actually perceived to be.

Quantitative first sequences begin with a quantitative finding (a measurement, a test result, or an exploratory finding) that a qualitative analysis then describes, frames, or explains. Identifying the underlying sequence of questions enables more granular distinctions. For example, using a more general quantitative → qualitative conceptualization obfuscates the differences between measuring → describing (e.g., illustrating a quantitative measure) and testing → generating (e.g., explaining a failed experiment).

6.2.4   Recursive Designs

Recursive designs entail an analysis that moves back and forth between methods. This design is pervasive in qualitative research (e.g., alternating between inductive describing and trying various theoretical frames), and it also occurs in quantitative research (e.g., moving back and forth between measuring and reliability testing when developing a measure). However, recursive designs are rare in mixed methods research, perhaps because each method tends to have separate datasets, which inhibits moving between methods.

Describing →← *measuring* can occur in intervention research, where the focus is on creating change by iteratively describing the situation, intervening, and then measuring the impact. A good example is provided by Nastasi and colleagues (2007), who developed a mental health improvement project in Sri Lanka. They designed an intervention and then iteratively modified it based on qualitative inductive descriptions of local responses and outcome measurement.

Framing →← *measuring* can occur during the development of a theoretically motivated measure, such as when qualitative data are being quantified. This is common in natural language processing when developing a textual measure indicative of a concept; the researchers recursively examine words in context and the properties of the overall measure (Boyd & Schwartz, 2021). The aim is to keep the emerging measure grounded in the particulars of the phenomenon.

Another example of framing →← measuring is Gillespie and Reader's (2016) development of a publicly available tool for measuring the nature and severity of patient complaints about healthcare services. Based on a systematic review of the literature (Reader et al., 2014), they identified several common categories of complaint. Starting with this framing from the literature, they then used iterative qualitative coding of samples of complaints to refine the coding scheme, recursively checking the qualitative validity and interrater reliability with each round of development. The emergent tool was subsequently used in quantitative and qualitative research to show the validity of patient-reported insights about healthcare services (Gillespie & Reader, 2018; Reader & Gillespie, 2021). In this example, the framing based on the literature, the qualitative and quantitative development, and the findings were all presented in separate research articles.

Exploring →← *generating* sometimes occurs when modeling big qualitative datasets, when the research alternates between exploring quantitative associations and generating explanations by examining qualitative particulars. Ideas generated qualitatively can be tested quantitatively in an exploratory mode, and quantitative relationships can be validated and explained by deep dives into the qualitative data. However, caution is required to prevent overfitting – picking up spurious correlations qualitatively and subsequently testing them (Calude & Longo, 2017). Confirmatory hypothesis testing requires a separate dataset (e.g., a holdout sample of the data). Any recursive design that involves hypothesis testing must therefore be embedded within a sequential design (i.e., a [generating →← exploring] → testing design).

Recursive designs have the maximum potential for synergy. Instead of relying on one-shot mixing (e.g., qualitative → quantitative), recursive designs can leverage synergies with each back-and-forth movement. This dynamic process is difficult to formalize, reproduce, and write up. The social world and the practice of social science are messier than the methods of social science (Feyerabend, 2001; Law, 2004), a misperception perpetuated by overly neat write-ups. Indeed, the replication crisis stems in part from recursive practices with many degrees of freedom being written up as single-shot confirmatory tests (Wicherts et al., 2016). Recursive designs have creative potential, but they must be conceptualized, formalized, and written up appropriately.

6.3 Integration Synergies

Conceptualizing integration in terms of research purposes gives specificity to the description of research designs, enabling a richer description of mixed methods research. For example, instead of describing Nisbett and Cohen's (1996) classic investigation of honor culture in the southern United States as alternating between qualitative and quantitative methods, we can be more precise about the underlying logic and the interrelation of different research purposes. Nisbett and Cohen began by recursively moving between ethnographic observation (e.g., violent children's games, no holds barred fist fighting) and descriptive statistics (e.g., homicide rates, participation in the military). Their abductive leap was to explain these qualitative descriptions and measurements in terms of an honor culture, that is, individuals' willingness to protect their reputation using violence. They then tested this theory using both surveys (southerners showed more endorsement of violence in response to an insult) and experiments (southerners showed more aggression when insulted). Accordingly, this design can be described as [describing →← measuring →← generating] → [testing (survey) + testing (experiment)].

Being specific about the research purposes helps to distinguish types of synergy. The first phase of Nisbett and Cohen's (1996) research leverages a *synergy of recursive generativity*. Questions arising from both description and measurement spur speculation and the search for additional descriptions and measurements – like a police investigation in search of a pattern. The second phase of the research leveraged a *synergy of consequent inquiry*, where the speculations arising from the first phase form a cumulative base that is built upon in the second testing phase. Moreover, this second testing phase used both surveys and laboratory experiments, thus demonstrating a *synergy of convergence*, where independent methods provide mutually supporting evidence that converges upon an interpretation. Conceptualizing integration in terms of research purposes brings the underlying logic of these synergies into clearer focus and helps us discuss both specific studies and much bigger long-term projects.

6.4   Creating Mixed Methods

An often-overlooked mark of mixed methods designs is creativity. As a methodological approach based on integrating methods and cultivating synergies between them, its outcomes should bear the creative marks of novelty and appropriateness (Stein, 1953). Yet any research design can become conventional and be used unreflectively. Especially in mixing methods, there are common combinations (e.g., surveys preceded or followed by interviews, experiments being also videotaped) that tend to be used unimaginatively. This is why recent discussions about innovation in mixed methods research are timely (e.g., Poth, 2018).

The pragmatist proposition of mixing methods to produce synergies is grounded in the idea that methods are constantly created and recreated to adapt to specific research purposes. The etymological root of the term "method" is a way or path; as such, methods can potentially provide many diverse paths for addressing research questions. To understand the potential creativity of these multiple paths, it is necessary to decouple method from purpose in the sense that a purpose can potentially be achieved by using multiple methods and a method could, when used in the right kinds of combinations, serve multiple purposes. This new form of flexibility helps us overcome functional fixedness (Duncker, 1945) when it comes to using methods for addressing practical problems and creating new knowledge. Also, it allows us to theorize the combinatorial dynamic of mixed methods by considering how each purpose relates to the other and becomes shaped by it (particularly in recursive and integrative designs).

The pragmatist approach to mixing methods supports calls for dialogue about mixed methods by Hesse-Biber (2010, pp. 417–418). Mixed methods dialoguing is not about winning but promoting conditions for dialogue, which will require several ingredients: (1) It is important to bring all stakeholders with an interest in this field to the dialogue table; we must also (2) confront our methodological and methods assumptions; (3) suspend immediate judgments; (4) embrace our differences; and (5) practice reflexivity by listening across our differences as a means toward building a new set of shared assumptions and, if not, at least a willingness to remain open to different points of view.

We should also not lose sight of the fact that different purposes and methods are born out of different human interests (Chapter 9), and often, the use of mixed methods comes out of a desire to create change, address pressing challenges, and drive processes of personal and societal transformation (Mertens, 2007; Poth, 2018). As such, creativity is called on to help researchers find new and innovative ways of aligning their purpose with their methodological tools and the kind of impact they want to create in the world. Mixing methods is particularly suited to world-making research, that is, research that engages with the world, is open to being challenged by the world, and aims to feed forward into a better world (Power et al., 2023). Mixing qualitative and quantitative methods offers good opportunities for creativity, from new ways to display data (McCrudden et al., 2021) to new designs. In Chapter 7, we will introduce new ways of displaying mixed methods data and propose a new research design based on the recursive restructuring of data between qualitative and quantitative forms.

6.5 The Contributions of a Pragmatist Approach

A pragmatist approach to the integration challenge starts with the insight that methods, just like theories (see Chapter 3), are tools for action and that research itself is a human activity, situated in material, social, and cultural terms. Instead of distinguishing methods from first principles or following a narrow understanding of quantitative versus qualitative research, a pragmatist approach differentiates methods in terms of their research purposes or what they help researchers "do." This clear differentiation enables theorization about how these different purposes are integrated. In this chapter, we have mapped out common ways of mixing qualitative purposes (describing, framing, generating) and quantitative purposes (measuring, testing, exploring) to produce synergies. This pragmatist approach to mixing methods makes six contributions.

First, the typology of purposes (Table 4.1) provides guidance on when to use qualitative, quantitative, and mixed methods. Scholars have characterized differences in epistemology (Denzin, 2012) and subject matter (Shweder, 1996) and distinguished family resemblances (Coxon, 2005; Morgan, 2018). But what is needed is a contingency theory of when to use qualitative, quantitative, and mixed methods (Johnson et al., 2007). To this end, we have argued that qualitative methods are suited to describing phenomena, theoretical framing, and generating explanations, whereas quantitative methods are suited to measuring phenomena, testing hypotheses, and exploring explanations. Differentiating these purposes can guide researchers in selecting the correct methods for their problem and aid mixed methods researchers in specifying their integrative strategy (Åkerblad et al., 2021).

Second, having clearly defined purposes for qualitative and quantitative research gives each approach separate domains of legitimacy. The paradigm wars encouraged researchers to choose between qualitative and quantitative research methods (Bryman, 2008), creating ontological uncertainty, with each group fearing being supplanted by the other. Grounding methods in different purposes gives each method clearly defined domains of legitimacy. This enables each approach to confidently focus on and refine what it does best – without fearing supplantation. Moreover, this creates a clear domain of legitimacy for mixed methods research, which arises whenever a research problem would benefit from mixing qualitative and quantitative purposes.

Third, differentiating qualitative and quantitative research purposes provides a more granular understanding of the integration challenge. The terms "qualitative" and "quantitative" are routinely used to conceptualize integration in terms of simultaneous (qualitative + quantitative), sequential (qualitative ←/→ quantitative), and recursive (qualitative →← quantitative) designs (Creswell & Creswell, 2018; Morse, 1991; Nastasi et al., 2007). But these terms are problematic because they encompass diverse research types and purposes (Coxon, 2005; Krippendorff, 2019), often without a proper reflection on how they relate to each other. Unpacking the underlying purposes enables a more precise specification of how methods combine to become more than the sum of the parts.

Fourth, the existing rationales for mixed methods research (validation, illustration, explanation, enrichment, etc.; Bryman, 2006; Clark & Ivankova, 2016; Greene et al., 1989) can be specified in greater detail. For example, instrument development entails both qualitative framing and quantitative measuring; illustration entails first measuring and then describing; and explaining starts with measuring or testing and then uses qualitative methods to generate explanations. Thus, using pragmatism to differentiate underlying research purposes contributes theoretical underpinnings to the existing and already nuanced rationales for mixed methods research.

Fifth, specifying the purposes underlying simultaneous, sequential, and recursive mixed methods designs (Creswell & Creswell, 2018; Nastasi et al., 2007) reveals three distinct sources of synergy. In simultaneous designs, the purposes allow similar or partially overlapping research questions. This leverages a synergy of convergence, either for validation or for enrichment. In sequential designs, the purposes arise in sequence, with the purpose of the second study growing out of the findings of the first study. This leverages a synergy of consequent inquiry, because the findings of the second study are dependent upon the purpose of the first study. Finally, in recursive designs, both purposes operate together, with each shaping the other, such that the questions being addressed by each study evolve in response to the other study. This synergy of recursive generativity arises from the rapid alternation between purposes and the openness of each method to the findings of the other method.

Finally, conceptualizing mixed methods in terms of chaining together qualitative and quantitative research purposes fosters methodological innovation. Traditional methodologies, particularly within the quantitative tradition, have always been keen to standardize their steps and procedures (see, for instance, discussions of "best practices" in Anguera et al., 2020) which, on the one hand, allowed researchers to claim "objectivity" but, on the other, made many of the established methods too rigid to be used without modification in the dynamic data landscape of today (see Chapter 5). Qualitative methods are traditionally more flexible, with considerable ongoing discussions precisely about the role of creativity in research (see Wegener et al., 2018). The challenge for mixed methods is to navigate this path between standardization and methodological innovation, an issue the field has engaged with seriously since its inception (after all, mixing methods and fostering synergies are creative acts). The pragmatist approach sharpens this innovative potential because it does not restrict methodological choices; instead, it focuses on the overarching aim of the research and then encourages researchers to work backward in terms of what tools are best suited for the given aim. It embraces any method that advances the guiding interest.

Alongside these contributions, there are also important limitations to consider. The terminology used to specify the six purposes is blunt. We have tried to balance accuracy, parsimony, and existing usage. Being primarily an analytical tool, the typology of purposes seems to create a discontinuity between qualitative and quantitative methods, when in research practice there is often a continuum (Johnson et al., 2007; Onwuegbuzie & Leech, 2005). The typology should be interpreted as "typifying" the extremes of both qualitative and quantitative purposes and also of inductive, deductive, and abductive purposes. Additionally, all paradigms both hide and reveal (Shannon-Baker, 2016), and using a transformative or critical realist paradigm would have focused on other nodes of integration (i.e., representation or causation). The present analysis uses a pragmatist paradigm to examine the role of research purposes in mixed methods research in-depth, and this approach foregrounds the relation between method and action, emergence, and creativity.

In conclusion, qualitative and quantitative methods can be integrated to produce insights irreducible to either method because these methods serve different purposes that can be synergistically combined. Returning to the metaphor of the carpenter's toolbox, each tool must be evaluated in terms of what it does (e.g., the purposes of sawing, sanding, hammering). Differentiating these purposes reveals integrative synergies, with superordinate outcomes irreducible to either tool (e.g., sawing → hammering = chair). Similarly, the proposed typology of research purposes provides a framework for deciding when to use qualitative and quantitative methods, for conceptualizing how these purposes can be combined in synergistic mixed methods designs, and for adding nuance to descriptions of mixed methods research.

CHAPTER 7

Multi-resolution Research

> There's something in the very small minutia of life that tells us something about the big, big picture that we see every day all over the place, and so I think the more specific and creative and revelatory you are in the micro, the more powerful the macro will be.
>
> Philip Seymour Hoffman

Big qualitative datasets, whether naturally occurring or created, have a depth and breadth that are rarely fully exploited. Too often, qualitative research focuses only on a small subset, while quantitative research focuses only on abstract measures. But big qualitative datasets can offer much more: They provide an opportunity to deeply integrate qualitative and quantitative methods *to analyze the same data.*

In this chapter, we develop the pragmatist proposition to *recursively restructure big qualitative data to enable both qualitative and quantitative analyses.* Big qualitative data can be transformed into excerpts, categories, and numbers, and we advocate recursively restructuring the raw data to avail of each. Specifically, we introduce "multi-resolution research" to conceptualize a mixed methods analysis that preserves the links between the macro (quantitative) and the micro (qualitative). Multi-resolution research is recursive; it uses qualitative analysis to "zoom in" revealing contextualized particulars and quantitative analysis to "zoom out" revealing statistical patterns.

Multi-resolution research is a mixed methods recursive transformation design. As with transformation designs, there is a focus on converting qualities into quantities, but this process is reversible throughout the analysis. As with recursive designs, the analysis moves back and forth between qualitative and quantitative analyses, but unusually for recursive designs, the qualitative and quantitative methods analyze the same data.

This chapter begins with a review of the growing number of empirical studies that use qualitative and quantitative methods to analyze the same data, arguing that this emerging method is inadequately theorized. Second, we use the mixed methods literature to conceptualize multi-resolution research in terms of qualitizing and quantitizing within the analysis phase of research. Third, we theorize the gains and losses of imposing different types of structure on raw data and argue that moving between data types can accrue gains and ameliorate losses. Finally, we introduce two research studies to illustrate how multi-resolution research can support abductive inference (i.e., theory creation) and increase research legitimacy. The pragmatist insight guiding multi-resolution research is that all human research and conceptualizing is anchored in concrete instances of human practice. In multi-resolution research, both the qualitative and quantitative analyses are anchored in the same raw data, the records of human practice.

7.1   Mixed Analyses of Big Qualitative Data

Many classic experiments in social psychology combined analyzing the data quantitatively to test outcomes and qualitatively to examine processes (Moscovici, 1991). Consider Darley and Latané's (1968) study of bystanders in which participants believed they were witnessing someone having a seizure. In addition to the experimental results, showing that four participants were less likely to intervene than two, they also reported the words of participants in the experiment (e.g., "It's just my kind of luck, something has to happen to me!" and "Oh God, what should I do?"). These quotes provide insight into the experiment and increase the legitimacy of the research. This mixing of experimentation with qualitative observation is also evident in Milgram's (1969) research on obedience, Asch's (1951) research on conformity, and the Stanford Prison Experiment (Haney et al., 1973). However, the qualitative element that characterized experiments during social psychology's "golden age" has largely disappeared. Experiments conducted online (using vignettes, primes, surveys, and reaction times) do not afford the same rich analysis. Accordingly, this approach to mixing methods within experimental research is now rarely mentioned in guides for experimental research (Stainton Rogers, 2011).

Beyond social psychology experiments, however, combining qualitative and quantitative methods to analyze the same data is increasing (Onwuegbuzie & Johnson, 2021). In addition to the long history of mixed analyses of interview and focus group data (Fakis et al., 2014; Vogl, 2019), it has recently burgeoned in big data studies of social media (Andreotta et al., 2019; Hamad et al., 2016; Rodriguez & Storer, 2020).

Mixing qualitative and quantitative analyses in big data research is inevitable because the bulk of big data is qualitative data (Salganik, 2019). Indeed, qualitative interpretation is routinely used in conjunction with computational techniques (Chen et al., 2018) – for example, to identify features to measure and model; create human-labeled data used for training and evaluating algorithms; interpret clustered output from unsupervised techniques; and create textual measures – as researchers recursively examine words in context alongside the overall properties of the measure (Boyd & Schwartz, 2021).

Qualitative and computational analyses have complementary strengths. Computational analysis is more efficient, reliable, and scalable, while manual analysis is more subtle, contextual, and evaluative (Chang et al., 2021; Ho et al., 2021; Lee et al., 2020). Automated techniques rely on lexical features within the data being analyzed, while manual analysis can interpret broader contextual cues beyond the text being analyzed (e.g., common sense; Rodriguez & Storer, 2020). Simply put, manual qualitative analysis is a high-value limited resource that should be targeted at subtle, contextual, or ill-defined phenomena.

Several step-by-step models have been proposed to support integrating computational methods with human interpretation (Andreotta et al., 2019; Chang et al., 2021; Shahin, 2016). These are generally two-step models that start with computation (e.g., natural language processing of a corpus of text) and end with an in-depth qualitative interpretation of excerpts. However, despite being useful, these step-by-step models continue to conceptualize quantitative and qualitative methods as separate (as indicated by occupying different steps in the process). This overlooks the opportunity for a more thorough integration of qualitative and quantitative methods afforded by big qualitative data (Guetterman et al., 2015; O'Halloran et al., 2021). Outstanding questions include: How can the same raw data be structured to enable both qualitative and quantitative analyses? What are the benefits and trade-offs of each type of data structure? And if the same data can be structured for both qualitative and quantitative analyses, what are the synergies of doing both?

7.2 Conceptualizing Multi-resolution Research

Multi-resolution research entails recursive data transformation (i.e., quantitizing and qualitizing) occurring during the analysis phase of research. This is unusual because, typically, integration occurs after the data analysis, when interpretations are built that integrate the separate qualitative and quantitative analyses (Fetters & Freshwater, 2015b). In contrast, multi-resolution research entails integrating methods when analyzing the same data.

Data restructuring entails transforming data from one type into another (Love & Corr, 2022; Vogl, 2019). There are two types of transformation (also called "conversion"): quantitizing and qualitizing (Teddlie & Tashakkori, 2009). Quantitizing entails converting qualities into quantities (Sandelowski et al., 2009). It is widespread: In observational studies, instances are counted; in field experiments, qualitative changes are categorized and scored; and in survey research, respondents have to convert feelings or experiences into ratings (Wagoner & Valsiner, 2005). Qualitizing entails converting quantities into qualities and has received much less attention (Nzabonimpa, 2018). Examples of qualitizing include creating a narrative summary of quantitative findings, characterizing scores within a range as being of a certain type, and reverting a number to its raw qualitative form to assess the validity (Creamer, 2017; van Velzen, 2018; Vogl, 2019). While quantitizing and qualitizing are opposites, they are combined within multi-resolution research. Quantitizing and qualitizing are commonly conceptualized as unidirectional, but in multi-resolution research they are put in a loop, such that there is a back-and-forth transformation between quantitizing (zooming out) and qualitizing (zooming in).

Multi-resolution research instantiates the pragmatist idea of anchoring all data and analysis in what is actually going on (i.e., the raw data). Population data and individual cases do not exist on different ontological planes; they are the same, except they are viewed at different scales (i.e., a single case up close or many cases at a distance). In this sense, multi-resolution research aims to cut across assumptions that disconnect the micro and the macro; it aims to see the micro in the macro and the macro in the micro.

Although multi-resolution research entails a recursive research design, it is atypical. Most recursive research designs entail moving between separate qualitative and quantitative datasets (e.g., Christ, 2007; Kerrigan, 2014; Nzabonimpa, 2018). A defining feature of multi-resolution research is that both qualitative and quantitative *analyses are performed on the same dataset.* This opens up a new type of synergy, because each datum (quantitative or qualitative) can be recontextualized into either its qualitative or quantitative form. Thus, the analysis moves recursively between assigning numbers to meanings and reverting the numbers to the underlying meanings.

Multi-resolution research recursively restructures data to gain the benefits of both exploratory and sequential designs (Creswell & Creswell,

2018). Exploratory sequence designs start with a qualitative analysis and then use the findings to guide the quantitative analysis; the qualitative method explores the phenomenon, and the quantitative measures or tests it. Explanatory sequence designs start with a quantitative analysis and then use the findings to guide the qualitative analysis; the qualitative analysis generates explanations for the quantitative findings. In multi-resolution research, both sequences occur: The quantitative analysis is grounded in qualitative details, and the qualitative analysis is situated within the larger quantitative patterns (e.g., frequencies, changes, associations). By recursively switching back and forth between qualitative and quantitative analyses, both exploratory and explanatory sequences are unlocked, enabling rapid iteration and development.

A benefit of multi-resolution research is that it integrates qualitative and quantitative methods at the level of data. Being anchored in the same data means that movement between analyses is frictionless (i.e., all qualitative data can be restructured as quantitative data and vice versa). Thus any discrepancies or tensions between the analyses will be more likely to be genuine – because they cannot be byproducts of data being collected at different times, in different contexts, or with different people (which might occur when mixing methods based on different datasets). Moreover, this frictionless movement between quantitizing and qualitizing enables recursive back and forth (in contrast to two-step qualitative–quantitative sequences), which, in turn, can enhance the creativity and legitimacy of the research.

7.3 Quantitizing and Qualitizing

All data in social science begin as traces of human activity (e.g., a measurement, observation, recording, document, artifact, or digital trace). This raw data can be structured (survey responses, experimental outcomes) or unstructured (recordings, transcripts, photographs). In either case, they usually require some structuring to become suitable for analysis (see Chapter 5). Multi-resolution research requires raw data that can be transformed into both qualitative and quantitative forms. We propose that this unstructured raw data can take three broad forms: excerpts, categories, and measures. We argue that these data types are not opposed or incompatible; instead, they can be based on the same underlying raw data.

Qualitative and quantitative data are often juxtaposed as fundamentally different types (e.g., Creswell & Creswell, 2018; Morgan, 2007) or even incommensurable (Guba & Lincoln, 1994). Qualitative data, it is argued, pertain to qualia, experiences, and meanings, while quantitative data pertain to quanta, frequencies, and statistical associations (Shweder, 1996). Although there is a difference between the quality of a red flower and a numeric representation of the flower (e.g., a beauty rating or its numeric values used by a computer), there is also a connection (which can be more or less valid). Indeed, oversharp distinctions between qualitative and quantitative data have been widely criticized (Bazeley, 2017; Coxon, 2005; Creamer, 2017). The main issue is that the distinction often does not hold in practice.

In qualitative research, there is often an element of quantification in frequency claims. Phrases such as "most interviewees," "some interviewees," "few interviewees," and "no interviewees" are widespread (Hammersley, 1996; Morgan, 2018). Such opaque phrasing does not undermine qualitative research or show that it is a poor attempt at quantification. Instead, quantitative claims often provide valuable background for interpreting qualitative data. Another more fundamental blurring within qualitative research is that most recent qualitative data are digital data (i.e., os and 1s combined to produce images and text). Thus, the image viewed on the computer screen is a numeric representation. This digitization of qualitative data enables researchers to search, sort, and filter qualitative data with increasing precision. It will also, we suspect, increasingly blur the lines between research based on qualitative interpretation and quantitative algorithms.

In quantitative research, qualitative elements are also widespread. Quantitative research often begins by converting qualitative phenomena (e.g., events, behaviors, feelings) into numbers (Berka, 1983; Trochim & Donnelly, 2021). Survey respondents quantify vague and ambiguous feelings using verbal anchors such as "sometimes" and "rarely" (French et al., 2007; Wagoner & Valsiner, 2005). Validation of quantitative measures also often relies upon qualitative judgment. For example, survey measures and textual measures are often generated and evaluated through qualitative assessment (e.g., expert raters, concept sorting, face validity checks, exit interviews; Gobo et al., 2022). Even in big data analysis, there is often a qualitative element, such as when supervised learning uses human-coded data as a gold standard or in interpreting the output from unsupervised algorithms (Kowsari et al., 2019).

The practical challenge of distinguishing qualitative and quantitative methods has prompted calls to abandon this oversharp and unhelpful dichotomy (Knappertsbusch, 2020). However, this would be rash (Morgan, 2018). Instead, we build upon the idea of data as a process

(Chapter 5) in order to reconceptualize the distinction. Qualitative and quantitative data are not ontologically different types of data; they are not opposed or incommensurable. Instead, they are two different transformations of the same raw data and, thus, two ways of looking at the data.

We propose that all quantitative data are theoretically (even if rarely practically) revertible to a qualitative form. Equally, we propose that all qualitative data are theoretically (even if not sensibly) convertible into a numeric form. To say that this bidirectional transformation is always possible is not to say that it should always be done. Some data are not suited for quantification and vice versa. Our argument is only that when suitable, zooming in and zooming out on the same data (i.e., bidirectional quantitizing and qualitizing) can add transparency, rigor, and validity to research, enhancing the opportunities for surprise and thus potentially spurring scientific progress.

Researchers increasingly need to choose how to structure their data (Chapter 5). Traditional methods (e.g., interviews, surveys) produced data with a structure that afforded specific analyses (e.g., thematic analysis, correlations). Thus, traditionally, choosing a method of data collection was implicitly also choosing a method of analysis. However, naturally occurring data afford multiple analyses. Big qualitative data can be used for both qualitative and quantitative analyses. Thus, these new sources of data force researchers to question what structure should be imposed on the data. And, if multiple structures are possible, then why not recursively restructure the data so as to avail of the full depth and breadth of the data?

Table 7.1 conceptualizes how human events are transformed into three broad data types: excerpts (e.g., quotes, images), categories (e.g., counts of excerpts), and measures (e.g., survey scales, textual measures). Each type of data has trade-offs. The framework specifies the added value provided by each data type and thus facilitates conceptualizing how using multiple data types can offset losses and accrue gains.

Events refer to what actually happened: either naturally occurring events (e.g., people talking, posting, behaving) or induced by the research (e.g., talking in an interview, selecting options in a survey). Each event "has an infinity of aspects or properties" (James, 1890, p. 332) and could be the basis for an infinity of analyses (e.g., a single utterance can be analyzed for content, context, pitch, pragmatics, motivation, cognition, addressivity, originality). These "predata" events are maximally rich, contextual, and particular; they are the world-as-it-is before being sampled, recorded, or curated. Indeed, events cannot be analyzed directly. Any analysis requires converting these events into raw data (e.g., a transcript of the talk, a record

Table 7.1 *Transformations of records of human activity*

Events
Activity that is either naturally occurring (talking, photographing, posting on social media, purchasing) or research-induced (interview, survey, experiment)

Raw data
Traces of events that are potentially analyzable and can be unstructured (documents, photographs, interview transcripts, social media posts) or prestructured (survey responses, experimental outcomes)

Data type	**Excerpts**	**Categorizations**	**Measures**
Transformation	Selection	Categorizing	Scaling
Definition	Excerpts are selections of records that illustrate a concept (e.g., qualitative coding).	Categorizations impose clearly defined inclusion and exclusion criteria to yield in/out category membership.	Measures convert records into ordinal (e.g., ranking from most to least), interval (e.g., 5-point scale), or ratio (e.g., amount) variables.
Example	A quote from a social media post	Social media posts categorized by topic	The sentiment of social media posts
Gains	Particular (excerpts are a subset of the original records) and contextual (excerpts can be viewed in the context of the original record)	Enables statements of equality (= and ≠), and thus counts and modes that can reveal differences between groups and changes over time	Enables mathematical operations (< and > for ordinal; + and − for interval; and * and / for ratio) and thus statistical modeling and generalization
Losses	Selective and put the broader data in the background (e.g., unclear sampling, risk of cherry-picking)	Loses some particularity and context, homogenizes differences within the category, and accentuates differences between categories	Generic (scores risk being disconnected from records) and decontextualized (difficult to retrieve the context for the score)
Illustrative analyses	Qualitative analysis, either bottom-up (e.g., grounded theory) or top-down using theoretical concepts	Counts, frequencies, mode, crosstabulations, and chi-square	Quantitative analysis, exploratory data analysis, confirmatory hypothesis testing, and statistical modeling
Multi-resolution research	Zooming in (qualitizing)		Zooming out (qualitizing)

of what was done). Any conversion of events into raw data necessarily entails a loss of resolution and a "conquest of abundance" (Feyerabend, 2001). Like Procrustes – who made every passerby fit his bed, either by stretching or amputating them – data collection forces the richness of lived life into a template (e.g., a transcript, record, digital trace, or document).

Raw data are the traces or records of human activity collected for research. Traditionally they have been prestructured during the data collection process as either qualitative (e.g., interviews, focus groups) or quantitative (e.g., Likert ratings, experimental outcomes) and thus affording only one type of analysis. However, naturally occurring data (i.e., the records and digital traces that are a byproduct of human activity) do not have any predefined structure. Naturally occurring data have high validity (it is part of what happens in society), but because it was not collected for research, it can be messy (unclear sampling, missing entries, and ambiguous). Accordingly, naturally occurring raw data require significant processing to become suitable for research. Consider a social media post, where the event is the person writing the post and the raw datum is the digital trace of the post: An excerpt could be selected and analyzed qualitatively for subtle signs of emotion, it could be reduced to one of five categories of emotion, or it could be measured using a sentiment algorithm. Each analysis entails a transformation and thus has both gains and losses. We propose that choosing between them is a self-imposed constraint; recursively restructuring the data enables all analyses and thus unlocks the full potential of the data.

Excerpts refer to a selection of raw qualitative data that forms the basis for an in-depth interpretative analysis (e.g., an image, a quote, a video segment). Excerpts are created when the researcher selects portions of raw data that best demonstrate a central theme or theoretical idea. Examples include identifying third-turn repairs in conversation (Schegloff, 1992), analyzing multivoicedness in texts (Aveling et al., 2015), and examining creativity in social interaction (Hawlina et al., 2019). Selecting excerpts entails a loss of data; not all the raw data can be selected, decisions need to be made about what is included and excluded, and another researcher might make different selections. Moreover, some concepts are inherently ambiguous, contextual, or multidimensional, what Cartwright and Bradburn (2011) term *ballung* concepts (the German word for cluster or congestion). For example, concepts such as "culture," "power," or "practices" are useful but also challenging to definitively and exhaustively identify in excerpts of raw data. Thus, despite being useful, it can be hard to justify why one excerpt was selected from the larger dataset (Gillespie & Cornish, 2014; Morse, 2010).

Categorizations entail rigorous operationalization with precise definitions and distinct inclusion and exclusion criteria. It is a more formal and conclusive process than selecting excerpts. All categorization is based on a judgment of equivalence (= and ≠). Everything within a category is equal, and everything outside the category is different. Examples of categorization include the topic of a news article, incidents in a complaint, people in a picture, and whether a product review is positive or negative. It is impossible to rank or order categorizations (e.g., topics, incidents, and people cannot be scaled without additional data). However, it is possible to count occurrences of a category. For example, one can count how many social media posts are related to topic X? How frequently does a speaker switch topics? Are the number of mentions of X increasing? One drawback of categorizations is that they necessarily obfuscate distinctions within categories (e.g., one can count people or countries, but no two people or countries are equivalent).

Measures entail linking the empirical qualities of a phenomenon with a conceptualization of what is being measured (Zeller et al., 1980). Different phenomena afford different types of measurement. For example, phenomena with zero values are measured using ratio scales (e.g., time taken, number of correct answers). Phenomena without zero values but with equal intervals are measured using an interval scale (e.g., date, location). And phenomena without a zero value and with unequal intervals are measured using ranks (e.g., preferring apples to oranges or agreement on a Likert scale). Finally, some phenomena are unsuited to measurement (Berka, 1983; Zeller et al., 1980), such as categorical phenomena (group membership), *ballung* concepts (e.g., heuristics, culture, power), and phenomenological experience (e.g., qualia, the taste of coffee). Powerful mathematical operations are gained by turning raw data into measurements (e.g., the ability to add, subtract, and multiply), but there is always a loss of specificity (subtle differences between units and intervals are obscured). Additionally, the transformed scores may become separated from the underlying raw data if the operationalization is not aligned with the phenomenon (e.g., power could be measured using assertive language, but this would miss many structural and material features of power).

These three types of data structure are evident in Milgram's (1969) classic experiment on obedience to authority, in which participants were instructed to shock a confederate learner. The *events* were participants' activities within the experiment – and no two participants behaved exactly the same way. The *raw data* were photographs, observations, transcripts, and audio recordings. These raw data captured some of the uniqueness of each participant's trajectory, such as the hesitations, stress behaviors, and utterances. *Excerpts* selected particular incidents (e.g., attempts at resistance, moments of obedience) and afforded qualitative analysis (e.g., how some acts of resistance were prompted by religion or growing up in Germany). These excerpts could be analyzed using *ballung* concepts such as obedience, power, authority, agency, politeness, resistance, and expectations within an experiment (Kaposi, 2017). *Categorization* was used to count the number of obedient participants (i.e., complied with the experimenter's request to continue to the maximum level of shock). This yielded the core finding, namely, that 66 percent of participants were obedient. However, while useful, such counts conceal the fact that each individual obeyed and resisted in their own unique ways. *Measurement* of obedience was done using the magnitude of the shock delivered (0–450 volts). This ratio metric is helpful (e.g., it allows us to analyze the minimum obedience, the average obedience, or regress variables on obedience), but it ignores discontinuities, like the crucial time at 150 volts when the confederate learner asked to leave the experiment. The question is not whether excerpts, categories, or measures are the "best," but what do the various data transformations (all built on the same raw data) reveal and conceal? Moreover, how might these different approaches to data structuring be coupled to provide more valid, reliable, and insightful findings?

Conceptualizing how raw data are converted into the three basic data structures helps explain what is gained and lost with each type of transformation. Excerpts gain contextual detail, enabling the analysis of specific data points in the context of the raw data. However, in isolation, excerpts have unknown sampling and frequency (e.g., potential cherry-picking; Morse, 2010). Categories gain the ability to count frequency (e.g., changes over time, differences between groups). However, these gains come at the expense of homogenizing differences within each category. Measures gain advanced mathematical operations (e.g., statistical modeling) and the ability to detect subtle patterns that are not easily evident in isolated excerpts (e.g., a bias across a population). However, measures force all their phenomenon onto a linear scale that may not be appropriate (e.g., some concepts are multidimensional and do not easily conform to the measurement assumptions). Recursive data restructuring aims to accumulate the advantages of each data structure while counteracting the losses. Because the same raw data can be converted into different types of data, affording different types of analysis, the idea is to move back and forth between these data types and associated forms of analysis.

Moving back and forth between different data types can also leverage mixed methods synergies. A common rationale for conducting a mixed methods analysis is that it yields synergies, where combining the analyses produces findings that are more than the sum of the parts. For example, mixing methods can offset weaknesses, provide a fuller analysis, aid a process analysis, provide explanations, and increase credibility (Bryman, 2006; Greene et al., 1989). Moving back and forth between different data structures, we argue, combines many established mixed methods synergies into two overarching benefits: (1) facilitating abductive inference and (2) increasing legitimacy. The following two sections will conceptualize and illustrate each of these synergies.

7.4   Abduction: Puzzle-Solving Investigation

One of the main rationales for using mixed methods is that it is more likely to produce creative insight (Greene et al., 1989). This creativity might explain why the practice of mixed methods research sometimes diverges from the planned research because the methodological synergy gains its own momentum (Bryman, 2006). Indeed, it has even been suggested that the write-ups of mixed methods research rarely convey the creative, nonlinear, and problem-solving nature of mixed methods research (Gobo et al., 2022; Poth et al., 2021). At the heart of mixed methods research is creating something irreducible to either method (Fetters & Freshwater, 2015a) – and formalizing and documenting this process are challenging.

There is much more literature on testing theories than on creating theories worth applying or testing (see Chapter 4). Methodology tomes have focused on induction (generalizing from data) and deduction (extrapolating from theory), rather than abduction (creating plausible theories). Abduction entails going beyond the data and existing theories to postulate a new explanation that can make sense of observations (Peirce, 1955; Tavory & Timmermans, 2014). Abduction is simultaneously central to many of the greatest scientific breakthroughs and also difficult to formalize. At best, there are heuristics for sensitizing researchers to the emergence of new theories. Specifically, McGuire (1997) recommends saturating oneself in the phenomenon of interest (i.e., having a grounded understanding of what is going on) and seeking out disruptive data, logical tensions, and empirical surprises (i.e., embracing contradictions as the gateway to insight).

Multi-resolution research spurs abductive inference because it retains access to the contextual particulars (i.e., excerpts of raw data), foregrounds tensions between particulars and generalities, and supports exploring plausible explanations. Being able to zoom down into the particulars, in terms of what went on (i.e., videos of the experiment, high-scoring sentences in text analysis, and outlying cases in a regression) enables contextual, subtle, and empathetic understanding. Also, juxtaposing qualitative and quantitative analyses of the same data increases the potential to discover meaningful puzzles and tensions (rather than being the artifacts of datasets collected at different time points or in different contexts). Finally, moving back and forth between the qualitative particulars and general findings enables a problem-solving approach to discrepancies, as tensions can be investigated by moving to a new type, or resolution, of data structure.

A study by de Saint Laurent and colleagues (2021a, 2022) on Covid-19 memes is an example of how recursive data restructuring can spur abduction. The project analyzed memes shared during the 2020 outbreak on a Reddit community (r/CoronavirusMemes) to understand what representations of the crisis they conveyed and what function the memes served.

Data. Nearly 35,000 memes were collected between January 23 and May 17, 2020. Considering the frequency with which memes were posted, as well as the upvotes for each meme, a subsample of 1,560 memes was created to examine: (1) how the emerging representations of the pandemic were anchored in more familiar objects (e.g., the Spanish flu); (2) how these representations were objectified in concrete artefacts (e.g., the image of the coronavirus); (3) what social groups were represented (e.g., political figures); and (4) the aims of the meme (e.g., humor or giving advice).

Analysis. The coding frame was based on a recursive process involving the three authors and two research assistants. Two hundred seventy-six memes were selected and used for this purpose, following the same criteria as the 1,560 memes set that was eventually subjected to content analysis; this qualitative analytical process of constructing a code book involved connecting theoretical constructs with new and surprising elements found in the data, resulting in a multidimensional coding frame. Once the entire sample of 1,560 memes was coded, various types of quantitative analysis were performed in order to study the evolution of the memes over time, what drove their success, and the associations between themes and functions.

Augmented coding. It is challenging to scale up in-depth qualitative analysis to handle large datasets. To solve this issue, a computer application was developed in Python to facilitate using the coding frame (see Figure 7.1). The application displayed the meme to code, tick boxes corresponding to the various categories in the coding frame, and a section for notes.

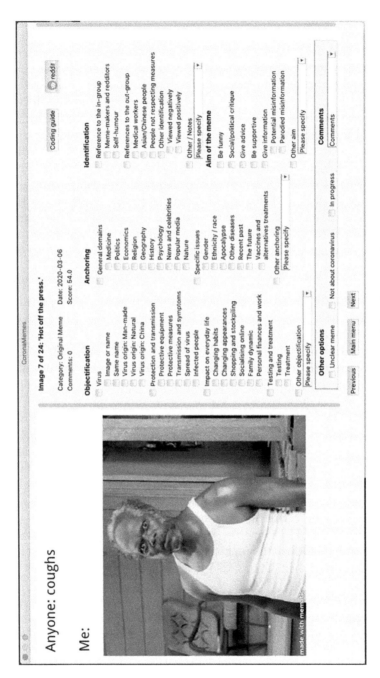

Figure 7.1 Computer-aided qualitative coding

The application and the resulting coding frame were an innovative use of computational means to enhance manual coding. This coding-augmented qualitative analysis enabled the researchers to refine the coding frame and, in a recursive manner, the overall analysis.

Findings. Some of the main findings related to the fact that the pandemic was most often objectified (i.e., represented in concrete terms) by displaying protective measures (e.g., social distancing) and the transmission of the virus (e.g., coughing, Figure 7.1). Memes also commonly referred to popular culture to anchor new meanings about a largely unknown, at the time, biological entity into an existing system of images, beliefs, and understandings very familiar to social media users. When it came to processes of identification, most memes depicted the self, the in-group, or people presumed to be most similar to the intended audience of internet users. Combining the in-depth qualitative and quantitative analyses also yielded some surprising abductive findings, especially regarding the political connotations of memes. While memes are often seen as primarily humorous, the quantitative analysis showed that political themes and critiques were a central part of the life of the Reddit community. However, it was zooming in on memes capturing political themes that revealed complex narratives beyond the depiction of specific politicians (for instance, some referred to supporters of different politicians, depicting them as gullible or even as dangerous). This led the researchers to the notion of role (e.g., Persecutor, Victim, Hero) in order to analyze the relationships between people or entities depicted in memes. The researchers then created a framework of roles (e.g., adding the role of the Fool) based on recursive moving between the individual memes and macro trends (e.g., sufficient frequency, coherent clustering).

Discussion. Within the research process, there was a continuous move back and forth between individual memes, the coding frame, and the larger dataset, which had been systematically coded. This zooming in on qualitative particulars and zooming out on macro trends gave the researchers confidence in the validity of their coding (e.g., by paying particular attention to counterexamples) and boosted their abductive insight. Abductive reasoning was fostered during the investigation by uncovering findings that challenged existing views of the pandemic (see also De Rosa & Mannarini, 2020). Individual memes that were surprising were used to challenge the statistical patterns, but also the quantitative findings helped to interpret individual memes. This recursive movement led to new insights about the characters and, at a deeper level, the roles portrayed in the memes. A typology of roles was developed, including the Persecutor, Victim, Hero, and

Fool. This typology recursively looped back into the data to prompt new questions: What kind of scenarios does the interaction between these roles reveal? What kinds of narratives do these roles create? These questions recursively fed into a novel analysis of the narrative content of these internet memes (de Saint Laurent et al., 2022).

7.5   Legitimacy: Doubly Constrained Interpretation

Recursively restructuring qualitative data can increase the legitimacy of findings by constraining interpretation. Both qualitative and quantitative analyses aim to constrain interpretation with empirical data, yet both have been criticized for having too many degrees of freedom. For example, excerpts can be selectively presented to suit a given interpretation (i.e., cherry-picking; Morse, 2010). Equally, quantitative measurement has many opaque degrees of freedom in cleaning data and choosing tests (Wicherts et al., 2016). Further constraining the degrees of freedom in both qualitative interpretation and quantitative analysis would produce more rigorous findings. Recursive data restructuring achieves this by constraining interpretation at both qualitative and quantitative levels.

Recursive data restructuring creates extra rigor by doubly constraining interpretation. The research is constrained by the quality criteria for both qualitative (i.e., the data should be credible, contextual, and richly described) and quantitative (i.e., the analysis should be reliable, valid, and generalizable) methods. Interpretations must convincingly operate both at a statistical level and at the level of specific cases (Seawright, 2016). Multi-resolution research thus uses the full qualitative depth and quantitative breadth of the data to constrain findings. The alternative is to base interpretation on a thin slice of the data (e.g., only excerpts, categories, or measures), which fails to leverage the full potential of the data.

This double qualitative–quantitative constraint is illustrated in a study reported by Noort and colleagues (2021c) that examined people withholding safety concerns, termed safety silence. In contrast to the vignette and survey methods that dominate the literature on voicing safety concerns (Noort et al., 2019a), the research team used a novel experimental paradigm in which participants interacted in-person with a confederate while confronting a safety issue (Noort et al., 2019b).

Data. Participants (n = 404) were asked to take part in a brainstorming task on the creative uses of a plank. The plank was about a meter long and could support only thirty kilograms. After listing their creative ideas, participants were asked to evaluate ideas ostensibly suggested by the previous participant. For each idea evaluated, the research assistant (the confederate) tested the idea in practice. All participants evaluated the same ideas, including a dangerous suggestion to use the plank as a footbridge between two chairs. What would the participants say when the research assistant (who weighed about sixty kilograms) finished assembling a wobbly footbridge and then began to walk across it?

Analysis. The quantitative analysis tested hypotheses using MANOVAs. The variables were survey measures, experimental outcomes, and textual measures of the participants' talk. In addition, all the participants' talk was recorded, transcribed, and made publicly available through an interactive visualization (Noort et al., 2021b). The visualization was created in Python using Scattertext (Kessler, 2017).

Visualization. Figure 7.2 is a static screenshot of an interactive visualization of participants' talk during the experiment. The figure combines categorizations (voice/silence, concerned/unconcerned), measures (how likely each word is to belong to each category), and excerpts (word use in context; the static plot only shows words, but, in the interactive plot, when clicked on, the words are shown in context). The figure plots the words that were most typical of participants who were concerned and voiced (top-right), concerned and silent (bottom-right), unconcerned and voiced (top-left), and unconcerned and silent (bottom-left). Words in the middle of the visualization were equally present across the categorizations.

The interactive visualization enables browsing participants' dialogue, and clicking on a word (or searching for it) displays the word use in context (split by the experimental outcome, voice/no voice). Thus, the visualization jointly displays excerpts, categories, and measures, enabling both the researchers and readers of the research to interrogate the full depth and breadth of the raw data. With advances in visualizing qualitative data, there is much potential for such mixed methods visualizations that reveal macro statistical patterns while keeping close to the raw data (Guetterman et al., 2015; O'Halloran et al., 2018; Sinclair & Rockwell, 2016).

Findings. Over half of the participants did not speak up about safety concerns despite being concerned. However, these concerned–silent participants (bottom-right of the figure) were not silent; they spoke with hesitation ("maybe," "guess," "uhm," "oh," "ah"). In contrast, participants who were concerned and voiced (top-right) referenced the safety critical information ("thirty," "kg," "maximum") and were assertive ("be careful," "because"). These qualitative particulars increase the validity and legitimacy of the findings.

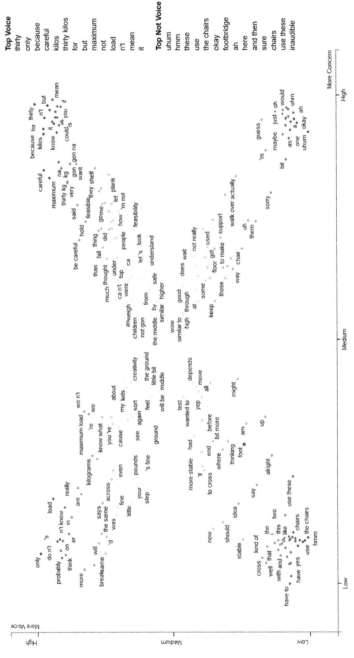

Voice document count: 187; word count: 8,949
Not Voice document count: 205; word count: 4,202

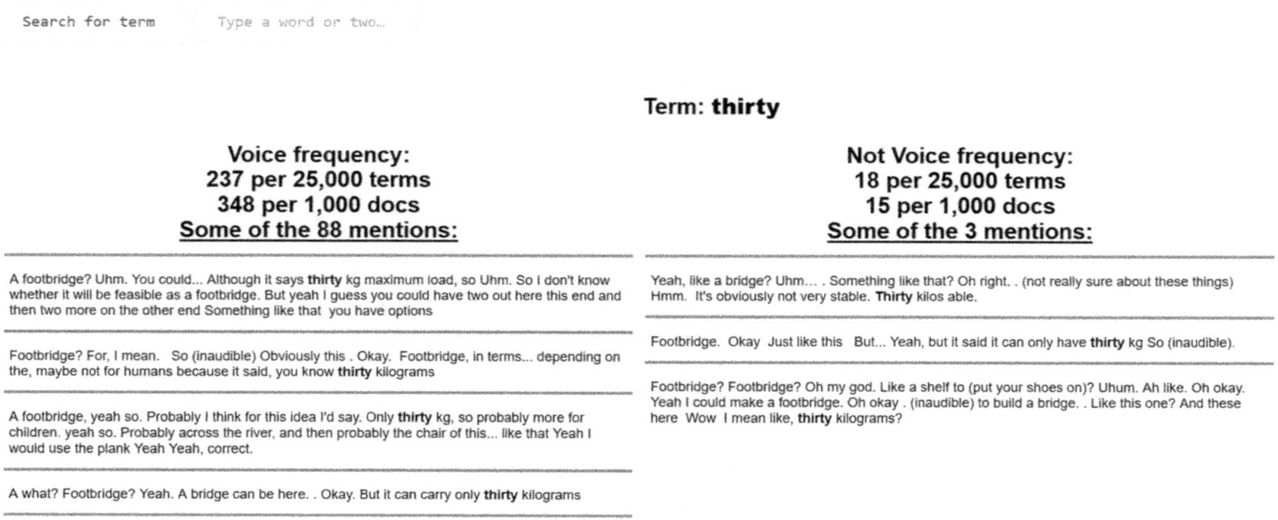

Term: **thirty**

Voice frequency:
237 per 25,000 terms
348 per 1,000 docs
<u>Some of the 88 mentions:</u>

A footbridge? Uhm. You could... Although it says **thirty** kg maximum load, so. Uhm. So I don't know whether it will be feasible as a footbridge. But yeah I guess you could have two out here this end and then two more on the other end Something like that you have options

Footbridge? For, I mean. So (inaudible) Obviously this . Okay. Footbridge, in terms... depending on the, maybe not for humans because it said, you know **thirty** kilograms

A footbridge, yeah so. Probably I think for this idea I'd say. Only **thirty** kg, so probably more for children.. yeah so. Probably across the river, and then probably the chair of this... like that Yeah I would use the plank Yeah Yeah, correct.

A what? Footbridge? Yeah. A bridge can be here. . Okay. But it can carry only **thirty** kilograms

Not Voice frequency:
18 per 25,000 terms
15 per 1,000 docs
<u>Some of the 3 mentions:</u>

Yeah, like a bridge? Uhm.... Something like that? Oh right. . (not really sure about these things) Hmm. It's obviously not very stable. **Thirty** kilos able.

Footbridge. Okay. Just like this But... Yeah, but it said It can only have **thirty** kg So (inaudible).

Footbridge? Footbridge? Oh my god. Like a shelf to (put your shoes on)? Uhum. Ah like. Oh okay. Yeah I could make a footbridge. Oh okay , (inaudible) to build a bridge. . Like this one? And these here Wow I mean like, **thirty** kilograms?

Figure 7.2   A screenshot of the interactive visualization showing that the word "thirty" was the most frequent among concerned–voicing participants and showing sentences in which the word "thirty" is used by participants who voiced or did not voice their concerns

Post hoc analysis, moving back and forth between the macro patterns and the qualitative particulars, yielded additional insights. The concerned–voicing participants often hesitate just prior to speaking up ("However, er. I think this is er just stands thirty kilograms," "But uhm… yeah I think it does. But I think it is not too safe"). This yields the abductive insight that hesitation might not be the opposite of assertively speaking up, but, instead, it might be the initial stage of speaking up, indicating either cognitive load or a communicative signaling discomfort. These early hesitations are, arguably, a form of "muted voice" (Noort et al., 2021c). This abductive insight adds legitimacy because it shows what is going on in particular cases, keeping the analysis close to the raw data. Also, the legitimacy is boosted because the same patterns were demonstrated both quantitatively (using participant statistics) and qualitatively (using freely browsable text).

Discussion. The ability to interrogate the verbatim transcripts of people voicing concerns (or not) within an experimental design reveals the potential synergies of mixing methods to analyze the same dataset. The same qualitative textual data can be analyzed as measures (likelihood of being said), categories (voice, silence), and excerpts (words in context). This increases the legitimacy of the research because (1) the interpretation has to account for qualitative particulars alongside quantitative patterns and (2) the resultant visualization is open to public scrutiny, with the verbatim transcripts being a powerful resource for anyone who wants to make a challenging interpretation. So far, calls for open data have focused on sharing numeric data (Shrout & Rodgers, 2018), but it is also increasingly possible to share the qualitative data that underpins the quantitative data (e.g., transcripts of what was said or done within an experiment; Glăveanu & Gillespie, 2021). Open data, which include the raw data linked to excerpts, categories, and measures, add legitimacy to the research through transparency and empowering secondary interpretations.

7.6   Data Requirements

Recursive data restructuring requires the qualitative and quantitative analyses to be applied to the same dataset. The simplest case is when exactly the same data are being used, for example, analyzing a corpus of text both qualitatively and quantitatively (e.g., when online posts are analyzed both quantitatively and qualitatively; Gillespie & Reader, 2022). More complex cases entail pairing qualitative and quantitative data by events or people. For example, quantitative metadata about geographic location could be paired with social media posts (same event), or a postexperiment interview could be paired with outcomes from the experiment. In the earlier example of the safety silence experiment, the experimental outcomes are paired with what participants said during the experiment. In all these cases of paired data, one can still zoom out to view overall patterns (geographic location, experimental outcomes) and zoom in to analyze specific excerpts (posts, utterances). However, if the qualitative and quantitative data are paired merely by topic (not data, events, or people), then they are unsuitable for recursive data restructuring. If data are only paired by topic (i.e., quantitative survey and qualitative interview on the same topic), then there is no way to transform one into the other (e.g., a one-to-one correspondence between survey responses and the interview excerpts is missing). Moreover, discrepancies might be artifacts of the different contexts and data collection procedures. In contrast, when the data are tightly paired, there are common data against which discrepancies can be reconciled.

Recursive data restructuring also requires data that meet the quality criteria for both qualitative and quantitative research (Buckley, 2018). From a qualitative standpoint, the data should comprise contextualized raw data (e.g., quotes, images, documents) that are credible, dependable, and afford thick description. From a quantitative standpoint, the data should be from a sufficiently known population and of sufficient scale and standardization to enable robust measurement. The data used in social research usually meet one or the other criteria but rarely both.

Most of the data created by researchers do not meet the requirements for recursive data restructuring because they are usually a thin slice (e.g., excerpts or measures). However, it is possible to create suitable data using traditional methods. Traditional qualitative methods (e.g., interviews, focus groups, observations, and video recordings) produce qualitative data that can be quantified, but they can be used in multi-resolution research only if there is a large volume of data – more than is traditionally used in qualitative research (Fakis et al., 2014; Vogl, 2019). Equally, one can add qualitative data collection to traditionally quantitative methods. For example, one can add talk-aloud protocols during survey completion, open-ended survey questions, video recordings during experiments, and postexperiment interviews to create tightly paired data (Moore & Gillespie, 2014; Niculae et al., 2015; Psaltis & Duveen, 2006).

In contrast, a lot of naturally occurring data are already suitable for multi-resolution research. Naturally occurring data exist independently of any research process and have not been prompted by the researchers. Instead of being elicited, they are part of the ongoing social processes in the world (i.e., instead of being reports about the world, they enable observations of the world). Naturally occurring big qualitative data are rapidly expanding and ideally suited to recursive data restructuring. Such data include online reviews (e.g., Glassdoor, TrustPilot, Care Opinion, Yelp), videos (YouTube, Vimeo), social media (Reddit, Twitter, TikTok), documents (formal complaints, earnings calls, incident reports, customer call transcripts), political speeches, cockpit voice recordings, parliamentary debates, closed-circuit television footage, and public inquiry data. These naturally occurring qualitative datasets are messy, but they have high validity because, in a pragmatist sense, they are what is going on.

7.7   The Benefits of Multi-resolution Research

Data have typically been either quantitative (e.g., population level) or qualitative (e.g., case study). However, with the growth in big qualitative data, we can access data that afford both quantitative population level and qualitative case study analyses. These big qualitative datasets force us to choose the data structure and subsequent analysis; the data were not made for either type of analysis and can be processed to enable both. We propose that no data structure is optimal in itself. Instead, we recommend leveraging the full breadth and depth of the data by recursively restructuring the data to move between excerpts, categories, and measures of the same data. Measurements can reveal differences, changes, comparisons, and statistical models. Excerpts reveal validity, contextual nuance, and challenging outliers. By analyzing only one slice of the data (i.e., excerpts, categories, or measures), the analysis is caught in an increasingly artificial trade-off between qualitative depth and quantitative breadth.

Expectations for research quality are rising. Large volumes of qualitative data are becoming easier and cheaper to record, transcribe, and analyze. Computing innovations allow for the analysis, visualization, and dissemination of deeply integrated qualitative and quantitative data side by side (Andreotta et al., 2019; Buckley, 2018; Chang et al., 2021; Shahin, 2016). Accordingly, the choice between depth (qualitative) and breadth (quantitative) is increasingly anachronistic; we should expect research to have both depth and breadth.

The advent of big qualitative data is also raising the bar for data quality regarding size, validity, and naturalism. However, these potentialities can be achieved only with a mixed methods approach. Computational approaches to qualitative data cannot supplant traditional qualitative methods (Bennett, 2015). Although, algorithms can reliably identify objects, actors, actions, quotations, sentiment, and various themes, human interpretation is required to frame questions, ensure validity, interpret findings, and understand limitations. In short, it is necessary to combine computation and interpretation to seize the potential of big qualitative data (Bazeley, 2017; Ho et al., 2021). Our point is that for big qualitative data, this combination of methods should occur at the level of data, with the same data being recursively transformed between qualitative and quantitative forms.

7.7.1 Increasing the Legitimacy of Quantitative Research

Recursive data restructuring can improve the legitimacy of quantitative research, which is currently grappling with the replication crisis (Shrout & Rodgers, 2018). Many experimental findings, especially in social psychology, do not replicate when tested independently (Open Science Collaboration, 2015). One reason for this problem is that there are many degrees of freedom in data collection, curation, and analysis (Wicherts et al., 2016). Recommendations to reduce the degrees of freedom include preregistering research, supporting replications, and making data open access (Shrout & Rodgers, 2018). Recursive data restructuring, we propose, can also further constrain the degrees of freedom by making visible the qualitative data that underpins the quantitative findings.

All quantitative research entails quantifying qualities. The risk is that the numeric values become disconnected from the phenomenon being measured. Accordingly, the best practice is to revert quantitative measures back to the qualitative data to ensure validity (Berka, 1983; Zeller et al., 1980). Recursive data restructuring takes this idea further, arguing that as far as possible quantitized data should be revertible to its qualitative form throughout the analysis and dissemination. This possibility of reverting measures to the underlying qualitative data has only recently become possible due to technological advances in collecting, storing, analyzing, and visualizing digital data.

Traditionally experimental and quantitative research has not recorded qualitative data; the numbers have been extracted at source (e.g., in experimental outcomes or rankings on a Likert scale). But as the costs of recording, storing, and analyzing data reduce, it is possible to include qualitative data. Surveys could include open-ended questions, talk-along interviews (Moore & Gillespie, 2014), and talk-aloud protocols (French et al., 2007; Wagoner & Valsiner, 2005). Equally, experiments that involve social interaction can include audio or video recordings of participants in the experiment (e.g., participants interacting, screen recordings), thus making the interactions that underpin the experimental findings analyzable (Psaltis & Duveen, 2007). The benefit of deepening the data in this way is that it would enable replications and reinterpretations (Glăveanu & Gillespie, 2021).

It is important to note that recursive data restructuring should not be used simultaneously with confirmatory hypothesis testing. Recursive analysis is an exploratory method, focused upon generating theory, finding explanations, and ensuring validity. Exploratory research is fundamentally different from confirmatory research (Stebbins, 2001; Tukey, 1980) and the data used for each should be kept separate. Exploratory research entails freely trying out various analyses on the data to find a good fit. Confirmatory research entails stating a hypothesis before analyzing the data. If recursive analysis is combined with confirmatory testing, then the recursive analysis should either be done on a training dataset (kept separate from the testing dataset) or be done on data after the confirmatory tests have been run. If confirmatory analysis were done on the same data as used to develop the hypothesis recursively, there would be a risk of overfitting, where the findings are peculiar to features of the dataset and thus fail to generalize.

7.7.2   Increasing the Impact of Qualitative Research

Recursive data restructuring can also make qualitative research more rigorous, efficient, and transparent. Qualitative research has been criticized for using small samples (Chang et al., 2021), "cherry-picking" excerpts (Morse, 2010), and lacking clarity on the sampling of excerpts. Augmenting qualitative research with computational analysis can address these challenges (Fielding, 2012; Leeson et al., 2019).

There are many software packages for qualitative research, but to date they have been elaborate filing systems for keeping track of manually labeled excerpts of text, image, or audio (Renz et al., 2018). In the near future, it is expected that this software will begin to incorporate more algorithms to boost qualitative analysis. First, algorithms are equivalent to humans for basic thematic analysis, and as such, this may become an automated first step in qualitative analyses (Chang et al., 2021; Ho et al., 2021; Lee et al., 2020). Second, search algorithms have improved significantly, such that text, image, and video can be searched reliably. These new search algorithms can return semantically similar results (i.e., beyond narrow word-matching) with surprising accuracy (Neuman, 2016). Again, it is expected that these advanced search algorithms will become embedded in qualitative research software, enabling searches for more subtle and analytic concepts – or having identified a particular excerpt, the algorithm will return excerpts that are semantically, compositionally, structurally, or visually similar. In these ways, there is likely to be a meeting of qualitative interpretation and advanced computational analysis that will embed recursive data restructuring in mainstream software.

Automating basic analyses would enable qualitative research to become more ambitious, tackle larger datasets, and provide more rigorous rationales for choosing excerpts to analyze in detail. Augmenting qualitative research with algorithms would reduce the burden on analysis and thus free up humans for in-depth and contextual interpretation – which is where the human element adds most value. The algorithms would be like tireless research assistants, working ceaselessly behind the scenes to analyze enormous amounts of data and produce comprehensible intermediate overviews that form the basis for in-depth manual interpretation (Janasik et al., 2009; Wiedemann, 2013). These algorithmic assistants would find similar excerpts, quantify the frequency of a certain type of excerpt, suggest patterns, and produce visualizations that enable the analysis to work on recursively restructured data – moving freely between the macro patterns and the micro details.

7.7.3 The Micro in the Macro and the Macro in the Micro

Human behavior has a fractal quality, revealing complexity at multiple levels of resolution. Charles Eames and Ray Eames (1977) made a short film zooming out from a couple having a picnic in Chicago to the edge of the known universe and then zooming back into the molecules within the man's hand, revealing patterns at the subatomic, atomic, cellular, human, planetary, solar system, and galaxy levels. Equally, zooming in and out of human behavior reveals patterns at different resolutions of analysis. For example, an utterance can be analyzed as the embodied production of sounds, as individual words, as a semantic web of associations, as consequential within a pragmatic context, as part of a genre, and as part of an institutional, cultural, or historical pattern. Recursive data restructuring aims to reconnect these levels of analysis.

We often talk about "levels" in social research (e.g., cognitive, individual, group, institutional, societal). But these levels are a simplifying heuristic. There is no ontological split between the individual and society; society is made up of individuals, and individuals are deeply societal. Our talk about levels can create problems: It obscures the way in which these so-called levels are not merely interdependent but actually one and the same. A statistical analysis of a text corpus is not on a different level to a qualitative analysis of one excerpt within the corpus; both pertain to the same data and, as such, are different views on the same underlying raw data. Recursive data restructuring, and the metaphor of zooming in with qualitative analysis and zooming out with quantitative analysis, enables one to study the social world as simultaneously micro and macro. For example, we can study excerpts within the context of macro discourses and macro discourses as comprising specific excerpts.

Multi-resolution research builds on the core pragmatist insight that all knowledge is anchored in human activity (Chapters 1, 2, and 3). Data are produced by transforming human activity into something suitable for analysis (Chapter 5). It follows that human activity can be converted into data for both qualitative and quantitative analysis. The abductive insight that guides multi-resolution research is converting the same events into multiple types of data suitable for multiple types of analysis. Multi-resolution research shows us that the taken-for-granted distinction between population-level research and case studies is an artificial byproduct of methods that have been unable to do both simultaneously.

In multi-resolution research, the micro and macro are examined as the *same phenomenon* viewed at different resolutions or scales; they are not two separate but "connected" phenomena. This insight about the macro and the micro being the same is obscured if raw data are thinly sliced into either excerpts, categories, or measures. Our traditional approach to separating qualitative and quantitative methods has made it difficult to conceptualize the macro in the micro and vice versa (Cornish, 2004). That is to say, the so-called disconnect between the micro and macro levels is an unhelpful byproduct of separating qualitative case studies from quantitative population studies. The methodological split between qualitative and quantitative methods has supported an unnatural carving of nature, separating the particular from the general. Multi-resolution research, via recursive data restructuring, seeks to make the micro (e.g., excerpts) and the macro (e.g., statistical patterns) ontologically whole – as two views of the same raw data.

CHAPTER 8

Ethics

A moral law, like a law in physics, is not something to swear by and stick to at all hazards; it is a formula of the way to respond when specified conditions present themselves. Its soundness and pertinence are tested by what happens when it is acted upon.

Dewey (1929, p. 222)

Ethical concerns permeate a pragmatist approach to methodology. We have already discussed ethical issues in Chapters 1, 3, 4, 5, 6, and 9. This is because, as Dewey's quote suggests, pragmatism is focused on action in and on the social world (Kilpinen, 2009). Whether we are planning a holiday or conducting research, human action is embedded in a field of norms, values, and standards. In so far as human action is consequential for other people, it is also moral. Thus, in so far as human action contributes, even in a small way, to the future of human relations, it requires responsibility.

Social science research has become increasingly aware of ethical issues since the mid-twentieth century. There are increasing guidelines covering an increasingly broad range of research contexts. This includes, for instance, the ethical standards set up by the American Psychological Association as well as international standards set up, for example, by the Declaration of Helsinki. The general principles of the former are (1) beneficence and nonmaleficence; (2) fidelity and responsibility; (3) integrity; (4) justice; and (5) respect for people's rights and dignity (American Psychological Association, 2023). The Declaration of Helsinki focuses more broadly on medical research involving human subjects. It starts from the premise that the health and well-being of participants are of paramount importance and, as such, that research should be guided by safeguarding the participant's interests (World Medical Association, 2022). These interests are served by following established research practices, including informed consent, privacy, confidentiality, and the right to withdraw. Consent forms typically list these rights and ask participants to acknowledge that they have been informed about the study and agree to participate.

The challenge, however, is how to move beyond ethics as "box ticking," a bureaucratic exercise that asks researchers to comply with formal requirements without necessarily engaging them in moral inquiry and deliberation. While the standards listed earlier are useful and morally sound (who would disagree with the idea of prioritizing a participant's health and sense of well-being?), they are rarely foregrounded for researchers or participants unless the investigation deals with a controversial topic or vulnerable populations. These guidelines preexist the encounter between researcher and participants and, beyond signing the consent form at the outset, rarely appear again in the research process. Pragmatism, with its emphasis on consequences, reflexivity, and sensemaking, insists that ethics is not a separate moment in research but an integral part of it (Baker & Schaltegger, 2015; Simpson & den Hond, 2022). Ethical deliberation should permeate the entire research process, from setting the aims to the consequences of the findings.

As such, pragmatism invites researchers to go beyond thinking of ethics only (or mainly) in terms of data collection and storage (through informed consent, confidentiality, right to withdraw, deleting data after the study, etc.). While these standards are important, the rituals associated with satisfying them (and, by extension, satisfying ethics review boards often faced with difficult tasks) risk becoming empty of meaning, in the worst case, or, at the very least, make researchers miss valuable opportunities for deeper forms of questioning (Schrag, 2011). For example, what do the participants, in contrast to the ethics committee, think about the research? Who is the knowledge created for? What does the knowledge "do"? What kinds of interests does it serve? Does the investigation promote prediction and control, or does it also empower its participants? Might there be unintended consequences of the research?

These questions should be central to any research project, from its conception and execution to its dissemination and impact. Unfortunately, it is much more likely for engaged ethical reflections to be part of doctoral dissertations (especially in the qualitative research tradition) than to appear in articles reporting empirical studies. The latter typically only briefly mention International Review Board approvals or the national or international guidelines followed, with little reflection on how ethics shaped the aims and approach of the research. The roots of this problem run deep. They concern a specific view of the relationship between science and ethics that pragmatist thinkers and researchers are eager to challenge.

In essence, a false opposition has been constructed between scientific discovery and the need to protect human subjects, a dichotomy that often places researchers in the uncomfortable position of negotiating what they see as competing pulls (Brendel & Miller, 2008). This view stems from the implicit assumption, in positivism, that scientific work should be "objective" and detached from "biased" human interests and concerns (see Chapters 2, 3, and 9). On the contrary, ethics foregrounds the individuals involved and rejects "an amoral position where 'facts' become separated from 'values', and are reduced to data, to variables whose numerical values are more important than their practical meanings" (Simpson & den Hond, 2022, p. 139). And yet, research participants have rarely been included in discussions about ethics (e.g., providing feedback on the ethical aspects of the study they participated in). In contrast, from a pragmatist standpoint, participants are on the front line of research ethics because they have the clearest view of the ethical implications of the research on those who participate in it. The point is that ethical concerns are too often reduced to a narrow version of "protecting human subjects" or the well-known "duty of care," which can be perceived as constraining by researchers, even leading them to abandon potentially impactful research. "Doing" science and being ethical risk being perceived as conflicting constraints rather than integrated practices and concerns.

Pragmatists are keen on dismantling this false opposition and bringing together science and ethics as part of a unitary process of inquiry, discovery, and moral deliberation. To achieve this, however, we need to consider research ethics as more than a series of guidelines and obligations. In the pragmatist tradition, ethics is conceived

> as a spirit of open inquiry and practically focused reasoning about ethical dilemmas. It can be described as a 'bottom up' approach to ethics in which moral and philosophical thinking is generated in response to (and is intended to resolve) day-to-day dilemmas. ... Pragmatic research ethics strives to carefully identify and analyze competing values in practical contexts of ... research, recognizing that moral trade-offs, pitting scientific validity and subject protection, are inevitable. (Brendel & Miller, 2008, p. 25)

In this chapter, we develop the pragmatist proposition that *social research creates both power and responsibility* – that ethics is an integral part of any research process, beginning to end, and that a pragmatist stance widens the role of ethics and shifts the focus from ethical boards and researchers to board, researchers, participants, and other stakeholders. We will also argue that moral inquiry is enhanced when using multi-resolution research given that it presents us with unique opportunities in both research and ethical terms.

The chapter is structured as follows: First, we frame the larger debate concerning universalism versus contextualism in ethics, largely mirroring the one between positivism and relativism in science. We propose that pragmatism transcends this dichotomy as well by considering the role of general (and particular) ethical norms and values in context. Then, we outline briefly what the pragmatist approach to ethics is founded on before discussing the ways in which ethical concerns and forms of reasoning accompany every phase of a research project. The practice of deception, widespread and controversial in social and psychological research, provides a case study. Finally, we end with considerations regarding mixed methods and multi-resolution research and their ethical commitments before offering some concluding thoughts.

8.1 Framing the Debate

The assumed opposition between science and ethics persists because of an oversharp distinction between objective "facts" versus human "values." The history of ethics is marked by numerous attempts to establish universal normative principles rather than operate with context-based moral judgments. From Plato to Kant, the main task has been to rationally derive moral guidelines that, once properly justified, could be applied across all contexts and situations. The alternative was considered to be irrational and dangerous: the fragmentation of ethics into a myriad of personal beliefs and self-serving conceptions. The normative approach inspired, among others, the creation of general ethical guidelines for researchers and their promotion by national and international bodies. According to Altman (1983, pp. 227–228), some key assumptions behind universalist ethics include the following:

1. There is some unique set of principles that specifies ethical conduct for any individual in any historical period.
2. There is some unique set of principles that specifies for all historical periods the ethical social order.
3. The task of fully justifying a set of ethical principles must proceed from an ethically neutral starting point.

The normative approach embraces universalism and rejects relativism in ethics (see also Chapters 2 and 3). Universalists judge the morality of other people's actions from an outside position by referring to transcendent ethical principles. The reason is that the origin of moral beliefs, be it God or Reason, is immovable and all-encompassing. Relativists, in contrast, "claim that because individuals are socially constructed, the types of people produced in these different cultures differ so widely as to render such judgment impossible" (Butt, 2000, p. 86); they see moral values as essentially constructed. As such, ethical principles – and especially dealing with ethical dilemmas – require interpretation and a great deal of local knowledge. One should not try to judge others "from the outside," without trying to understand their position and worldview from the inside. The risk with this position, as Butt also notes, is that what is moral or immoral becomes a question of societal practices. This can become problematic, for example, when dealing with something like universal human rights. Should they be pursued with no consideration for historical differences and local knowledge? Relativists would not necessarily argue against extending human rights, and certainly neither would pragmatists (Hoover, 2016), but their approach would be guided by doubt and questioning rather than an unexamined reliance on norms.

Pragmatists are promoters of moral deliberation and, as such, might seem to be on the side of relativism rather than universalism in ethics. Yet it would be wrong to assume this. In fact, the uniqueness of the pragmatist standpoint is that it tries to integrate normative-universalist and contextual-relativist positions. Pragmatism tries to move the debate beyond these oppositions by proposing moral pluralism (Graham et al., 2013). In contrast to both universalists and relativists, pragmatists privilege the voice of the participants in the research (and, more broadly, those who will be on the receiving end of the knowledge produced). When giving these stakeholders a voice in research ethics, it is expected that their ethical judgments will be shaped by their culture and norms (i.e., aspects of relativism), but there will also be absolute constraints that researchers cannot ignore (i.e., aspects of universalism).

One of the main problems with universalism is that once a commitment is made to general principles, then anything that opposes or questions those principles considered "right" risks being deemed unfounded or even unethical; otherwise, the principles themselves must be revised. One of the main problems with relativism is overlooking how important the notion of universal values is for local discussions of ethics. In practice, universal and contextual arguments are brought to bear on any ethical deliberation, and precisely the interplay and articulation of these positions lead to nuanced, ethical, and workable conclusions. This pragmatist position is useful for Institutional Review Board discussions of specific research proposals (Brenneis, 2005). These boards are necessarily guided by some general ethical principles, reminiscent of universalism, while their reason for existing is an understanding that each research project has some unique elements and, as such, needs to be considered in its own right. It is precisely this openness to debate and discussion that is at the heart of pragmatist ethics. This enables ethics to adapt and respond not only to changing practices of research but also to changing cultural norms. However, in addition to this, pragmatists also emphasize that these debates should not be isolated to ethics boards or researchers but should also involve research participants and other stakeholders.

Johansen and Frederiksen (2021) refer to a pragmatic-dualist approach to research ethics. Similarly, Morgan (2014b, p. 142), aiming to reach a synthesis leading to "ethical solidarity," writes about pragmatic humanism as an approach concerned

> with cultivating a sensitized mindset (in those who are willing to listen) to a deeper consideration of the sameness that can be found even within our differences, and in particular, of the sameness that exists in our shared capacity to suffer, to cause suffering, and also to relieve suffering.

What matters most are not universal principles or local values but sensitivity to human interests and giving stakeholders voice within discussions of ethics. A focus on our shared humanity can be such a starting point, one which places differences against a background of commonalities. Bringing research stakeholders into the discussions about ethics may reveal that there is less opposition between science and ethics than has hitherto been assumed.

8.2   Pragmatism and Ethics

One of the aims of pragmatism is to transcend unhelpful dichotomies. We carry this aim forward by seeking to transcend the structured–unstructured data dichotomy (Chapter 5) and the qualitative–quantitative methods dichotomy (Chapters 6 and 7). The divides between science and ethics and, within ethics, between normative-universal and contextual-relativist standpoints are other dichotomies that we want to challenge. Instead of reinforcing the old terms of these debates, a pragmatist approach shifts the focus from ethical principles to the processes through which they emerge, clash, and transform – from universal laws to how power and responsibility manifest in research practice. Such critical reflection is possible only when people are presented with moral dilemmas whereby two or more courses of action are imagined as possible. Thus, at the heart of this enacted ethics is the experience of doubt.

"Wherever there is doubt," Simpson and den Hond (2022, p. 140) note, "there will also be a moral choice to be made; the resultant action is deemed moral if the situation is transformed and growth results." In other words, the ultimate criterion for assessing what is "good" and "bad" considers the entire situation, the actors and actions involved, and their short-term and long-term consequences. Morality does not reside in prejudgment but precisely in the acts of choosing, deliberating, and doubting (Senghor & Racine, 2022). In a broader sense, such actions are based on expectation and, thus, by definition, on uncertainty. Ethics does not deal in certainties because it considers the future of human action and its fundamentally uncertain consequences (see Chapter 9). The morality of any act (just like the truth value of knowledge) is in the future: what it does, who is impacted by it, and what future it contributes to. This makes the work of Institutional Review Boards and ethics committees even more challenging. They are tasked with prejudging something that has not occurred, and while there are actions whose consequences are almost certainly negative, many occupy a much greyer area when it comes to anticipated futures. This raises the prospect of evaluating ethics not only before a research project is conducted but also at the end of it, when the actual consequences on participants can be assessed (later in this chapter, we will discuss using postassessments for research that entails deception).

Assessing the risks associated with research activities is an essential part of the process. Normative universalism tries to eliminate risk by resting on immovable laws; relativism avoids it by refraining from reaching a final ethical conclusion. Pragmatism, in contrast, engages the risk head-on: It brings participants and stakeholders who experience the practical consequences of the research into the discussion to make an informed, but necessarily uncertain, assessment of the ethical implications of the research. It embraces the fact that "moral trade-offs between competing values may entail nuanced and fallible judgments" (Brendel & Miller, 2008, p. 25). Also, just like actions are shaped by failures and obstacles, ethical reasoning needs to be flexible enough to shift direction and learn from the ever-present possibility of getting things wrong. The fallibility of ethical judgments is not a sign of weakness or an indication that they should be abandoned; on the contrary, it reflects the condition of human action as always anticipating and constructing a future that should never be taken for granted.

This open-endedness makes it difficult to construct a unitary or singular pragmatist ethical theory. In fact, given that the pragmatist does not follow antecedent principles and rejects the logic of foundationalism – rather building the foundations in the actual interaction, in the practical consequences of what is being done as well as by following closely human action in its diversity – the lack of consensus is not surprising. In the words of Serra (2010, p. 7), "instead of proposing a specific theory, pragmatism describes itself as a method for understanding better – or reconstructing – already existing theories, and more generally, as a method that enables greater awareness of our actual moral life." Pragmatist ethics offers a way of dealing with ethical questions, not necessarily answering these questions.

It is perhaps more appropriate, then, to discuss the ethical theory of specific authors. To take a concrete example, John Dewey's work inspired numerous (neopragmatist) elaborations. For instance, Fesmire (2003, p. 4) emphasized Dewey's interest in the moral imagination and his thesis that "moral character, belief, and reasoning are inherently social, embodied, and historically situated" and that "moral deliberation is fundamentally imaginative and takes the form of a dramatic rehearsal." Since the impact of action is, at least in part, in the future, we need the help of imagination in order to build anticipations of what is to come (Zittoun & Gillespie, 2018). We can also imaginatively rehearse actions and their consequences, something that should not be the solipsistic activity of isolated researchers but a topic of discussion and collective deliberation. Serra (2010) points out that, for Dewey, ethical reflection starts whenever the person encounters morally problematic situations, those that have incompatible ends and, thus, require reflexivity and choice. "Moral experience is bound to not knowing what to do among several demands" (Serra, 2010, p. 4). Importantly, these acts of deliberation are not intrapersonal as much as they are interpersonal, communicative, and socially engaged. "In deliberating, we not only imagine and reflect on the consequences for ourselves but also try to figure out the responses of others" (Serra, 2010, p. 5). This is where imagination and perspective-taking become important for ethical conduct by facilitating the "playing out" of impulses, courses of action, and potential outcomes. Deliberation is dramatic and active; it is not a cold mathematical calculation; it is personal, embodied, and empathetic. Ethics is lived through rather than detached from everyday living and its myriad of experiences, including the experience of research.

A more radical stance on this is provided by Emmanuel Levinas, who, although not a pragmatist, did privilege the face-to-face moment of interaction. Levinas (1991) argued that ethics begins by being confronted with the actual face of the other, making it lived and personal rather than detached and abstract. While other philosophers put Truth first, Levinas put ethics first. He argued that our responsibility for one another comes before questions of ultimate truth. We are, he argued, created through social interaction, and as such, there is nothing before encountering the other. These relations to each other, he argued, are the basis of ourselves, and without these ethical interdependencies, and taking responsibility for these interdependencies, truth has no value for humans. One key insight that Levinas provides is that the Other always exceeds Self. The Other has a perspective that can never be fully understood by Self (see the idea of surplus of the Other in Gillespie, 2003). This means that devolving ethics entirely to an ethics committee, which is not impacted by either the research process or outcome, could give false security. The ethics committee cannot fully know the participants in the research or the people impacted by the knowledge. In short, Levinas' ideas prompt us toward engaging more actively with our participants and end-users of knowledge or stakeholders in a research project – to give them voice in assessing the ethicality of the research.

While there might not be any definitive pragmatist theory of ethics, there is enough "family resemblance" between the thinking of pragmatists and neopragmatists to allow the abstraction of some general features of the overall approach. For example, LaFollette (1997) identified four key characteristics of pragmatist ethics: (1) It employs criteria without being criteriological; it refers to moral principles but foregrounds deliberation; (2) it is objective without being absolute; it tries to separate what is ethically good and bad but admits fallibility in the process; (3) it recognizes that ethical judgments are relative without being relativist, because ethical judgments need to engage lived contexts but also compare across contexts; and (4) it is pluralist without being indecisive; pragmatism recognizes moral differences but also tries to decide about them based on open dialogue (see also Serra, 2010). These four characteristics overlap with what Arras (2001) described as "freestanding pragmatism" in ethics. This entails (1) contextualism, namely, reasoning about ethical dilemmas in context; (2) instrumentalism, namely, focusing on practical outcomes; (3) eclecticism, namely, using multiple theoretical approaches in ethical decision-making; (4) theory independence, or the avoidance of "top-down" deliberation; (5) reflective equilibrium, or the continuous reexamination of one's own assumptions; and (6) searching for consensus through inclusive deliberation. For both LaFollette and Arras, ethics is neither an individual nor an institutional practice. Ethical judgments occur in a space created by human actions and interactions involving various actors, interests, experiences, and expectations. This plurality invites a reflective stance on the morality of specific research activities and what is understood by ethics in each given context.

What are the strengths and weaknesses of this broad pragmatist stance? Because pragmatism has its roots in an empirical and experimental approach to knowledge construction while, at the same time, acknowledging the relation of knowledge with human interests and concerns, it is well placed to navigate the ethics of research. The activity of Institutional Review Boards could undoubtedly be enriched by taking a pragmatist stance. One of the main challenges comes from fully grasping the context around moral deliberation: Who is part of this context? Whose interests are being represented (or made invisible)? Why are participants and other stakeholders so rarely involved in discussions about ethics? How can we ultimately decide where to draw the line in our ethical analysis, and when to end our ethical deliberation? (See also Altman, 1983.) For instance, Mead (1934, p. 387) wrote that "when we reach the question of what is right … the only test … is whether we have taken into account every interest involved." The interests involved depend upon the consequences, and the consequences are in the future and inherently uncertain (although we can have more or less confidence), and as such, it is impossible to fully take account of all the interests involved before the consequences are realized (see also Chapter 9). Saying that the outcomes of this process vary, pragmatically, context to context, might not suffice. At the same time, we should avoid developing a fatalistic or agnostic outlook on ethical decision-making. There will always be unanticipated consequences (Merton, 1936), and the risk of "getting things wrong" (as with any human activity) is ever-present. The quality of an ethics preprocess depends on whether the relevant stakeholders have been taken into account – which is most easily achieved with genuine stakeholder participation.

8.3   A Pragmatist New Look at Research Ethics

How do these different pragmatist ethics (in plural) apply to research? How can we translate an open system into a list of guidelines, even if advisory rather than mandatory? Brendel and Miller (2008) offered a useful proposal in this regard, namely, a set of guidelines for a pragmatist approach to ethics in research. Their context is clinical research, but their guidelines are broadly applicable:

1.   The importance of focusing on case-by-case moral problem solving to balance the drive toward scientific discovery with the need to protect human subjects in clinical research.
2.   A conceptualization of ethical principles in clinical research as a set of working hypotheses – rather than pre-determined, fixed moral

rules – about how to promote research while protecting human subjects in concrete situations.

3. The need for open-minded engagement of ethical inquiry with the specific contextual details of proposed research projects.

4. Acknowledgment of the fallibility of principled judgments about clinical research and of the appropriateness of revising basic assumptions, decisions, and policies based on new information and analysis, including experimental evaluation.

5. The importance of open-minded debate and deliberation, as well as respect for minority viewpoints, amongst a diversity of individuals reviewing clinical research proposals. (Brendel & Miller, 2008, pp. 25–26)

We uphold all these general guidelines and consider them essential for research with human participants in any field; what could be added to them is an "ethics from the inside" approach in which the perspective and interests of those involved or impacted by the research come to the fore. Taken together, these principles show that ethical concerns are not reserved for specific "moments" within the research process like data collection and data reporting. There is much more to ethical engagement than considering what kind of information participants are given, what debriefing is set in place, or how confidentiality is safeguarded, as important as these concerns are. Within pragmatism, ethics permeates the whole process of research, from why the topic is chosen out of the infinity of possible topics to the guiding questions and interests to how the findings are built upon theoretically and practically.

The typical image of the "trade-off" between science and ethics is replaced here by a unifying goal of producing knowledge that works for the humanity and dignity of those involved and, thus, that improves the human condition. For pragmatism, there is no trade-off because truth and values are assessed in the same way, namely, in terms of consequences. The trade-off, if we are to speak of one, is not between science and ethics. The only trade-off is between the interests of self and others (i.e., when the interests of different groups are in conflict or the consequences of the research for self and others are markedly different). This is why pragmatist researchers reflect on much more than what kind of methodological devices are reliable, valid, or trustworthy. They start by considering what the study and its conceptual framing "do" in relation to how we consider human beings. Are participants depicted as agentic or nonagentic, creative or uncreative, active or passive? Are the findings going to be used to empower or control others? Does the study add or take away from the complexity of human existence? Will the research produce knowledge that empowers people? Or that makes them predictable and controllable – limiting some people's degrees of freedom while increasing the action capacity of others (e.g., companies, groups in power)?

Research ethics often focuses on the duties and responsibilities of the researcher (i.e., how, for example, duty of care is framed). Pragmatism shares this concern for consequences (i.e., mental, physical, and well-being impacts of the research on participants), but it also encourages us to respect the human dignity and agency of research participants, topics that are not always at the forefront of how we design and conduct research. The broader implication is that humans are intrinsically creative and reflective, and as such, it is ethically questionable to treat them as mere data points without any concern for the motivation and context of their participation in research. This goes well beyond informed consent and points to a more profound notion of accountability in research (Bauer & Gaskell, 2000). It also connects to empowerment and the need for researchers to reflect more deeply on what kind of human interests are advanced or hindered by their studies (see Chapter 9).

The pragmatist proposition guiding our conceptualization of research ethics is that all social research entails both power and responsibility. The power of the researcher comes from their role in designing the research situation and inviting participants to comply with his or her instructions. It also derives from the knowledge being produced; useful knowledge holds power as it creates change. Whether this change is positive or not raises the second issue, that of responsibility. Responsibility is associated with the consequences of the study, for researchers and participants, consequences that follow from how the study is designed and carried out. Researchers must make many ethical decisions along the way, with imperfect information and uncertain outcomes, but decisions that can nonetheless be informed by using stakeholders to stimulate self-reflection. In the end, whoever is impacted by the knowledge produced within the study has a stake in the process. Pragmatism invites us to consider this aspect as an ethical dilemma in and of itself and, as with any dilemma, to use it as an opportunity for rethinking our assumptions and questioning our commitments. In the words of Johansen and Frederiksen (2021, p. 280):

> Dilemmas regarding research ethics cannot be contained in a sentence or two in the introduction or conclusion of a research paper stating that proper research ethics have been observed. Research ethics are not some appendage that can be identified, prepared and implemented once and for all. On the contrary, they are an epistemological condition embedded in the whole

research project – from introductory considerations about theme and issue to the concluding thoughts about facilitation and dissemination. They must be considered and reconsidered, negotiated and re-negotiated, throughout the entire research process.

These dilemmas are not always the most obvious. For example, a salient dilemma might be whether subjecting research participants to moderate stress is compensated by the usefulness of the knowledge obtained. However, sometimes the unproblematized aspects of research might carry significant ethical implications. For example, the way a research question is set carries specific assumptions, some of which concern research participants (e.g., their abilities, knowledge, interest, and level of agency). The way participants are approached and incentivized to participate in the research project betrays assumptions about what might motivate them and how these motivations can be used to persuade them to take part in the study. The coding frames employed by researchers capture their expectations about the data and about what is important to them, which is rarely the same as what is important to their participants. Even the analysis performed involves choices such as emphasizing unity or variability, highlighting positive or negative aspects, and displaying trust in the participants' accounts or suspicion. Last but not least, writing up a piece of research involves choices, especially about what is to be included and to be left out of the account, including which participant perspectives are "important" or "valuable" and need to be foregrounded as part of the findings. Writing up the research also brings into focus the potential uses and abuses of the research findings and entails choices about how to frame these. Other dilemmas, like the use of deception, present researchers with both explicit and implicit moral dilemmas and, as such, present an interesting case study to demonstrate the utility of a pragmatist approach.

8.4 The Case of Deception

Deception has posed a long-standing dilemma for research, especially in social psychology. Many of the classic experiments on obedience (Milgram, 1969), conformity (Asch, 1955), bystander effects (Darley & Latané, 1968), and the power of the situation (Haney et al., 1973) used deception, and it is difficult to imagine how these studies could have been conducted without deception. These studies produced much concern at the time (Baumrind, 1964), and subsequently, deception in experiments was curtailed (American Psychological Association, 2010; British Psychological Society, 2010).

The debate about using deception in research continues today (Baumrind, 2013; Just, 2019; Weiss, 2001). The core problem with deception is that it violates the foundational idea of informed consent: How can participants consent to be deceived? If they are told about the research, then they will not be deceived. But if they are not told about the deception, then they cannot give consent. Accordingly, one might assume that research using deception is at an impasse.

The pragmatist response to this impasse focuses on the participants who have gone through the research and thus experienced its consequences. Instead of getting consent before the deception, the idea is to obtain consent after the deception. Crucially, this entails giving participants the power to halt the research if they believe it to be unethical. In this sense, each participant endorses the next participant to go through the research. From a pragmatist standpoint, these participants are particularly well placed to assess the ethics of the research because they have experienced the research. Moreover, giving participants the power to halt the research genuinely empowers them, such that they are more likely to be treated with respect in the research and fully debriefed.

One example of this pragmatist approach to the ethics of deception is research on cyranoids, namely, people who speak words given to them by a hidden other in real time (Gillespie & Corti, 2016). In the classic variant of this research, run by Milgram (1992), participants were asked to interview a boy aged eleven. Unbeknownst to the participants, there was a university professor (Milgram) who heard their questions and told the answers to the boy via a concealed wireless transmission to the boy's ear. The boy was trained to repeat the words heard fluidly, even when he did not understand the content of the words. How would the interviewers assess the depth and breadth of the boy's conversational skills? Milgram found that the physical appearance of the boy (age eleven) was more powerful in determining attributions than the content of what the boy said (the words of a professor).

In replications and extensions of this cyranoid research (Corti, 2015; Corti & Gillespie, 2015a, 2015b, 2016), the ethical problem of deception was addressed by giving each participant in the research the right to halt the research. After participants were debriefed, they were asked if they would object to someone else like themselves taking part in the study and being deceived, just like they had been deceived. The participants' responses were revealing: They acknowledged that they had sometimes felt awkward during the experiment, but they also appreciated the importance of understanding how appearance shapes our judgments. In the end, no participant halted the research. Moreover, some participants thanked the researchers, saying that they had learned about their own biases (Corti, 2015).

This approach to ethics is pragmatist because any research, no matter how carefully it has been mapped out ethically, can have unintended consequences (Merton, 1936). Just like there can be no guarantee in advance that our theories or knowledge will work (see Chapter 3; Peirce, 1955), equally, there can be no guarantee in advance of research that the consequences will be ethical for all participants. Accordingly, just like pragmatism puts the truth in the future, it equally puts the ethicality of research in the future. This, of course, is not to say that there should not be prior ethical scrutiny – there should. Ethics committees utilize prior experience to make informed expectations about how the research will be received and the potential consequences it might have. Rather, it is to say that the "final" arbiter of whether the research is ethical is in the actual consequences – not the expected ones.

This pragmatist approach to the ethics of using deception in research (which could, of course, be extended to all research) illustrates a key pragmatist move: to champion the people directly impacted by the research. By giving these participants the power to halt the research, one is empowering participants. When participants are thus empowered, the debrief and the explanation of the motivation and rationale for the research cease to be a formality; they become an earnest, even existential, activity. In line with Levinas' (1991) ethics, this locates ethics in the point of contact between the researcher and the participants. It builds on broader ethical and safety thinking because it allows each research participant to "stop the line" (Bell & Martinez, 2019). Thus, it keeps the research, throughout the data collection process, on alert for deviations from the expected impact on participants; it remains open to the possibility of surprise and disruption.

8.5 Ethics in Mixed Methods Research

Mixed methods research entails mixing various ethical commitments. Each method, and especially its application, presents the researcher with specific opportunities and challenges in the moral domain. Besides general guidelines formalized by national and international bodies, different methods bring their own ethical requirements. For example, experiments are grounded in control and standardization, and as such, they call for a deeper reflection on what kind of impact the control exercised by the experimenter might have over the participants. Beyond highly visible and ethically questionable studies like Zimbardo's Stanford Prison Experiment (Perlstadt, 2018), we need to acknowledge the power of experimental authority in every single study of this kind and how it impacts participants. Interviews, in contrast, are more accommodating of participants' interests because they have less standardization and more openness to participants' own views. And yet, even in interviews, there is a power dynamic and a struggle for meaning and recognition (Tanggaard, 2007). In observational studies, there is much variability in how researcher and participant interact, depending on whether the observation is overt or covert, participatory or not. Specific ethical issues in observational methods relate to the trust built between the observer and the observed and avoiding the numerous ways in which this trust can be broken. Last but not least, doing research with online data raises its own series of ethical dilemmas, key among them being the difficulty (sometimes impossibility) of gaining informed consent (Eynon et al., 2008). Naturally occurring data can be public, but this does not automatically mean it is ethical to use these data for research.

Mixed methods research often combines one or more of the aforementioned methods and others (see Chapter 6) and thus brings together different ethical concerns. Mixed method studies are acknowledged for increasing the complexity of ethical decision-making while, at the same time, offering a wider range of flexible tools for tackling ethical dilemmas in multifaceted real-world contexts (Preissle et al., 2015). In recent years, there has been growing interest in how mixed methods researchers discuss their ethical decisions and the distinctive reflexivity that mixed methods research might foster. A systematic review of these issues by Cain and colleagues (2019) found, disappointingly, that researchers do not tend to discuss ethics topics at length within mixed methods research. When they do, discussions of ethics fall under four main categories: (1) ethics as defined by an Institutional Review Board; (2) data quality as a measure of ethics; (3) ethics as defined by theory; and (4) social justice-minded ethics. The first two can be considered surface considerations given that they transfer ethical responsibility onto others, in the form of either institutions or data themselves. The last two, however, point to the role of theory and social impact, the latter resembling pragmatist criteria. The authors called for more transparency in reporting on ethics and more reflexivity in moral decision-making, linking these with the credibility and legitimation of the research itself.

Worryingly, studies have found that many mixed methods investigators do not consider their ethics training useful for planning, conducting, and reporting their research (Stadnick et al., 2021). These findings raise the important issue of how to prepare mixed methods researchers to recognize, seize, and address ethical dilemmas. In the absence of such training, researchers might not notice when such dilemmas present themselves and misguidedly see themselves as better at managing them than they are. A more substantial ethics education for mixed methods researchers should include five issues.

First: *one should know one's epistemological position and the epistemological underpinning of using different methods in specific ways.* Epistemology is deeply intertwined with ethics (see also Chapters 1 and 2), given the fact that it organizes our worldview and addresses key questions, such as what counts as valid, reliable knowledge. Pragmatism connects its theory of truth and its ethics by pointing to the consequences of our actions. In contrast, epistemologies like positivism contribute to the perceived separation between science and ethics, discussed at the outset of the current chapter.

Second: *one should consider the ethical implications of theories and conceptual frameworks.* Mixing methods often, but not always, leads to mixing theories as well. Given that, as we argued in Chapter 3, theories are similar to maps or models, this means that researchers either work with a more complex and detailed guide or are confused by what different maps are telling them about the data and their interpretation. In pragmatism, theories are not abstract constructions but tools that help researchers discover, select, and act in relation to the phenomena they are interested in, and therefore, ethical questions follow logically. For instance, theories assist researchers in making specific analytical choices: When does the phenomenon of interest start or end? What counts as data and what is irrelevant information? What records should be kept and transformed for analysis and what can be disregarded? Which participants should be included and excluded in the research? These questions involve ethical reasoning because they relate to participants' participation, representation, and visibility.

Third: *one should reflect on the ethical dimension of research questions*, especially when these questions are very different from each other within the same mixed methods study. In Chapter 4 we proposed a typology of questions that differentiated between and within qualitative and quantitative approaches to the data. This typology showed that there is more to scientific research than induction and deduction because it emphasized the role of abduction and the creativity involved in coming up with new questions. These questions need to be considered in terms of soundness, feasibility but also impact, and ethics.

Fourth: *moving from raw to various forms of transformed data, and back again, poses its own ethical dilemma.* This is because, as shown in Chapter 4, structuring data involves simplifying, summarizing, or categorizing exist-ing data. Particularly when working with data that reflect human perspec-tives or experiences, structuring should be guided by ethical concerns as to how these perspectives and experiences are represented and what might be lost when focusing on data at only one stage in their transformation process. Conducting research with big qualitative data presents us with its own challenges, described in more detail toward the end of Chapter 4.

Finally: *mixing methods can lead to synergistic effects also in the area of eth-ics.* It does not suffice to avoid complexity by following, separately, the eth-ical guidelines for each method; the combination might have unexpected consequences and help researchers implement traditional ethics advice in a new key. For example, experimentalists can gain a new understanding of trust by conducting interviews or can appreciate the role of consent differently when combining their study with online or internet research. Of course, there can be a tension and even conflict between the moral demands of different methods. But these are opportunities to become reflective and creative in dealing with moral dilemmas.

8.6   Ethics in Multi-resolution Research

Multiple resolution research presents us with an interesting case for ethics because the ethical demands placed on researchers are different in quanti-tative and qualitative studies. In quantitative research, the need for control and even deception comes to the fore (see the earlier discussion of ethics; Weiss, 2001), while in qualitative research, ethics often focuses on how participants are portrayed and how much room there is for their "voice" (Ashby, 2011). Pushed to the limit, some recommend that studies use no deception or as little as possible (Just, 2019) and are very critical of find-ings from prior research that do not meet contemporary ethical standards (Baumrind, 2013). For qualitative studies, a radical proposal is to give par-ticipants the power to veto either part of the data or the interpretation derived from the data they provided (see the discussion of participant vali-dation in Bauer & Gaskell, 2000). At the very least, participants should be asked whether the perspectives they offered were understood correctly or whether the researcher misunderstood their views. On a practical level, this means creating channels of communication between researcher and participants that allow participants to be part of the research process after data collection has been completed. Such longer-term relations between researcher and participants contribute to building trust (Christopher et al., 2008) and ensuring that the research and its outcomes do not have a detrimental impact on participants, and maybe even have a positive impact.

As shown throughout this book, in multi-resolution research we need to balance multiple constraints; in particular, multi-resolution research is doubly constrained by the demands placed on it by both quantitative and qualitative research. In being so, it needs to find new and innovative ways for solving some traditional tensions between these two types of research. Take, for instance, the issue of surprise. The quality of qualitative studies is judged, at least in part, by whether the analysis managed to add to or trouble the initial assumptions of the researchers (something Gaskell and Bauer, 2000, refer to as "local surprise"). In contrast, quantitative research is pushed toward adopting practices like preregistration, that is, specifying and submitting one's research plan and expected findings to a registrar (Nosek et al., 2019). This is useful for clearly separating hypothesis-generating (exploratory) from hypothesis-testing (confirmatory) research and reducing uncertainty and surprise in the latter (which is the bulk of studies conducted within an experimental paradigm). Pragmatically, multi-resolution research requires navigating this tension and being able to foresee – and perhaps preregister – certain aspects of the study while making sure that the generative dynamics coming out of zooming in and out of the same corpus of data, and the "surprises" associated with it, are not stifled by open science practices (Kaufman & Glăveanu, 2018). Fundamentally, multi-resolution research remains an exploratory type of design and any kind of confirmatory or hypotheses-testing practices are limited in scope and value.

Doubly constrained ethics refers to balancing different and sometimes conflicting ethical demands that arise out of analyzing data both quantitatively and qualitatively. These demands include, among others, a concern for issues of voice and representation (a marker of quantitative studies) alongside standardization and making meaningful analytical cuts (a marker of quantitative research). Some of these constraints apply at different moments of the research cycle; for instance, widening participation is important during data collection, while analytical frames are devised before or during data analysis. Other times, some of these demands might seem incompatible. For example, the requirement of allowing the voice of the participants to be heard – the basis of calls for "thick description" (Geertz, 1973) – could conflict with the need for bold analytical distinctions or quantification. We could move even further in this regard and, following a pragmatist stance, we could imagine giving participants a veto on how they are portrayed in research. Multi-resolution research considers these trade-offs pragmatically and asks for the researcher to constantly engage in reflective deliberation as to the costs and benefits of each methodological decision taken. Fortunately, because of the recursive and multiscalar nature of multi-resolution research, what appear as trade-offs when one has to choose between either a qualitative or quantitative approach turn into an exercise of establishing priorities for a given segment of the study (with the possibility of reversing these priorities in another). Pragmatically, we should develop and use theory without foundational assumptions, and therefore, we should be able to use different, even incompatible, theoretical and ethical frames within the same research project to genuinely expand the range of ethical insights we use for one and the same study.

The presence of constant deliberation in multi-resolution research offers researchers the opportunity to think about ethical issues in deeper and more comprehensive ways. In doing so, they will necessarily have to consider the interests being served by the production of knowledge and raise the important questions of "who is the study for" and "what does the study do." Does the study impoverish or enrich our view of people as engaged, agentic, and reflective? Thus, the implications of multi-resolution research go beyond the validity, reliability, or surprise embedded in one's findings and address, at a broader level, what kind of image of fellow human beings, human interactions, and human society we are advancing through our studies, theories, and methodological innovations. One could criticize research for oversimplifying humans, for denying the richness of human experience and diversity, for "mechanizing" humans, and prioritizing control over agency. Such impoverishing models of human beings do not do justice to them, suppress all sorts of diversity, and feed forward into building impoverishing and even oppressive institutions, which, in turn, shape the kind of people we become. In contrast, research that empowers both researcher and participants is based on a commitment to difference, agency, and fairness. Pragmatism fosters research that does not merely describe social life but is reflective about being an intervention in social life. Such research begins by recognizing that all social research implies both power and responsibility.

8.7   Conclusion

Pragmatist approaches to research ethics aim to transcend unhelpful dichotomies by focusing on the development of research that serves human purposes (Wicks & Freeman, 1998). By considering the interests at stake and the action-based nature of scientific inquiry, pragmatists envision research as an inherently ethical activity (Simpson & den Hond, 2022). At the same time, the emphasis is placed on moral deliberation and decision-making rather than an appeal to fixed and absolute moral laws that should govern human behavior, including in research. Pragmatism focuses on who is impacted by the research, the stakeholders, and it gives them an important role in assessing the ethicality of research.

Currently, the ethicality of research tends to be assessed by researchers and ethics committees (which may have lay membership but rarely any actual research participants). By involving research participants and other stakeholders in deliberating the ethical dilemmas posed by research, we can distribute agency within the entire research system. Social research entails both power and responsibility, but these should not be concentrated at one point in the system. By giving voice to participants, we would be empowering not only them but also researchers themselves. What might seem like a reduction of researcher agency is actually an opportunity for authentic forms of dialogue and moral deliberation. Researchers would be the first to benefit from such engagement, given the fact that ethical dilemmas are, as discussed earlier, both social and contextual. They would develop a deeper and richer understanding of the research situation and, with it, a more diverse set of perspectives from which to conduct research that is ethically anchored in substantial issues. In this way, research, including its ethical dimensions, is not conducted by the researcher *on* but *with* human participants. Bringing research participants into the decision-making will help researchers create knowledge that is useful beyond academia.

The metaphor of building knowledge without foundations (introduced in Chapter 2) is applicable to research ethics. Like a ship that is patched at sea, our ethical guidelines are keeping us afloat, and should not be abandoned, but they also need patching as we encounter new contexts and challenges. As Serra (2010, p. 11) writes: "[T]he task of a pragmatist ethics … is not to provide final solutions, but rather to indicate that it is only via the testing and communication of experiences that the superiority of one moral idea over another can be demonstrated." This is not a relativistic stance; it is a progressivist stance. Although our ethical considerations will never be perfect, they can always be better. Research ethics is always uncertain – until after the research is completed. The final arbiter, or truth, of ethicality lies with the participants (who are heterogeneous, culturally embedded, and changing). A pragmatist approach to ethics brings together researchers, participants, and all people impacted by the knowledge, by focusing on the consequences of the research (for participants, stakeholders, the researchers, and society). This approach fosters hope, "an optimism about the possibilities for the future and a disposition to experimenting with alternative ways of living that hold some promise to better realize human aspirations" (Wicks & Freeman, 1998, p. 130). Thus, for pragmatism there is no opposition between truth and ethics: Both are evaluated by the same criteria, namely, whether they create a better world, enrich humanity, and expand possibility.

CHAPTER 9

Expanding Human Possibilities

Knowledge falters when imagination clips its wings or fears to use them. Every great advance in science has issued from a new audacity of imagination. What are now working conceptions, employed as a matter of course because they have withstood the tests of experiment and have emerged triumphant, were once speculative hypotheses.

Dewey (1929, p. 294)

In this last chapter, we raise what typically is an opening question: What is the purpose of research? Of course, what is meant by purpose here goes well beyond the aims, objectives, research questions, and hypotheses in any given study (Doody & Bailey, 2016). These are all generally made explicit (see Chapter 4). What is less explicit is the reason we engage in research; what is research for? For some, this interrogation could sound trivial: Through research, we gain knowledge about ourselves and the world (discovering Truth). If this knowledge is valid, then research is a worthy achievement in and of itself. But what exactly counts as valid knowledge, and how do we judge it so? The positivist view, dominant in many areas of the human and social sciences (even if not always convergent with the thinking of early positivists; Bailey & Eastman, 1994), is that research's true purpose is to reveal what is the case and do so by organizing the messiness of life-as-we-find-it and abstracting, from it, a transcendental and universal Truth. To this end, positivist research tries to rise above the changing realm of human needs, values, and biases. In contrast, constructionist research prefers to dwell within the messiness of human life and anchors all knowledge to human contingencies (Holstein & Gubrium, 2013). This implies a plurality of truths, potentially as many as there are perspectives in and on the world.

Pragmatism avoids the pitfalls of considering research either as the discovery of objective Truth or the multiplicity of subjectivities. Research is not merely an exercise of knowing the world (or one's version of it) but one of world-making and future-building (Gergen, 2015; Power et al., 2023). This does not mean that every piece of research gets to change the world, yet doing research means engaging in human, most often collaborative, activity that transforms the present given an anticipated future. This future not only includes the acquisition of new knowledge, it considers its impact, use, and renewal. When we understand research as an activity, we acknowledge its material, social, cultural, and political embeddedness. The perspectives enacted and coconstructed during the research process are not the God's eye view of positivism nor the relativism of constructionists. For pragmatism, perspectives are bound to positions in the world and actively construct the world (i.e., change it) through dialogue, interaction, and position exchange, all of which are possibility-expanding processes. In this chapter, we develop the implications of our final pragmatist proposition that *social research should aim to expand human possibility.*

We will argue, with Dewey (1929), that research depends on and should foster human imagination, agency, and possibility. These creative elements permeate the research cycle, from epistemology to data analysis. In this chapter, we will trace the role of possibility in human research, from human interests through methodology and into the overall aims of social research.

9.1   Human Interests

A pragmatist discussion of research purposes starts from human interests. Human interests refer to people's needs and wants. People's actions in the world are initiated by their interests and aim to satisfy their interests. Social research, as an activity, is motivated by the interests of researchers, funders, and governments. From a positivist standpoint, the connection between human interests and research is problematic because it undermines assumptions about impartiality, objectivity, and absolute certainty. From a constructionist standpoint, this is further evidence of research serving vested or idiosyncratic interests. Between the Scylla of naïve realism and the Charybdis of extreme relativism, pragmatists turn the problem of human interests into a guiding light for social research.

From a pragmatist standpoint, truth that is independent of human interests (if it could exist) would be meaningless and uninteresting. Any truth that is not "for us," that serves no human purpose and contributes nothing to our future, is simply inconceivable. In James's words:

> The trail of the human serpent is thus over everything. Truth independent; truth that we 'find' merely; truth no longer malleable to human need; truth incorrigible, in a word; such truth exists indeed superabundantly, but then

it means only the dead heart of a living tree ... grown stiff with years of veteran service and petrified in men's regard by sheer antiquity. (James, 1907, pp. 64–65)

The beating heart of knowledge is at the intersection with human interests. It is these interests that make knowledge important, interesting, and useful. There is no "useful" without a guiding interest. Instead of suppressing human interests, pragmatism builds them into knowledge production to such an extent that they become the criteria for evaluating knowledge. Does the knowledge work? Does it fulfil the goal? Does it satisfy the interest that fueled the research project? In this way, the problem of human interests is transformed into the solution to both naïve realism and extreme relativism. The question is not "is this true" but, instead, whether this enables us to act more effectively (Rorty, 1999). The knowledge that enables us to land on the moon, run the Internet, and handle a pandemic is true in so far as it works. Equally, anti-vaccine beliefs are false in so far as they will not serve the human interest of avoiding infection – although it might serve other interests (de Saint Laurent et al., 2021b).

Habermas (1968) analyzed the human interests underlying the production of knowledge. In a radical move, criticizing the focus on creating reliable knowledge (as knowledge independent of human activity), Habermas proceeded to classify knowledge in terms of the interests that it addresses. Thus, he marks an important shift in focus from "how do we know this knowledge is accurate?" to "what interests are being served by this knowledge?" His theory identifies three basic human interests.

Technocratic interests are served by knowledge that predicts, guides interventions, and, in general, acts upon the world, including other people. For example, big data can be aggregated to create predictive models, based on vast numbers of correlations, without any clear theory (Coveney et al., 2016), and these models can serve technocratic interests (including surveillance; Andrejevic, 2014). Technocratic interests do not require understanding, merely prediction and control. In the social sciences, technocratic interests often entail one group (e.g., companies, governments, health services) creating knowledge to predict the behavior of another group (e.g., consumers, citizens, patients) and sometimes to change it for personal advantage (increasingly with advanced computational techniques; Hunter, 2018). Many popular theories in social science serve technocratic interests (e.g., nudge theory; Thaler & Sunstein, 2009), even when the outcomes are intended to benefit society.

Hermeneutic interests are served by knowledge that provides understanding, makes phenomena explicable, and, in short, tells a good story.

This interest seeks insight into the world, history, and the human condition (Brockmeier & Meretoja, 2014; Martin & Sugarman, 2001). From a hermeneutic standpoint, purely predictive models (e.g., based on big data) will be unsatisfying and uninsightful because they cannot explain the "why" of human activity (Coveney et al., 2016; Wise & Shaffer, 2015) or help us to make sense of the future (Jäger, 2016). Pure prediction fails because it bypasses interpretation – data are considered to contain, within themselves, the "finding" or "result" the researcher is looking for when, in reality, any act of research should be an act of making new meaning. Knowledge answering to hermeneutic interests does not need to predict or control anything; it only aims to explain in human terms, such as through narrative and metaphor (see Chapter 3; Bruner, 1990).

Emancipatory interests are served by knowledge that enables people to act, especially upon themselves (rather than other people). Emancipatory research leads to personal transformation and/or the transformation of one's world. Habermas (1968) argued that emancipatory knowledge entails reflective reason grasping itself as interested and attempting to transcend its own limitations. He gave the example of psychoanalysis, which provided people with concepts that could be used to liberate themselves from their unconscious tendencies (Madison, 2005). Another example is what Paolo Freire (1970) referred to as conscientization, namely, the liberating act of coming to terms with one's (sometimes oppressed) position in the world and striving toward a better, more equal, and just future. From an emancipatory standpoint, a big data predictive model could be emancipatory if it was put in the hands of people who used it to better predict and thus master their own behavior. Any knowledge can be emancipatory if it liberates people from their biases, habits, or societal condition (Mantelero, 2018; Montiel & Uyheng, 2022).

Habermas emphasized the emancipatory interest, which he saw as arising in the reflective act of reason grasping itself and thus transcending the very interests it started from. He believed that the emancipatory interest, driven by critical reflection, can produce nonideological knowledge (Habermas, 1989). This might sound like an overly optimistic aim for research, given the cultural, historical, and political dimensions of scientific knowledge. The emancipatory interest should not be considered an end state but a means for developing studies that consider the hopes, needs, and life contexts of those involved in the research. It is research that foregrounds awareness, critical thought, and ethical concerns. Last but not least, it is research that produces knowledge for the sake of people rather than for the sake of knowledge itself. This does not mean that technocratic or hermeneutical interests are not valuable. Indeed, in trying to build something efficiently, we might need to increase control or be ready to predict the outcomes of our actions. At the same time, emancipatory interests should allow for a hermeneutic analysis of the situation before trying to implement change. The overarching point is that researchers should be aware of, and critically reflect on, the main interests that guide their research.

From a methodological standpoint, there is no one-to-one correspondence between the human interests being pursued and the methods used (Bauer & Gaskell, 2000). Although technocratic interests gravitate toward quantitative methods, so that the insights scale to larger groups, qualitative methods can also be employed for this purpose. For example, during the colonial era, qualitative anthropological studies were used for intelligence gathering on subjugated populations (Gosden, 2004). Today, qualitative studies could be employed to understand what people like or do not like about e-cigarettes (Pokhrel et al., 2015) and thus better target advertising. Equally, although hermeneutic and emancipatory interests gravitate toward qualitative methods, quantitative methods can be used (e.g., quantitative changes in how people use language; Moretti, 2013) and provide emancipatory insights (e.g., documenting inequality and social immobility; Breen & Jonsson, 2005).

To some extent, the human interest underpinning a particular research project is revealed by the topic and declared aim of the study. For instance, research questions (see Chapter 4) that aim to measure, examine associations, or establish cause and effect typically follow a control and prediction logic specific to technocratic interests. But these might be secondary outcomes of the study itself, with the researcher primarily motivated to understand a set of events (hermeneutical) or give voice to participants rarely represented in research (empowering). Conversely, questions oriented toward uncovering human experience, a key aim in qualitative studies, may be only superficially hermeneutical if they are motivated by a desire to better predict how people will behave in a given context (technocratic).

The picture becomes even more complex when we consider mixing methods because different human interests can be served by various subcomponents or substages of the research, regardless of whether there is an overall interest that guides the entire investigation. This reflects the synergistic quality of mixing methods (see Chapter 6) and can lead, for example, to technocratic and hermeneutic concerns being subordinated to emancipatory aims or the other way around (for a discussion of paradigmatic perspectives in this type of research, see Shannon-Baker, 2016). Such potentially entangled interests should prompt mixed methods researchers to be extra reflective about their topic and methodological choices (Cain et al., 2019; Feilzer, 2010). Using mixed methods, especially in a recursive manner (i.e., quantifying and qualitizing the same raw data; Chapter 7), can stimulate this reflection because the raw data usually reflect the interest of the people being studied (e.g., their words verbatim) while the highly transformed data increasingly reflect the interests of the researchers (e.g., codified or quantified using the researchers' chosen constructs). Thus moving between these data transformations ensures that these interests are forced into contact. Moreover, such recursive transformations mean that the interests embedded in the raw data cannot be completely forgotten, but they remain salient and evident throughout the analysis process. A pragmatist standpoint does not prescribe which interest to pursue but it does demand reflexivity about the interests at stake.

9.2   Hierarchies of Knowledge and Interests

A question that students of research methodology sometimes ask is: Which is the best method to use? Teachers are quick to point out, in line with pragmatist views, that this question is incomplete without specifying "best for what." And yet the positivist tradition does imply a hierarchy of methods, knowledge, and human interests. While the social sciences use a wide array of methods (e.g., randomized control trials, narrative analysis, experiments, experience sampling, and computational text analysis), they are not all considered equal. Some methods are viewed as intrinsically "better" than others. This approach proposes "hierarchies of evidence" that rank methods in terms of their rigor, reliability, and validity (Elamin & Montori, 2012; Evans, 2003). Usually, meta-analyses and systematic reviews are at the top of the hierarchy, closely followed by randomized control trials. Further down are descriptive studies with decreasing sample sizes and case studies at the bottom. While these hierarchies have been criticized for devaluing qualitative research and overvaluing quantitative methods (e.g., Creswell et al., 2007), a pragmatist lens provides additional insight into why these hierarchies are problematic.

From a pragmatist standpoint, different research methods are suited not only for different problems but also for different interests. For example, randomized control trials often serve a technocratic interest in determining precisely which specified intervention (e.g., a medicine, vaccine, or nudge) is effective in producing a predetermined outcome for a specific population (Birnie et al., 2015; Wilson et al., 2017). This method effectively answers questions such as: Should medicine X be approved by regulators?

Is medicine X more effective than medicine Y for condition Z? Does having chocolate near the checkout counter increase chocolate purchases? Are people more likely to agree to organ donation if they have to opt out compared to opting in? Randomized control trials are particularly effective in the social context of "evidence-based policy" because they adjudicate between interventions. They aid policymakers in deciding which medicine, intervention, or policy is likely to have the desired outcome (Sanderson, 2002). But there is more to human life than evidence-based policy (for a critique, see Greenhalgh & Russell, 2009).

Many valuable bodies of knowledge have developed without randomized control trials (Cornish & Gillespie, 2009). Theories of self-presentation (Goffman, 1959) and language use (Schegloff, 2007) are insightful, revealing the incredible subtlety of human interaction. Their validity hinges upon good description and astute interpretation. A randomized trial in these domains would add little because the aim is hermeneutic understanding. Feminism does not rely upon experimental trials, yet it contributes to society by answering to an emancipatory interest (Fahy, 1997). Heuristics for living with mental illness (e.g., using headphones to block out hearing voices, reminder technologies for dementia; Gillespie et al., 2012; Shergill et al., 1998) are also emancipatory. They are documented and circulated as potential resources, and it makes little sense to experiment to determine which is "best" because some work fully for some people but not for others. Similarly, we do not use experiments to determine which carpentry tool or mnemonic heuristic is "best" and remove the rest. The diversity of tools and heuristics is valuable; it is the fertile soil for future developments and a resource we can use for adapting to unforeseen contexts.

A pragmatist approach recognizes the diversity of human interests and values the diversity of methodological tools. However, it is critical of universal hierarchies (of evidence, knowledge, or interests). It asks the questions: Why have randomized control trials been conceptualized as superior to research focusing on the tactics of daily living and cultural critique? What purposes does this hierarchy serve? What do these hierarchies imply about the relation between research, methods, and human existence?

The hierarchy of evidence idea reveals that there is a hierarchy of human interests; it suggests that contemporary science is in the service of technocratic interests, not hermeneutic, and much less emancipatory interests. Positivism, grounded in the technocratic interests of prediction and control (Merchant, 2015), is widespread and assumes that predictive tools like experiments define what science is (Hendrick, 1977). Hermeneutic traditions, often associated with qualitative and constructionist approaches, had a resurgence during the heyday of postmodernism, in the late 1980s and 1990s (with earlier roots in the more materialist approach of Berger & Luckmann, 1966), but have come under considerable criticism recently in the wake of post-truth scholarship (D'Ancona, 2017; McIntyre, 2018). Emancipatory research, while far from dominant, has been growing, fueled by Marxist, feminist, and postcolonial, and decolonial critiques (Sandoval, 2013). Nevertheless, these emancipatory approaches struggle against the hierarchies of knowledge that enshrine the positivist interests of prediction and control.

Health psychologists have filled many library shelves with technocratic research, for example, on whether attitudes predict smoking, exercise, taking medication, ethical consumption, and so on. This research shows that despite well-intentioned attitudes, behavioral follow-through is more challenging (e.g., De Leeuw et al., 2008). The neglected emancipatory questions that need to be asked are: What heuristics do people use to change their behavior? How can health psychologists create empowering heuristics to enable people to follow through on their attitudes? How can people be supported to design their lives so that their behavior can be consistent with their attitudes? And, more structurally, how can we collectively design societies to support human health and wellbeing? For example, might the societal structures of consumerism be fueling the growing epidemic of perfectionism (with the associated tendencies toward anxiety, self-harm, and suicide) among young people (Curran, 2023)? These health-related questions do not depend on control and prediction or on understanding lived experience. What motivates (or demotivates) actions in this area reflects people's networks of participation and the agency they derive from them (see Campbell & Jovchelovitch, 2000).

Similarly, social psychologists have spent much effort examining the technocratic conditions for creating persuasive messages (e.g., Bergkvist & Zhou, 2019; Chaiken, 1979). Obviously, this research is beneficial to commercial and political interests. The neglected emancipatory questions include: What discursive tactics do people use to resist peer pressure and speak up? What heuristics and tactics could be created that might support people in critically evaluating and resisting persuasive advertisements? What knowledge might enable employees, politicians, and even regulators to speak up about problems? And, more structurally, what are the social and societal conditions that empower people to speak up about problems and voice concerns? What are the societal and organizational supports that enable people to listen to and act upon concerns raised? Again, these are uncommon research questions because they address a nonprioritized set of emancipatory human interests. They also challenge a long-standing negative bias when it comes to social psychological research that is extensively invested in the study of the loss of agency (e.g., conformity and obedience, the bystander effect, crowds and deindividuation, the automatic nature of stereotypes) rather than how individuals, groups, and societies gain agency, including as part of the research process (e.g., Christens, 2019; Trott, 2019).

In summary, the research questions we ask reveal the interests we serve. There is an infinity of research questions – no question is self-evident. All research questions entail a *choice*. We can choose to ask different questions. Instead of asking primarily "does X predict Y?" and "how can we make people do Z?" emancipatory questions ask "what do people want to do?" "what are their problems of living?" "what would enrich their lives?" and "how can we enable people to do what they want to do?" The point is not to replace technocratic questions and interests altogether but to realize that many other valid research questions and interests exist.

A pragmatist approach does not advocate for hermeneutic or emancipatory interests over technocratic interests; this would uphold an inverted hierarchy but a hierarchy nonetheless. Pragmatism only insists that diverse human interests are at the heart of knowledge production. And, with this realization, we are forced to address the challenge at the center of all science: Choosing one question out of an infinity of possible questions entails prioritizing one interest over others. This challenge cannot be addressed within science (i.e., science cannot tell us which questions to ask; see Chapter 4). There is no "True" interest or research question we should pursue. The choice of a research question is an ethical choice. Our choice reveals what we want to do, whom we want to empower, and what type of society we want to create.

9.3 Empowering Human Activity

Pragmatism accepts the contingency and uncertainty of knowledge (Dewey, 1929; Rorty, 1989). The only facts we have belong to the past; the future is an expectation that will become a fact, whether surprising or expected (Miller, 2010). Knowledge is our attempt to generalize past experience into useful expectations (Peirce, 1955). Knowledge is our attempt to guide human action into a fundamentally uncertain future. However, this fundamental uncertainty does not mean that we should give up on knowing or become skeptical of it. Useful knowledge can reduce future surprises and make the future more, rather than less, expected, even if never entirely predictable. In this sense, there is a close affinity between pragmatism and recent propositions that all life (from cells to humans to societies) aims at surprise reduction and, thus, at maximizing expectation (Friston, 2010; Friston et al., 2012). From a pragmatist standpoint, studying human action means engaging with the future-making and world-building potentialities of individuals and societies. It implies research that is sensitive to uncertainty, contingency, and surprise. We live in irreversible time (Valsiner, 2014), in a world made and remade through differences (Glăveanu & Gillespie, 2014), material engagement (Malafouris, 2019), and dialogues with alterity (Marková, 2016).

Human beings are actively constructing the future, both for themselves and others. Reducing surprise is not merely a cognitive act. We build shelters, check the weather forecast, and put on sun cream to avoid the surprise of sunburn (see also the role of anticipation; Poli, 2017). That is to say, the future we encounter does not merely happen, it is also something that we contribute to making (Thompson & Byrne, 2022; Wenzel, 2022). We are not passive in the face of the future – we use knowledge to prepare ourselves for various eventualities. This is not to say that we are always in control of the future we create; even our unintended actions contribute to the future we encounter (Gillon, 2001; Merton, 1936; Tenner, 1996). We are often in the predicament of being responsible for a future that we did not intend to make. But, again, the lack of certainty, the disjunction between expectation and the reality of our future situation, should not lead us to abdicate responsibility. We can create knowledge that enables us to understand the consequences of our actions better and thus be more responsible (Baldwin, 1979; van der Duin, 2019). Our knowledge is necessarily imperfect, but it is better than nothing, and it is incrementally improving (including through scientific research and the Popperian principle of falsification; Popper, 1969). Creating useful knowledge – the pragmatist marker for truth – entails not only making the future less surprising but also enhancing human coordination, empowering human action, and creating ideas, situations, and resources that bring out the best in humanity.

The pragmatist emphasis on the relation between action, knowledge, and responsibility invites a reflection on morality. From a pragmatist standpoint, to the extent that knowledge is consequential it is also moral (Brinkmann, 2010). Knowledge is necessarily moral because changing the possibilities for action changes the status quo (Mach et al., 2020). If knowledge makes a difference for human life, then it is not merely a matter of Truth, it is also a matter of what future we want to create (i.e., the

"Truth" of climate change, medical error, and famine are determined by human choices). This leads to the idea that we can evaluate knowledge not in terms of whether it is True but in terms of whether it enriches our collective future (de Saint Laurent et al., 2018). Thus, the discussion of human interests in this chapter goes beyond choosing between questions or methods; it fundamentally concerns the kinds of futures we envision, cultivate, and enact through doing social research. Is it the causal and orderly world of technocratic interests, focused on control and efficiency? Or are we cultivating intersubjectivity and lived experience, such that the future is built on understanding oneself and others? Or, yet, are we supporting agentic action in which participation is empowered for the construction of inclusive, just, and equitable futures?

As researchers, we hold additional responsibility for the world we live in and the world we bring into being through knowledge production (Glerup et al., 2017; Leonelli, 2016). Even the smallest decisions we take in a research process contribute to this future in the making, whether we are aware of it or not, whether this is the future we intend or not. Gergen (2015) argued against a mirroring view of knowledge and for a more active future-making paradigm. Instead of observing reality to report on it "as is," he proposed we see research as a value-based exploration of what could be. The question is, then, what exactly do we want this world to be like? Science is a methodology that can make the world more predictable (technocratic interests), understandable (hermeneutic interests), and actionable (empowerment interests). But science cannot tell us what we should try to predict, understand, or act upon. Science is a method that cannot be used to determine the goals it should be directed toward. Deciding what to do with science is a decision that lies outside of science, in ethics, common sense (Marková, 2016), or public deliberation (Christiano, 1997). Science can help us achieve goals, but there is no scientific determination of which goals we should pursue; that is a choice and, thus, a moral decision.

9.4 Methodologies of the Possible

We have argued for a pragmatist approach to key methodological issues such as epistemology, theory, questions, data, analysis, and ethics. It is important to emphasize that pragmatism, at heart, entertains *any* approach to these issues that makes a contribution. Pragmatism is inherently pluralistic (deVries et al., 2017; Melles, 2008). It does not take a fundamentalist stance on any of these issues; the only thing it will not relinquish is the focus on the consequences. Pragmatism not only evaluates knowledge in terms of its consequences but it also conceptualizes methodology as a way to make new knowledge that opens up new (and hopefully desirable) consequences. This pluralistic approach to methodology opens new possibilities for research.

Possibilities come out of differences and dialogues of perspective (Glăveanu, 2020a; Glăveanu & Gillespie, 2014). We are all positioned in the world in material, social, cultural, and historical ways, and we develop perspectives on self, others, and society from the different positions we occupy (Gillespie, 2012; Martin & Gillespie, 2013, 2020). Equally, researchers are positioned in a material sense when conducting a study – from the tools used to the way in which bodies, roles, and places are engaged during an investigation – where they acquire different knowledge and identities based on the projects they work on and the institutions they belong to, each one with its own rights, responsibilities, and power relations. Importantly, researchers also occupy symbolic positions from which they enact symbolic perspectives on the problem at hand. These perspectives can be understood in general terms (e.g., theory, epistemology, and human interests) or specific ones (e.g., the way key constructs are defined, variables measured, and conclusions drawn). This is where methods emerge as both enablers and constrainers of possibility. When adopting a specific method, the researcher commits, at least to some extent, to its premises, approach, and worldview (Christ, 2013; Kuhn, 1962; Marková, 1982; Mulej, 2007). Each method is a perspective that highlights specific qualities of the data, context, or findings and brings them to the fore. At the same time, it works to obscure other qualities and insights that would have become apparent to a researcher using a different method. Some possibilities are gained, some are lost (see Chapter 7 for the gains and losses of transforming data into excerpts, categories, and numbers). No method encapsulates the Truth; each method is incomplete but each can also be useful.

Possibility expands when a person, or a researcher, takes distance from and steps outside a singular perspective (Gillespie, 2007b, 2018). New possibilities arise in the space between perspectives or methodological approaches. This does not mean abandoning any particular perspective or method altogether. It is the capacity to relate the space of possibilities (and constraints) specific to one data type, method, or approach with alternatives that is crucial. Going back to pragmatist theory, it is an act of repositioning and, more specifically, exchanging positions (Gillespie, 2012; Gillespie & Martin, 2014) that holds the key to understanding the dynamics of the possible. In practical terms, this means moving between physical, social, and symbolic positions in ways that enrich one's perspective and understanding of the situation. Each movement can potentially leverage new insight into the problem at hand. For example, in the game of hide and seek, mastering the two positions (hiding, seeking) and their associated perspectives and being able to even hold them simultaneously (i.e., hiding with the view of the seeker in mind, and the other way around) is crucial for a player's success. And children learn to play hide and seek by alternating between doing hiding and doing seeking (Gillespie, 2006b). Agency and creativity within the game come not from taking the role and the associated perspective of either the hider or the seeker but from integrating both.

In methodological terms, this means that new spaces of possibilities open not only when we use multiple methods in the same research project – the metaphorical equivalent of occupying multiple positions – but especially when we can seamlessly move between these methods and the perspectives they offer. Multi-resolution research (Chapter 7) is meant to achieve precisely this aim. Within it, while distinct analytical steps can still be differentiated, what matters more is the repositioning offered by zooming in and out of the same dataset, the simultaneity of grasping overall patterns (zooming out) and individual detail (zooming in). The recursiveness vis-à-vis the data, reminding of position exchange, is a feature embedded in multi-resolution research. It scaffolds possibility-enabling processes within research by fostering repositioning via position exchange (e.g., moving between qualitative and quantitative positions in relation to the same raw data) and dialogues of perspective (e.g., showcasing potential tensions between raw and transformed data). At the same time, multi-resolution research is not a specific form of analysis. Thus, it is less prescriptive than most other methods, and in the spirit of pragmatism, it allows researchers the freedom to choose between specific analytical tools regarding their data, problem, and question. This increased agency evokes empowerment as a human interest when applied to the choice of methodology. Whether the exact topics under investigation help or empower people depends, of course, on each project. However, by offering the opportunity to retrieve the particular within the general (and the general in the particular), multi-resolution research makes it easier to recover participant voices, stories, and experiences and let them support, nuance, and often contradict the overall pattern, thus increasing the chances of discovering surprise and having our expectations disrupted.

An overarching theme running through each chapter of this book is the idea that differences (between theories, questions, methods, and research traditions) can expand the possibilities for research. Whether discussing epistemology, theory, data, or analysis, the emphasis falls on how diverse perspectives can be brought together and how this dialogue of difference can enable creative synergies. Pragmatism is inherently pluralistic, and while such pluralism can make some researchers recoil with the fear that "anything goes," pragmatism cuts through with a clear-headed focus on consequences.

Chapter 1 outlined seven propositions for a pragmatist approach to methodology in social research – each developed further in the subsequent chapters. This pragmatist approach starts with action and its consequences. From the start, what is specific for human action is that it can have multiple motivations and be guided by various interests and concerns (see also Boesch, 1991). Research is no exception, and any viewpoint, datum, or analysis is welcomed if it can contribute to the problem at hand; there is no fundamentalism beyond the commitment to being useful and making a contribution. However, to fully appreciate the consequences of knowledge necessarily requires engaging with the perspectives of multiple stakeholders (e.g., research colleagues, participants, ethics committees, and institutions). Human possibility is expanded not by being trapped in one perspective but by evaluating the consequences of knowledge from a diversity of standpoints.

Chapter 2 developed the epistemological proposition that *truth is in its consequences*. Historically, the debate has been between, on the one hand, realist and positivist views and, on the other hand, constructionist, relativist, and postmodern views (Jovchelovitch, 2019). Pragmatism emerges, historically and methodologically, as a third epistemology that avoids the pitfalls of a transcendental Truth and hopelessly subjective and fragmented truths. Pragmatism focuses on the future rather than only the present or past; it focuses on the world as it becomes, and not only the world as it is or was. Simplistically, positivism is an epistemology anchored in the past; it emphasizes underlying causes as the push from the past. It uses the metaphor of the universe as a mechanical clock set in motion by initial conditions. Constructionism is an epistemology anchored in the present. It risks trapping researchers in an eternal present of subjective experience without being able to say anything confidently about the past or the future. Pragmatism is an epistemology anchored in the future; it takes ideas and expectations from the past, acts in the present, and evaluates everything by the consequences in the future.

Chapter 3 developed the proposition that *theories are tools for action*. The idea is that theories crystallize past experiences into guides or maps to the future, which can be more or less useful. From a pragmatist standpoint, we use theories to make the world more predictable, hospitable, and actionable. Theories are lenses through which we make sense of ongoing events and the data derived from them; theories lean into the future (Davis, 2021). This pragmatist realization is empowering because it enables researchers to take advantage of moving between the bricolage of theoretical positions to acquire more tools to act on their data. From a pragmatist standpoint, theories are rarely competing alternatives (e.g., to be tested between) and are more often akin to a collection of tools, with each tool being useful in certain cases. Instead of separating theory from data collection and analysis, as is common, pragmatism sees the value of theory throughout the research process. Placing the researcher at a meta-level and, as such, developing theories about one's own theoretical tools and constructs can be empowering by creating a much-needed space for choice and deliberation about theories and methods.

Chapter 4 developed the proposition that *research is as much about creating questions as answering questions.* To this end, we outlined a typology of research questions and conceptualized these questions as bridges between theories and research practice. If theories are tools, then research questions connect these tools to the particularities of the problem at hand. Following the pragmatist principle of plurality, in this typology, quantitative and qualitative lines of questioning are not only intrinsically diverse but they can and do often complement each other, supporting theoretical development and empowering researchers to create new questions (Fetters & Molina-Azorin, 2017b). What is possibility-enabling at this level is the capacity to mix and match research questions, aware of the different human interests and theoretical commitments they embody. This is empowering for researchers to the extent to which they can then innovate at the level of method and pragmatically adapt their analytical procedures to the new questions being created. Creating new questions entails being open to surprise and being sensitive to disruptive data. We argued that one way to search for such disruptions is to move back and forth between theories, methods, and modes of analysis. Tensions revealed by such movement are the seeds of possibility – new theories, questions, and paths of action.

Chapter 5 developed the idea of *data as a process.* In contrast to static classifications of "types" of data, we examined different "states" of data. The idea is that raw data can be transformed into different types of data, and thus they can be continuously restructured into multiple types. Data emerged, thus, as a process rather than a fixed state, very much in line with the pragmatist emphasis on repositioning in order to develop new perspectives. And, indeed, working with data has different affordances depending on where these data are in their transformation (Hogan, 2015). Most of all, the reversibility of data transformations reflects the principle of position exchange and, as such, has the potential to expand researcher agency. But, of course, there are also powerful constraints on data collection, including data accessibility, that can hinder possibilities in this area. Data have been described as the new oil, and thus companies increasingly want exclusive access to the data they collect. Often researchers are locked out under the guise of protecting personal data. This undermines the possibility of researchers scrutinizing how these data, concealed within the corporate vaults, are (and could be) used.

Chapter 6 developed the proposition that *qualitative and quantitative methods are synergistic*. Mixed methods research is a clear example of "methodologies of the possible" because of the creative synergies that can be produced. The literature on mixing methods is vast and continuously expanding (Molina-Azorin & Fetters, 2022), and, at its core, it offers researchers an expanded horizon of possibilities regarding topics under study, methodological procedures, and the depth and usefulness of research findings. Often driven by a pragmatist type of logic, even if only implicitly, mixed methods cut across old divides, especially the one between qualitative and quantitative data and analyses. Although mixed methods research often fails to yield synergies, when it does, the results can be dramatic, with each method reinforcing, enriching, and even challenging the other. The key theoretical issue for mixed methods research is the integration challenge (Fetters & Freshwater, 2015a), namely, the challenge of specifying how mixing methods can yield outcomes that are more than the sum of the parts. We showed how a pragmatist approach can contribute to this debate, by showing how qualitative and quantitative research have different purposes and how these purposes can be combined in synergistic and empowering ways.

Chapter 7 developed the idea of *analyzing big qualitative data both qualitatively and quantitatively*. The key insight here is that big qualitative datasets do not have a fixed data type; they can be converted into both qualitative (e.g., excerpts) and quantitative (e.g., numeric) forms. Recursively repositioning vis-à-vis the raw data can improve rigor, spur theoretical development, and expand the possibilities for analysis. Zooming in and out of the same body of data provides more legitimacy to the findings while, at the same time, increasing the possibility of abductive insights (Mitchell, 2018). This intrinsic creativity of multi-resolution research, in terms of its outcomes, resonates with the agency of researchers applying this new methodology. This is because, besides some general guidelines, multi-resolution research does not overconstrain the types of analyses (quantitative or qualitative) that can be applied to the data. At the same time, working with data at different stages of structuration allows for the kind of repositioning that is fundamental for agency and possibility. This opens the ethical question of whether the new possibilities experienced by researchers are translated into expanded fields of opportunities for participants or other stakeholders.

Chapter 8 elaborated on the pragmatist proposal that *social research creates both power and responsibility*. A pragmatist approach to ethics moves away from universal principles toward contextual moral deliberation. This view reveals the deep connections between pragmatism and democracy as a sociocultural practice (Brinkmann, 2013; Caspary, 2000). From this standpoint, the emphasis is placed on dialogue and participation rather than preestablished and decontextualized moral laws, something that is also at the heart of emancipatory human interests (i.e., being able to understand and value marginal perspectives and local knowledge, and measure them against their consequences for individuals, groups, and society). Conducting social research requires engagement with issues of participation, deliberation, and responsibility. If we bring futures into existence through our research and methods, we hold responsibility for how these futures affect others, not only in the short term. Ethics is, thus, not a one-time concern, typically at the start of the research process, but an ongoing practice of reflection on the present in the horizon of multiple possible futures.

Finally, we get to the uniting proposition of this chapter, that *social research should aim to expand human possibility*. Pragmatism views science as a means to create useful knowledge. What counts as useful, however, is determined by the guiding research interests (e.g., technocratic, hermeneutic, or emancipatory). No scientific method can determine which interest social researchers "should" pursue; it is a choice. Our choice, along with the early American pragmatists, is unashamedly emancipatory: social research should be used to increase people's capacity to act, to improve lives, to make the future more predictable and desirable, and to be reflective about who is using which knowledge to do what to whom.

9.5 Conclusion

In this final chapter, we argued that social scientists are not mere servants of Truth, they are social, cultural, and political actors making choices, following human interests, and advancing toward their preferred futures

(Voros, 2003). Research is never the neutral pursuit of Truth, regardless of how much realists and positivists would want it to be. But neither is it the mere cataloging of subjectivities and social conventions, as it is sometimes portrayed by constructionists. From a pragmatist standpoint, research is an activity animated by human interests that is part of the activities of today that will shape the lives of tomorrow (McNamee, 1988; Schratz & Walker, 2005).

Given that "knowledge is power" (Mead, 1936, pp. 350–351), we should also evaluate it in terms of the interests advanced or hindered by it. Is the research producing effective, insightful, or emancipatory knowledge? Pragmatism invites us to reflect on this question but does not determine what interests we should pursue. For some, this might be a glaring hole at the heart of classical pragmatism. In trying to avoid hierarchies and dichotomies, pragmatism also avoids prescribing courses of action and considers each human interest potentially useful, depending on what we might want to achieve with it. How should we decide which interest to follow? Are all of them equally valid? What if the interest motivating the research leads to the domination of others or environmental destruction? Where do we draw the line? Faced with the multiple global challenges of today, it seems irresponsible not to take a stand on this issue.

The early positivists, such as Comte (1858), recognized these issues. Comte saw the transformative potential of social science for society but argued that it needed to be given direction by a secular religion that itself was outside science. The pragmatists, in contrast, put their faith in democracy (Addams, 2002). This link between democracy and science is odd for many realists, but, from the standpoint of pragmatism, which sees no clear separation between values and knowledge, it is essential (Brinkmann, 2013; Putnam, 1995). Social science needs steering in terms of what questions to ask, what interests to enhance, and how to evaluate the consequences of the knowledge produced. It is only through deep democracy, permeating the public sphere and institutions, that the interests of the many can be addressed and the most broadly beneficial consequences of knowledge can be achieved.

In this book, we have developed pragmatism into a possibility-expanding approach to methodology. The pragmatist insight is to use consequences to bypass relativism and reconceptualize all knowledge as moral. This approach is grounded in notions of difference, plurality, and dialogue. The strength of this approach lies in the value of considering traditional topics such as epistemology, research questions, data, analyses, and human interests as intrinsically plural. There is no universally better question to ask or method to use; creativity and agency are embedded in the myriad of choices researchers have to make along the research process (see also Wegener et al., 2018). Mixing methods, an eminently pragmatist exercise, is especially amenable to reflection, deliberation, and discovering new synergies and possibilities.

A pragmatist approach to refining our methodologies of the possible can help social researchers to seize the emerging potentials created by the exponential increase in new forms of data and, in particular, big qualitative data (see Chapter 5). Besides the opportunities and challenges associated with using this mainly – for now – public resource, there are a few methods out there that can use these data to reach useful and meaningful conclusions. Moreover, any single method, in isolation, risks giving us only a partial picture when it comes to this kind of data (think, for instance, about the advantages and disadvantages of natural language processing vs. discourse analysis). Possibilities abound when it comes to creatively devising new tools for research, and this book advanced one such idea in the form of multi-resolution research (Chapter 7). Such methodologies have the potential to create more valid and robust findings that are useful because they are simultaneously connected to particulars while also leveraging vast quantities of data.

Although we were not born into a universe with the simple certainties often craved (Dewey, 1929), we have the potential and the responsibility to improve the world we find ourselves in. What is often sought "behind" human experience needs to be created through human experience. Certainties, agency, and social justice are made, not found. Pragmatism entails a project of world-making (Gergen, 2015; Power et al., 2023). It eschews grand plans and simple narratives in favor of concrete incremental improvements to the human condition (Dewey, 1910a). A pragmatist approach to research methodology starts from where we are, with the world as we find it, and aims to improve upon it. As James eloquently wrote, the world is "unfinished, growing in all sorts of places, especially in the places where thinking beings are at work" (1907, p. 116). To support this collective project, the role of research is not simply to describe the world as it is but to help imagine the world as it could be.

References

Abbott, A. (2000). *Chaos of disciplines*. University of Chicago Press.

Abend, G. (2008). The meaning of "theory". *Sociological Theory*, 26(2), 173–199. https://doi.org/10.1111/j.1467-9558.2008.00324.x

Adams, D. (2017). *The ultimate hitchhiker's guide to the galaxy*. Pan Macmillan.

Addams, J. (1990). *Twenty years at Hull-House*. University of Illinois Press.

Addams, J. (2002). *Democracy and social ethics*. University of Illinois Press.

Adnan, K., Akbar, R., Khor, S. W., & Ali, A. B. A. (2020). Role and challenges of unstructured big data in healthcare. *Data Management, Analytics and Innovation*, 1042, 301–323. https://doi.org/10.1007/978-981-32-9949-8_22

Åkerblad, L., Seppänen-Järvelä, R., & Haapakoski, K. (2021). Integrative strategies in mixed methods research. *Journal of Mixed Methods Research*, 15(2), 152–170. https://doi.org/10.1177/1558689820957125

Al-Ababneh, M. M. (2020). Linking ontology, epistemology and research methodology. *Science & Philosophy*, 8(1), 75–91.

Aldewereld, H., Boissier, O., Dignum, V., Noriega, P., & Padget, J. A. (2016). *Social coordination frameworks for social technical systems*. Springer.

Alexander, J. C. (1982). *Positivism, presuppositions, and current controversies*. University of California Press. https://doi.org/10.4324/9781315815855

Allemang, B., Sitter, K., & Dimitropoulos, G. (2022). Pragmatism as a paradigm for patient-oriented research. *Health Expectations*, 25(1), 38–47. https://doi.org/10.1111/hex.13384

Allport, G. (1954). *The nature of prejudice*. Addison-Wesley.

Altman, A. (1983). Pragmatism and applied ethics. *American Philosophical Quarterly*, 20(2), 227–235.

American Psychological Association. (2010). *Ethical principles of psychologists and code of conduct*. American Psychological Association. www.apa.org/ethics/code/principles.pdf

American Psychological Association. (2023). *Ethical principles of psychologists and code of conduct*. American Psychological Association. www.apa.org/ethics/code

Anderson, C. (2008, June 23). *The end of theory: The data deluge makes the scientific method obsolete*. Wired. www.wired.com/2008/06/pb-theory/

Andrejevic, M. (2014). Surveillance in the big data era. In K. B. Pimple (Ed.), *Emerging Pervasive Information and Communication Technologies (PICT): Ethical challenges, opportunities and safeguards* (pp. 55–69). Springer.

Andreotta, M., Nugroho, R., Hurlstone, M. J., et al. (2019). Analyzing social media data: A mixed-methods framework combining computational and qualitative text analysis. *Behavior Research Methods*, 51(4), 1766–1781. https://doi .org/10/gfxzv2

Anguera, M. T., Blanco-Villaseñor, A., Jonsson, G. K., Losada, J. L., & Portell, M. (2020). Best practice approaches for mixed methods research in psychological science. *Frontiers in Psychology*, 11, 590131. https://doi.org/10.3389/ fpsyg.2020.590131

Ansell, C., & Boin, A. (2019). Taming deep uncertainty: The potential of pragmatist principles for understanding and improving strategic crisis management. *Administration & Society*, 51(7), 1079–1112. https://doi .org/10.1177/0095399717747655

Arras, J. D. (2001). Freestanding pragmatism in law and bioethics. *Theoretical Medicine and Bioethics*, 22(2), 69–85. https://doi.org/10.1023/A:1011495624471

Asch, S. E. (1951). Effects of group pressure upon the modification and distortion of judgment. In H. Guetzkow (Ed.), *Groups, leadership and men* (pp. 177–190). Carnegie Press.

Asch, S. E. (1955). Opinions and social pressure. *Scientific American*, 193(5), 31–35.

Asghar, M. R., Lee, T., Baig, M. M., et al. (2017). A review of privacy and consent management in healthcare: A focus on emerging data sources. In *2017 IEEE 13th International Conference on E-Science (e-Science)* (pp. 518–522). https://doi .org/10.1109/eScience.2017.84

Ashby, C. E. (2011). Whose "voice" is it anyway? Giving voice and qualitative research involving individuals that type to communicate. *Disability Studies Quarterly*, 31(4), 26. https://doi.org/10.18061/dsq.v31i4.1723

Aveling, E.-L., Gillespie, A., & Cornish, F. (2015). A qualitative method for analysing multivoicedness. *Qualitative Research*, 15(6), 670–687. https://doi .org/10.1177/1468794114557991

Axley, S. R. (1984). Managerial and organizational communication in terms of the conduit metaphor. *The Academy of Management Review*, 9(3), 428–437.

Backett-Milburn, K., Mauthner, N., & Parry, O. (1999). The importance of the conditions and relations of project design for the construction of qualitative data: Some experiences from collaborative team working. *International Journal of Social Research Methodology*, 2(4), 297–312. https://doi .org/10.1080/136455799294970

Bacon, F. (1620). *Novum organum*. P. F. Collier & Son.

Baggini, J. (2017). *A short history of truth: Consolations for a post-truth world*. Quercus.

Bailey, J. R., & Eastman, W. N. (1994). Positivism and the promise of the social sciences. *Theory & Psychology*, 4(4), 505–524. https://doi .org/10.1177/0959354394044003

Baker, G., & Morris, K. J. (1996). *Descartes' dualism*. Routledge.

Baker, M., & Schaltegger, S. (2015). Pragmatism and new directions in social and environmental accountability research. *Accounting, Auditing & Accountability Journal*, 28, 263–294. https://doi.org/10.1108/AAAJ-08-2012-01079

Bakhtin, M. (1981). *The dialogic imagination: Four essays.* University of Texas Press.

Bakhtin, M. (1986). *Speech genres & other late essays.* University of Texas Press.

Baldwin, T. (1979). Foresight and responsibility. *Philosophy*, 54(209), 347–360. https://doi.org/10.1017/S0031819100048750

Ball, J. (2017). *Post-truth: How bullshit conquered the world.* Biteback Publishing.

Bateson, G. (1972). *Steps to an ecology of mind.* Ballantine Books.

Baucal, A., Gillespie, A., Krstić, K., & Zittoun, T. (2020). Reproducibility in psychology: Theoretical distinction of different types of replications. *Integrative Psychological and Behavioral Science*, 54(1), 152–157. https://doi.org/10.1007/s12124-019-09499-y

Bauer, M. W., & Gaskell, G. (2000). *Qualitative researching: With text, image and sound.* SAGE.

Baumrind, D. (1964). Some thoughts on ethics of research: After reading Milgram's "Behavioral study of obedience". *American Psychologist*, 19, 421–423.

Baumrind, D. (2013). Is Milgram's deceptive research ethically acceptable? *Theoretical & Applied Ethics*, 2(2), 1–18.

Bazeley, P. (2017). *Integrating analyses in mixed methods research.* SAGE.

Bazeley, P., & Kemp, L. (2012). Mosaics, triangles, and DNA: Metaphors for integrated analysis in mixed methods research. *Journal of Mixed Methods Research*, 6(1), 55–72. https://doi.org/10.1177/1558689811419514

Becker, H. S. (1998). *Tricks of the trade: How to think about your research while you're doing it.* University of Chicago Press.

Beckwith, C. I. (2017). *Greek buddha: Pyrrho's encounter with early Buddhism in Central Asia.* Princeton University Press.

Beer, D., & Burrows, R. (2013). Popular culture, digital archives and the new social life of data. *Theory, Culture & Society*, 30(4), 47–71. https://doi.org/10.1177/0263276413476542

Bell, S. K., & Martinez, W. (2019). Every patient should be enabled to stop the line. *BMJ Quality & Safety*, 28, 172–176. https://doi.org/10.1136/bmjqs-2018-008714

Bennett, A. (2015). Found in translation: Combining discourse analysis with computer assisted content analysis. *Millennium*, 43(3), 984–997. https://doi.org/10.1177/0305829815581535

Berentson-Shaw, J. (2018). *A matter of fact: Talking truth in a post-truth world* (Vol. 67). Bridget Williams Books.

Berger, P., & Luckmann, T. (1966). *The social construction of reality: A treatise in the sociology of knowledge.* Penguin.

Berger, P., & Luckmann, T. (1967). *The social construction of reality.* Doubleday New York.

Bergkvist, L., & Zhou, K. Q. (2019). Cause-related marketing persuasion research: An integrated framework and directions for further research. *International Journal of Advertising*, 38(1), 5–25. https://doi.org/10.1080/02650487.2018.1452397

Berka, K. (1983). *Measurement.* Springer.

Bhaskar, R. (1975). *A realist theory of science.* Leeds Books.

Biesta, G., & Burbules, N. C. (2003). *Pragmatism and educational research.* Rowman & Littlefield.

Billig, M. (1985). Prejudice, categorization and particularization: From a perceptual to a rhetorical approach. *European Journal of Social Psychology*, 15, 79–103.

Birnie, K. A., Chambers, C. T., Taddio, A., et al. (2015). Psychological interventions for vaccine injections in children and adolescents: Systematic review of randomized and quasi-randomized controlled trials. *The Clinical Journal of Pain*, 31(Suppl 10), S72–S89.

Bjerg, O., & Presskorn-Thygesen, T. (2017). Conspiracy theory: Truth claim or language game? *Theory, Culture & Society*, 34(1), 137–159. https://doi.org/10.1177/0263276416657880

Blackburn, S. (2005). *The Oxford dictionary of philosophy*. Oxford University Press.

Blumer, H. (1969). *Symbolic interactionism*. University of California Press.

Boeije, H., Slagt, M., & van Wesel, F. (2013). The contribution of mixed methods research to the field of childhood trauma: A narrative review focused on data integration. *Journal of Mixed Methods Research*, 7(4), 347–369. https://doi.org/10.1177/1558689813482756

Boesch, E. E. (1991). *Symbolic action theory and cultural psychology*. Springer-Verlag.

Bohannon, J. (2015). Torture report prompts APA apology. *Science*, 349(6245), 221–222. https://doi.org/10.1126/science.349.6245.221

Bolla, S., & Anandan, R. (2018). Contemporary review on technologies and methods for converting unstructured data to structured data. *International Journal of Engineering and Technology (UAE)*, 7(3), 527–530. https://doi.org/10.14419/ijet.v7i3.27.18476

Borges, J. L. (1999). *By Jorge Luis Borges Collected Fictions*. Penguin Books.

Boyd, D., & Crawford, K. (2012). Critical questions for big data. *Information, Communication & Society*, 15(5), 662–679. https://doi.org/10.1080/1369118X.2012.678878

Boyd, R. L., & Schwartz, H. A. (2021). Natural language analysis and the psychology of verbal behavior: The past, present, and future states of the field. *Journal of Language and Social Psychology*, 40(1), 21–41. https://doi.org/10.1177/0261927X20967028

Breen, R., & Jonsson, J. O. (2005). Inequality of opportunity in comparative perspective: Recent research on educational attainment and social mobility. *Annual Review of Sociology*, 31, 223–243. https://doi.org/10.1146/annurev.soc.31.041304.122232

Brendel, D. H., & Miller, F. G. (2008). A plea for pragmatism in clinical research ethics. *The American Journal of Bioethics*, 8(4), 24–31. https://doi.org/10.1080/15265160802166025

Brenneis, D. (2005). Documenting ethics. In L. Meskell & P. Pels (Eds.), *Embedding ethics* (pp. 24–31). Routledge.

Brinkmann, S. (2009). Facts, values, and the naturalistic fallacy in psychology. *New Ideas in Psychology*, 27(1), 1–17.

Brinkmann, S. (2010). *Psychology as a moral science: Perspectives on normativity*. Springer Science & Business Media.

Brinkmann, S. (2013). *John Dewey: Science for a changing world*. Transaction Publishers.

British Psychological Society. (2010). *Code of conduct, ethical principles, and guidelines*. British Psychological Society.

Brockmeier, J., & Meretoja, H. (2014). Understanding narrative hermeneutics. *Storyworlds: A Journal of Narrative Studies*, 6(2), 1–27. https://doi.org/10.5250/storyworlds.6.2.0001

Brown, A. J. (2020). "Should I stay or should I leave?": Exploring (dis) continued Facebook use after the Cambridge Analytica scandal. *Social Media+ Society*, 6(1), 2056305120913884.

Brown, M. E. L., & Dueñas, A. N. (2020). A medical science educator's guide to selecting a research paradigm: Building a basis for better research. *Medical Science Educator*, 30(1), 545–553. https://doi.org/10.1007/s40670-019-00898-9

Bruner, J. S. (1990). *Acts of meaning*. Harvard University Press.

Bryman, A. (2006). Integrating quantitative and qualitative research: How is it done? *Qualitative Research*, 6(1), 97–113. https://doi.org/10.1177/1468794106058877

Bryman, A. (2008). The end of the paradigm wars. In P. Alasuutari, J. Brannen, & L. Bickman (Eds.), *The SAGE handbook of social research methods* (13–25). SAGE.

Brynjolfsson, E., & McAfee, A. (2011). The big data boom is the innovation story of our time. *The Atlantic*, 21, 30.

Buckley, R. (2018). Simultaneous analysis of qualitative and quantitative social science data in conservation. *Society & Natural Resources*, 31(7), 865–870. https://doi.org/10.1080/08941920.2018.1446232

Butt, T. (2000). Pragmatism, constructivism, and ethics. *Journal of Constructivist Psychology*, 13(2), 85–101. https://doi.org/10.1080/107205300265892

Byrne, D., & Callaghan, G. (Eds.). (2013). *Complexity theory and the social sciences: The state of the art*. Routledge. https://doi.org/10.4324/9780203519585

Cain, L. K., MacDonald, A. L., Coker, J. M., Velasco, J. C., & West, G. D. (2019). Ethics and reflexivity in mixed methods research: An examination of current practices and a call for further discussion. *International Journal of Multiple Research Approaches*, 11(2), 144–155. https://doi.org/10.29034/ijmra.v11n2a2

Calude, C. S., & Longo, G. (2017). The deluge of spurious correlations in big data. *Foundations of Science*, 22(3), 595–612. https://doi.org/10/gfkk82

Campbell, C., & Jovchelovitch, S. (2000). Health, community and development: Towards a social psychology of participation. *Journal of Community & Applied Social Psychology*, 10(4), 255–270. https://doi.org/10.1002/1099-1298(200007/08)10:4<255::AID-CASP582>3.0.CO;2-M

Campbell, J., & Cassam, Q. (2014). *Berkeley's puzzle: What does experience teach us?* Oxford University Press.

Caputo, J. D. (2016). *Truth, the search for wisdom in the postmodern age*. Penguin Books.

Carolan, M. (2003). Reflexivity: A personal journey during data collection. *Nurse Researcher* (through 2013), 10(3), 7–14.

Cartwright, N., & Bradburn, N. (2011). *A theory of measurement*. Unpublished manuscript.

Caspary, W. R. (2000). *Dewey on democracy*. Cornell University Press.

Cassell, C., Cunliffe, A. L., & Grandy, G. (2017). *The SAGE handbook of qualitative business and management research methods*. SAGE.

Chaiken, S. (1979). Communicator physical attractiveness and persuasion. *Journal of Personality and Social Psychology*, 37(8), 1387–1397. https://doi.org/10.1037/0022-3514.37.8.1387

Chambers, S. (2021). Truth, deliberative democracy, and the virtues of accuracy: Is fake news destroying the public sphere? *Political Studies*, 69(1), 147–163. https://doi.org/10.1177/0032321719890811

Chang, T., DeJonckheere, M., Vydiswaran, V. G. V., et al. (2021). Accelerating mixed methods research with natural language processing of big text data. *Journal of Mixed Methods Research*, 15(3), 398–412. https://doi.org/10.1177/1558689821021196

Chen, N.-C., Drouhard, M., Kocielnik, R., Suh, J., & Aragon, C. R. (2018). Using machine learning to support qualitative coding in social science: Shifting the focus to ambiguity. *ACM Transactions on Interactive Intelligent Systems (TiiS)*, 8(2), 1–20.

Chomsky, N. (1995). *The minimalist program* (Vol. 28). Cambridge University Press.

Christ, T. W. (2007). A recursive approach to mixed methods research in a longitudinal study of postsecondary education disability support services. *Journal of Mixed Methods Research*, 1(3), 226–241. https://doi.org/10/chxs3r

Christ, T. W. (2013). The worldview matrix as a strategy when designing mixed methods research. *International Journal of Multiple Research Approaches*, 7(1), 110–118. https://doi.org/10.5172/mra.2013.7.1.110

Christens, B. D. (2019). *Community power and empowerment*. Oxford University Press.

Christensen, T. C., Barrett, L. F., Bliss-Moreau, E., Lebo, K., & Kaschub, C. (2003). A practical guide to experience-sampling procedures. *Journal of Happiness Studies*, 4(1), 53–78. https://doi.org/10.1023/A:1023609306024

Christiano, T. (1997). The significance of public deliberation. In J. Bohman & W. Rehg (Eds.), *Deliberative democracy: Essays on reason and politics* (pp. 243–278). Massachusetts Institute of Technology Press.

Christopher, S., Watts, V., McCormick, A. K. H. G., & Young, S. (2008). Building and maintaining trust in a community-based participatory research partnership. *American Journal of Public Health*, 98(8), 1398–1406.

Clark, A. (2018). A nice surprise? Predictive processing and the active pursuit of novelty. *Phenomenology and the Cognitive Sciences*, 17(3), 521–534. https://doi.org/10.1007/s11097-017-9525-z

Clark, V. L. P., & Ivankova, N. (2016). Why use mixed methods research? Identifying rationales for mixing methods. In V. L. P. Clark & N. V. Ivankova (Eds.), *Mixed methods research: A guide to the field* (pp. 79–104). SAGE Publications.

Cleland, C. E. (2011). Prediction and explanation in historical natural science. *The British Journal for the Philosophy of Science*, 62(3), 551–582.

Comte, A. (1858). *The positive philosophy of Auguste Comte* (H. Martineau, Trans.). Blanchard.

Constant, A., Ramstead, M. J. D., Veissière, S. P. L., & Friston, K. (2019). Regimes of expectations: An active inference model of social conformity and human decision making. *Frontiers in Psychology*, 10. https://doi.org/10.3389/fpsyg.2019.00679

Conway, E. M., & Oreskes, N. (2012). *Merchants of doubt*. Bloomsbury Paperbacks.

Cooke, N. A. (2017). Post truth, truthiness, and alternative facts: Information behavior and critical information consumption for a new age. *The Library Quarterly*, 87(3), 211–221. https://doi.org/10.1086/692298

Corley, K. G., & Gioia, D. A. (2011). Building theory about theory building: What constitutes a theoretical contribution? *Academy of Management Review*, 36(1), 12–32. https://doi.org/10.5465/amr.2009.0486

Cornish, F. (2004). Making "context" concrete: A dialogical approach to the society-health relation. *Journal of Health Psychology*, 9(2), 281–294.

Cornish, F. (2020). Communicative generalisation: Dialogical means of advancing knowledge through a case study of an "unprecedented" disaster. *Culture & Psychology*, 26(1), 78–95. https://doi.org/10.1177/1354067X19894930

Cornish, F. (2021). "Grenfell changes everything?" Activism beyond hope and despair. *Critical Public Health*, 31(3), 293–305. https://doi.org/10.1080/0958159 6.2020.1869184

Cornish, F., & Gillespie, A. (2009). A pragmatist approach to the problem of knowledge in health psychology. *Journal of Health Psychology*, 14(6), 800–809. https://doi.org/10.1177/1359105309338974

Corti, K. (2015). *Developing the cyranoid method of mediated interpersonal communication in a social psychological context: Applications in person perception, human-computer interaction*. London School of Economics.

Corti, K., & Gillespie, A. (2015a). A truly human interface: Interacting face-to-face with someone whose words are determined by a computer program. *Frontiers in Psychology*, 6, 634. https://doi.org/10.3389/fpsyg.2015.00634

Corti, K., & Gillespie, A. (2015b). Revisiting Milgram's cyranoid method: Experimenting with hybrid human agents. *The Journal of Social Psychology*, 155(1), 30–56. https://doi.org/10.1080/00224545.2014.959885

Corti, K., & Gillespie, A. (2016). Co-constructing intersubjectivity with artificial conversational agents: People are more likely to initiate repairs of misunderstandings with agents represented as human. *Computers in Human Behavior*, 58, 431–442. https://doi.org/10.1016/j.chb.2015.12.039

Coveney, P. V., Dougherty, E. R., & Highfield, R. R. (2016). Big data need big theory too. *Philosophical Transactions of the Royal Society A: Mathematical, Physical and Engineering Sciences*, 374(2080), 20160153. https://doi.org/10.1098/rsta.2016.0153

Coxon, A. P. M. (2005). Integrating qualitative and quantitative data: What does the user need? *Forum Qualitative Sozialforschung / Forum: Qualitative Social Research*, 6(2), Article 2. https://doi.org/10.17169/fqs-6.2.463

Craig, R. T. (2007). Pragmatism in the field of communication theory. *Communication Theory*, 17(2), 125–145. https://doi.org/10.1111/j.1468-2885.2007.00292.x

Crano, W. D., Brewer, M. B., & Lac, A. (2014). *Principles and methods of social research*. Routledge.

Creamer, E. G. (2017). *An introduction to fully integrated mixed methods research*. SAGE.

Cresci, S., Di Pietro, R., Petrocchi, M., Spognardi, A., & Tesconi, M. (2020). Emergent properties, models, and laws of behavioral similarities within groups of twitter users. *Computer Communications*, 150, 47–61. https://doi.org/10.1016/j.comcom.2019.10.019

Creswell, J. W., & Creswell, J. D. (2018). *Research design: Qualitative, quantitative, and mixed methods approaches*. SAGE.

Creswell, J. W., Hanson, W. E., Clark Plano, V. L., & Morales, A. (2007). Qualitative research designs: Selection and implementation. *The Counseling Psychologist*, 35(2), 236–264. https://doi.org/10.1177/0011000006287390

Csikszentmihalyi, M. (1990). *Flow: The psychology of optimal experience*. Harper & Row.

Curran, T. (2023). *The perfection trap*. Penguin.

Damasio, A. R. (2006). *Descartes' error*. Random House.

D'Ancona, M. (2017). *Post-truth: The new war on truth and how to fight back*. Random House.

Darley, J. M., & Latané, B. (1968). Bystander intervention in emergencies: Diffusion of responsibility. *Journal of Personality and Social Psychology*, 8(4), 377–383.

Darwin, C. (1859). *The origin of species*. Dent, Rowman & Littlefield.

Darwin, C. (2001). *Charles Darwin's Beagle diary*. Cambridge University Press.

Daston, L. (1992). Objectivity and the escape from perspective. *Social Studies of Science*, 22(4), 597–618. https://doi.org/10.1177/030631292022004002

Davis, C. (2021). Sampling poetry, pedagogy, and protest to build methodology: Critical poetic inquiry as culturally relevant method. *Qualitative Inquiry*, 27(1), 114–124. https://doi.org/10.1177/1077800419884978

De Leeuw, R. N., Engels, R. C., Vermulst, A. A., & Scholte, R. H. (2008). Do smoking attitudes predict behaviour? A longitudinal study on the bi-directional relations between adolescents' smoking attitudes and behaviours. *Addiction*, 103(10), 1713–1721. https://doi.org/10.1111/j.1360-0443.2008.02293.x

De Rosa, A. S., & Mannarini, T. (2020). The "invisible other": Social representations of COVID-19 pandemic in media and institutional discourse. *Papers on Social Representations*, 29(2), 5–1.

de Saint Laurent, C. (2014). "I would rather be hanged than agree with you!": Collective memory and the definition of the nation in parliamentary debates on immigration. *Outlines. Critical Practices Studies*, 15(3), 22–53. https://doi.org/10.7146/ocps.v15i3.19860

de Saint Laurent, C., Glăveanu, V. P., & Chaudet, C. (2020). Malevolent creativity and social media: Creating anti-immigration communities on Twitter. *Creativity Research Journal*, 32(1), 66–80.

de Saint Laurent, C., Glăveanu, V. P., & Literat, I. (2021a). Internet memes as partial stories: Identifying political narratives in coronavirus memes. *Social Media + Society*, 7(1), 2056305121988932. https://doi.org/10.1177/2056305121988932

de Saint Laurent, C., Glăveanu, V. P., & Literat, I. (2022). Mimetic representations of the COVID-19 pandemic: An analysis of objectification, anchoring, and identification processes in coronavirus memes. *Psychology of Popular Media*. https://doi.org/10.1037/ppm0000370

de Saint Laurent, C., Murphy, G., Hegarty, K., & Greene, C. (2021b). Measuring the effects of misinformation exposure on behavioural intentions. https://doi.org/10.31234/osf.io/2xngy

de Saint Laurent, C., Obradović, S., & Carriere, K. R. (2018). *Imagining collective futures: Perspectives from social, cultural and political psychology*. Springer.

Deacon, T. W. (2011). *Incomplete nature: How mind emerged from matter*. W. W. Norton & Company.

Dennett, D. (1991). *Consciousness explained*. Penguin Press.

Denscombe, M. (2021). *The good research guide: For small-scale social research projects*. McGraw-Hill Education (UK).

Denzin, N. K. (1970). *The research act*. Aldine.

Denzin, N. K. (2012). Triangulation 2.0. *Journal of Mixed Methods Research*, 6(2), 80–88. https://doi.org/10.1177/1558689812437186

DeRosa, D. M., Smith, C. L., & Hantula, D. A. (2007). The medium matters: Mining the long-promised merit of group interaction in creative idea generation tasks in a meta-analysis of the electronic group brainstorming literature. *Computers in Human Behavior*, 23(3), 1549–1581.

Descartes, R. (1637). Discourse on the method for rightly conducting one's reason and for seeking truth in the sciences. In D. Weissman (Ed.), *Discourse on method: And, Meditations on first philosophy* (pp. 3–48). Yale University Press.

Descartes, R. (1641). Meditations on first philosophy. In J. Cottingham, R. Stoothoff, & D. Murdoch (Eds.), *The philosophical writings of Descartes* (Vol. II). Cambridge University Press.

Devers, K. J., & Frankel, R. M. (2000). Study design in qualitative research–2: Sampling and data collection strategies. *Education for Health*, 13(2), 263.

deVries, W., Jackman, H., Aikin, S. F., & Talisse, R. B. (2017). *Pragmatism, pluralism, and the nature of philosophy*. Routledge.

Dewey, J. (1896). The reflex arc concept in psychology. *Psychological Review*, 3(July), 357–370.

Dewey, J. (1903). *Studies in logical theory* (Vol. 11). Chicago University Press.

Dewey, J. (1905). The postulate of immediate empiricism. *The Journal of Philosophy, Psychology and Scientific Methods*, 2(15), 393–399.

Dewey, J. (1910a). Science as subject-matter and as method. *Science*, 31(787), 121–127. https://doi.org/10.1126/science.31.787.121

Dewey, J. (1910b). *The influence of Darwin on philosophy and other essays*. Henry Hold and Company.

Dewey, J. (1917). Duality and dualism. *The Journal of Philosophy, Psychology and Scientific Methods*, 14(18), 491–493. https://doi.org/10.2307/2940462

Dewey, J. (1920). Reconstruction in philosophy. In J. A. Boydston (Ed.), *John Dewey the middle works 1899–1924* (Vol. 12). Southern Illinois University Press.

Dewey, J. (1922). *Human nature and conduct*. Henry Holt.

Dewey, J. (1929). *The quest for certainty*. Minton, Balch & Company.

Dewey, J. (1934). *Art as experience*. Minton, Balch & Company.

Dewey, J. (1958). *Experience and human nature*. Dover Publications.

Dewey, J. (1997). *How we think*. D.C. Heath.

Dewey, J., & Bentley, A. F. (1946). Interaction and transaction. *The Journal of Philosophy*, 43(19), 505–517.

Dick, P. K. (1962). *The man in the high castle*. Penguin UK.

Dingemanse, M., Roberts, S. G., Baranova, J., et al. (2015). Universal principles in the repair of communication problems. *PLOS ONE*, 10(9), e0136100. https://doi.org/10.1371/journal.pone.0136100

Doody, O., & Bailey, M. E. (2016). Setting a research question, aim and objective. *Nurse Researcher*, 23(4). https://doi.org/10.7748/nr.23.4.19.s5

Douglas, K. M., Uscinski, J. E., Sutton, R. M., et al. (2019). Understanding conspiracy theories. *Political Psychology*, 40, 3–35. https://doi.org/10.1111/pops.12568

Doyle, A. C. (1892). *The adventures of Sherlock Holmes*. George Newnes.

Duncker, K. (1945). On problem-solving. *Psychological Monographs*, 58(5), 1–113.

Eames, C., & Eames, R. (Directors). (1977). *Powers of ten*. The Eames Office.

Earp, B. D., & Trafimow, D. (2015). Replication, falsification, and the crisis of confidence in social psychology. *Frontiers in Psychology*, 6. https://doi.org/10.3389/fpsyg.2015.00621

Edwards, M., Tuke, J., Roughan, M., & Mitchell, L. (2020). The one comparing narrative social network extraction techniques. In *2020 IEEE/ACM international conference on Advances in Social Networks Analysis and Mining (ASONAM)* (pp. 905–913). https://doi.org/10.1109/ASONAM49781.2020.9381346

Einstein, A. (1982). How I created the theory of relativity. *Physics Today*, 35(8), 45–47.

Eisenhardt, K. M. (1989). Building theories from case study research. *The Academy of Management Review*, 14(4), 532–550. https://doi.org/10.2307/258557

Elamin, M. B., & Montori, V. M. (2012). The hierarchy of evidence: From unsystematic clinical observations to systematic reviews. In J. G. Burneo (Ed.), *Neurology: An evidence-based approach* (pp. 11–24). Springer.

Emadian, A., England, C. Y., & Thompson, J. L. (2017). Dietary intake and factors influencing eating behaviours in overweight and obese South Asian men living in the UK: Mixed method study. *BMJ Open*, 7(7), e016919. https://doi.org/10.1136/bmjopen-2017-016919

Evans, D. (2003). Hierarchy of evidence: A framework for ranking evidence evaluating healthcare interventions. *Journal of Clinical Nursing*, 12(1), 77–84. https://doi.org/10.1046/j.1365-2702.2003.00662.x

Eynon, R., Fry, J., & Schroeder, R. (2008). The ethics of internet research. In G. Blank, N. G. Fielding, & R. M. Lee (Eds.), *The SAGE handbook of online research methods* (pp. 23–41). SAGE.

Fahy, K. (1997). Postmodern feminist emancipatory research: Is it an oxymoron? *Nursing Inquiry*, 4(1), 27–33. https://doi.org/10.1111/j.1440-1800.1997.tb00134.x

Fakis, A., Hilliam, R., Stoneley, H., & Townend, M. (2014). Quantitative analysis of qualitative information from interviews: A systematic literature review. *Journal of Mixed Methods Research*, 8(2), 139–161. https://doi.org/10.1177/1558689813495111

Falk, H. (2003). Digital archive developments. *The Electronic Library*, 21(4), 375–397. https://doi.org/10.1108/02640470310491603

Farr, R. (1987). The science of mental life: A social psychological perspective. *Bulletin of the British Psychological Society*, 40, 2–17.

Farr, R. (1984). Interviewing: The social psychology of the inter-view. In C. L. Cooper & P. Makin (Eds.), *Psychology for Managers*, 2nd edition (pp. 182–200). Macmillan and British Psychological Association.

Farr, R. (1997). The significance of the skin as a natural boundary in the sub-division of psychology. *Journal for the Theory of Social Behaviour*, 27(2–3), 305–323.

Faugier, J., & Sargeant, M. (1997). Sampling hard to reach populations. *Journal of Advanced Nursing*, 26(4), 790–797. https://doi.org/10.1046/j.1365-2648.1997.00371.x

Feilzer, Y. M. (2010). Doing mixed methods research pragmatically: Implications for the rediscovery of pragmatism as a research paradigm. *Journal of Mixed Methods Research*, 4(1), 6–16. https://doi.org/10.1177/1558689809349691

Feltham-King, T., & Macleod, C. (2016). How content analysis may complement and extend the insights of discourse analysis: An example of research on constructions of abortion in South African newspapers 1978–2005. *International Journal of Qualitative Methods*, 15(1), 1–9. https://doi.org/10.1177/1609406915624575

Ferretti, A., Ienca, M., Sheehan, M., et al. (2021). Ethics review of big data research: What should stay and what should be reformed? *BMC Medical Ethics*, 22(1), 1–13. https://doi.org/10.1186/s12910-021-00616-4

Fesmire, S. (2003). *John Dewey and moral imagination: Pragmatism in ethics.* Indiana University Press.

Festinger, L. (1956). *When prophecy fails: A social psychological study of a modern group that predicted the destruction of the world.* University of Minnesota Press.

Festinger, L. (1957). *A theory of cognitive dissonance.* Stanford University Press.

Fetters, M. D., & Freshwater, D. (2015a). The 1 + 1 = 3 integration challenge. *Journal of Mixed Methods Research*, 9(2), 115–117. https://doi.org/10.1177/1558689815581222

Fetters, M. D., & Freshwater, D. (2015b). Publishing a methodological mixed methods research article. *Journal of Mixed Methods Research*, 9(3), 203–213. https://doi.org/10/gcsfkr

Fetters, M. D., & Molina-Azorin, J. F. (2017a). The Journal of Mixed Methods Research starts a new decade: Principles for bringing in the new and divesting of the old language of the field. *Journal of Mixed Methods Research*, 11(1), 3–10. https://doi.org/10/gf23fh

Fetters, M. D., & Molina-Azorin, J. F. (2017b). The Journal of Mixed Methods Research starts a new decade: The mixed methods research integration trilogy and its dimensions. *Journal of Mixed Methods Research*, 11(3), 291–307. https://doi.org/10.1177/1558689817714066

Feyerabend, P. (2001). *Conquest of abundance: A tale of abstraction versus the richness of being.* University of Chicago Press.

Fielding, N. G. (2012). Triangulation and mixed methods designs: Data integration with new research technologies. *Journal of Mixed Methods Research,* 6(2), 124–136. https://doi.org/10.1177/1558689812437101

Filstead, W. J. (1979). Qualitative methods: A needed perspective in evaluation research. In T. D. Cook & C. S. Reichardt (Eds.), *Qualitative and quantitative methods in evaluation research* (pp. 33–48). SAGE.

Fisher, A. J., Medaglia, J. D., & Jeronimus, B. F. (2018). Lack of group-to-individual generalizability is a threat to human subjects research. *Proceedings of the National Academy of Sciences,* 115(27), E6106–E6115. https://doi.org/10.1073/pnas.1711978115

Flick, U. (2002). *An introduction to qualitative research.* SAGE.

Fong, A., Hettinger, A. Z., & Ratwani, R. M. (2015). Exploring methods for identifying related patient safety events using structured and unstructured data. *Journal of Biomedical Informatics,* 58, 89–95. https://doi.org/10.1016/j.jbi.2015.09.011

Foster, I., Ghani, R., Jarmin, R. S., Kreuter, F., & Lane, J. (2016). *Big data and social science: A practical guide to methods and tools.* Chapman and Hall/CRC.

Foucault, M. (1973). *Madness and civilization.* Vintage Books.

Foucault, M. (1975). *Discipline & punish: The birth of the prison.* Vintage Books.

Freire, P. (1970). *Pedagogy of the oppressed* (M. B. Ramos, Trans.). Continuum.

French, D. P., Cooke, R., McLean, N., Williams, M., & Sutton, S. (2007). What do people think about when they answer theory of planned behaviour questionnaires? A "think aloud" study. *Journal of Health Psychology,* 12(4), 672–687.

Friston, K. (2010). The free-energy principle: A unified brain theory? *Nature Reviews Neuroscience,* 11(2), 127. https://doi.org/10.1038/nrn2787

Friston, K., Thornton, C., & Clark, A. (2012). Free-energy minimization and the dark-room problem. *Frontiers in Psychology,* 130. https://doi.org/10.3389/fpsyg.2012.00130

Galenson, D. W. (2008). *Old masters and young geniuses: The two life cycles of artistic creativity.* Princeton University Press.

Gallese, V., & Goldman, A. (1998). Mirror neurons and the simulation theory of mind-reading. *Trends in Cognitive Sciences,* 2(12), 493–501.

Gaskell, G., & Bauer, M. W. (2000). Towards public accountability: Beyond sampling, reliability and validity. In M. W. Bauer & G. Gaskell (Eds.), *Qualitative researching with text, image and sound: A practical handbook for social research* (336–350). SAGE.

Geertz, C. (1973). *The interpretation of cultures.* Fontana Press.

Gergen, K. J. (1973). Social psychology as history. *Journal of Personality and Social Psychology,* 26, 309–320.

Gergen, K. J. (2015). From mirroring to world-making: Research as future forming. *Journal for the Theory of Social Behaviour,* 45(3), 287–310. https://doi.org/10.1111/jtsb.12075

Gerring, J. (2012). Mere description. *British Journal of Political Science,* 721–746. https://doi.org/10.1017/S0007123412000130

Gillespie, A. (2003). Supplementarity and surplus: Moving between the dimensions of otherness. *Culture & Psychology*, 9(3), 209–220.

Gillespie, A. (2004). The mystery of G. H. Mead's first book. *Theory & Psychology*, 14(3), 423–425.

Gillespie, A. (2005a). G.H. Mead: Theorist of the social act. *Journal for the Theory of Social Behaviour*, 35(1), 19–39.

Gillespie, A. (2005b). Malcolm X and his autobiography: Identity development and self-narration. *Culture & Psychology*, 11(1), 77–88.

Gillespie, A. (2006a). Descartes' demon: A dialogical analysis of Meditations on First Philosophy. *Theory & Psychology*, 16(6), 761–781.

Gillespie, A. (2006b). Games and the development of perspective taking. *Human Development*, 49(2), 87–92.

Gillespie, A. (2007a). Collapsing Self/Other positions: Identification through differentiation. *British Journal of Social Psychology*, 46(3), 579–595.

Gillespie, A. (2007b). The social basis of self-reflection. In J. Valsiner & A. Rosa (Eds.), *The Cambridge handbook of sociocultural psychology* (pp. 678–691). Cambridge University Press.

Gillespie, A. (2012). Position exchange: The social development of agency. *New Ideas in Psychology*, 30, 32–46. https://doi.org/10.1016/j.newideapsych.2010.03.004

Gillespie, A. (2018). Distinguishing two processes of self-reflection. In J. Valsiner & A. Rosa (Eds.), *The Cambridge handbook of sociocultural psychology* (pp. 245–259). Cambridge University Press.

Gillespie, A. (2020a). Disruption, self-presentation, and defensive tactics at the threshold of learning. *Review of General Psychology*, 24(4), 382–396. https://doi.org/10.1177/1089268020914258

Gillespie, A. (2020b). Semantic contact and semantic barriers: Reactionary responses to disruptive ideas. *Current Opinion in Psychology*, 35, 21–25. https://doi.org/10.1016/j.copsyc.2020.02.010

Gillespie, A., Best, C., & O'Neill, B. (2012). Cognitive function and assistive technology for cognition: A systematic review. *Journal of the International Neuropsychological Society*, 18, 1–19. https://doi.org/10.1017/S1355617711001548

Gillespie, A., & Cornish, F. (2014). Sensitizing questions: A method to facilitate analyzing the meaning of an utterance. *Integrative Psychological and Behavioral Science*, 48(4), 435–452. https://doi.org/10.1007/s12124-014-9265-3

Gillespie, A., Cornish, F., Aveling, E.-L., & Zittoun, T. (2007). Conflicting community commitments: A dialogical analysis of a British woman's World War II diaries. *Journal of Community Psychology*, 36(1), 35–52.

Gillespie, A., & Corti, K. (2016). The body that speaks: Recombining bodies and speech sources in unscripted face-to-face communication. *Frontiers in Psychology*, 1300. https://doi.org/10.3389/fpsyg.2016.01300

Gillespie, A., Corti, K., Evans, S., & Heasman, B. (2017). Imagining the self through cultural technologies. *Handbook of Imagination and Culture*, 301–318.

Gillespie, A., & Martin, J. (2014). Position Exchange Theory: A socio-material basis for discursive and psychological positioning. *New Ideas in Psychology*, 32, 73–79.

Gillespie, A., & Reader, T. W. (2016). The Healthcare Complaints Analysis Tool: Development and reliability testing of a method for service monitoring and organisational learning. *BMJ Quality & Safety*, 25(12), 937–946. https://doi.org/10.1136/bmjqs-2015-004596

Gillespie, A., & Reader, T. W. (2018). Patient-centered insights: Using health care complaints to reveal hot spots and blind spots in quality and safety. *The Milbank Quarterly*, 96(3), 530–567. https://doi.org/10.1111/1468-0009.12338

Gillespie, A., & Reader, T. W. (2022). Online patient feedback as a safety valve: An automated language analysis of unnoticed and unresolved safety incidents. *Risk Analysis*, n/a(n/a). https://doi.org/10.1111/risa.14002

Gillespie, A., & Zittoun, T. (2010). Using resources: Conceptualizing the mediation and reflective use of tools and signs. *Culture & Psychology*, 16(1), 37–62. https://doi.org/10.1177/1354067X09344888

Gillon, S. M. (2001). Unintended consequences [Why our plans don't go according to plan]. *The Futurist*, 35(2), 49–53.

Glăveanu, V. P. (2010). Paradigms in the study of creativity: Introducing the perspective of cultural psychology. *New Ideas in Psychology*, 28(1), 79–93.

Glăveanu, V. P. (2011). Is the lightbulb still on? *Social representations of creativity in a western context. International Journal of Creativity and Problem Solving*, 21(1), 53–72.

Glăveanu, V. P. (2014). Revisiting the "art bias" in lay conceptions of creativity. *Creativity Research Journal*, 26(1), 11–20. https://doi.org/10.1080/10400419.2014.873656

Glăveanu, V. P. (2020a). *The possible: A sociocultural theory*. Oxford University Press.

Glăveanu, V. P. (2020b). *Wonder: The extraordinary power of an ordinary experience*. Bloomsbury Academic.

Glăveanu, V. P., & Gillespie, A. (2014). Creativity out of difference: Theorising the semiotic, social and temporal origin of creative acts. In V. P. Glăveanu, A. Gillespie, & J. Valsiner (Eds.), *Rethinking creativity* (pp. 25–39). Routledge.

Glăveanu, V. P., & Gillespie, A. (2021). Cognition stays wild: A commentary on Ross and Vallée-Tourangeau's rewilding cognition. *Journal of Trial & Error*, 2(1). https://doi.org/10.36850/r4

Glăveanu, V. P., Gillespie, A., & Karwowski, M. (2019). Are people working together inclined towards practicality? A process analysis of creative ideation in individuals and dyads. *Psychology of Aesthetics, Creativity, and the Arts*, 13(4), 388–401. https://doi.org/10.1037/aca0000171

Glerup, C., Davies, S. R., & Horst, M. (2017). "Nothing really responsible goes on here": Scientists' experience and practice of responsibility. *Journal of Responsible Innovation*, 4(3), 319–336. https://doi.org/10.1080/23299460.2017.1378462

Gobo, G., Fielding, N. G., La Rocca, G., & van der Vaart, W. (2022). *Merged methods: A rationale for full integration*. SAGE.

Goertzel, T. (1994). Belief in conspiracy theories. *Political Psychology*, 731–742. https://doi.org/10.2307/3791630

Goffman, E. (1959). *The presentation of self in everyday life*. Penguin.

González-Bailón, S. (2013). Social science in the era of big data. *Policy & Internet*, 5(2), 147–160. https://doi.org/10.1002/1944-2866.POI328

Goodman, R. B. (1995). *Pragmatism: A contemporary reader*. Routledge.

Goodman, R. B. (2012). William James's pluralisms. *Revue Internationale de Philosophie*, 260(2), 155–176. https://doi.org/10.3917/rip.260.0155

Gosden, C. (2004). The past and foreign countries: Colonial and post-colonial archaeology and anthropology. In L. Meskell & R. W. Preucel (Eds.), *A companion to social archaeology* (pp. 161–178). Blackwell.

Gould, S. J. (1981). *The mismeasure of man*. W. W. Norton & Company.

Graham, J., Haidt, J., Koleva, S., et al. (2013). Moral foundations theory: The pragmatic validity of moral pluralism. *Advances in Experimental Social Psychology*, 47, 55–130.

Graham, J., Haidt, J., & Nosek, B. A. (2009). Liberals and conservatives rely on different sets of moral foundations. *Journal of Personality and Social Psychology*, 96(5), 1029. https://doi.org/10.1037/a0015141

Greene, J. C., Caracelli, V. J., & Graham, W. F. (1989). Toward a conceptual framework for mixed-method evaluation designs. *Educational Evaluation and Policy Analysis*, 11(3), 255–274. https://doi.org/10/cjqt52

Greenhalgh, T., & Russell, J. (2009). Evidence-based policymaking: A critique. *Perspectives in Biology and Medicine*, 52(2), 304–318. https://doi.org/10.1353/pbm.0.0085

Guastello, S. J., Koopmans, M., & Pincus, D. (2008). *Chaos and complexity in psychology: The theory of nonlinear dynamical systems*. Cambridge University Press.

Guba, E. G., & Lincoln, Y. S. (1994). Competing paradigms in qualitative research. *Handbook of Qualitative Research*, 2(163–194), 105.

Guess, A., Lyons, B., Nyhan, B., & Reifler, J. (2018). Avoiding the echo chamber about echo chambers: Why selective exposure to like-minded political news is less prevalent than you think. Knight Foundation White Paper.

Guetterman, T. C., Fetters, M. D., & Creswell, J. W. (2015). Integrating quantitative and qualitative results in health science mixed methods research through joint displays. *The Annals of Family Medicine*, 13(6), 554–561. https://doi.org/10/f7zj9r

Guetterman, T. C., Molina-Azorin, J. F., & Fetters, M. D. (2020). Virtual special issue on "integration in mixed methods research". *Journal of Mixed Methods Research*, 14(4), 430–435. https://doi.org/10.1177/1558689820956401

Gupta, M., Rahman, A., Dutta, N. C., et al. (2020). Impact of a rural drowning reduction programme in Bangladesh on gender equity, norms and behaviour: A mixed-method analysis. *BMJ Open*, 10(12), e041065. https://doi.org/10.1136/bmjopen-2020-041065

Haack, S. (1976). The pragmatist theory of truth. *The British Journal for the Philosophy of Science*, 27(3), 231–249. https://doi.org/10.1093/bjps/27.3.231

Habermas, J. (1968). *Knowledge and human interests*. Polity Press.

Habermas, J. (1989). *The structural transformation of the public sphere*. Polity Press.

Hacking, I. (1995). The looping effects of human kinds. *Causal Cognition: A Multidisciplinary Approach*, 351–383.

Hacking, I. (1999). *The social construction of what?* Harvard University Press.

Hagan, T. L., Rosenzweig, M. Q., Zorn, K. K., van Londen, G. J., & Donovan, H. S. (2017). Perspectives on self-advocacy: Comparing perceived uses, benefits, and drawbacks among survivors and providers. *Oncology Nursing Forum*, 44(1), 52–59. https://doi.org/10.1188/17.ONF.52-59

Hagues, R. (2021). Conducting critical ethnography: Personal reflections on the role of the researcher. *International Social Work*, 64(3), 438–443. https://doi.org/10.1177/0020872818819731

Haig, B. D. (2005). An abductive theory of scientific method. *Psychological Methods*, 10(4), 371–388.

Hamad, E. O., Savundranayagam, M. Y., Holmes, J. D., Kinsella, E. A., & Johnson, A. M. (2016). Toward a mixed-methods research approach to content analysis in the digital age: The combined content-analysis model and its applications to health care twitter feeds. *Journal of Medical Internet Research*, 18(3), e5391. https://doi.org/10.2196/jmir.5391

Hammersley, M. (1996). The relationship between qualitative and quantitative research: Paradigm loyalty versus methodological eclecticism. In J. T. E. Richardson (Ed.), *Handbook of qualitative research methods for psychology and the social sciences* (pp. 159–174). BPS Blackwell.

Hammersley, M. (2002). Research as emancipatory. *Journal of Critical Realism*, 1(1), 33–48. https://doi.org/10.1558/jocr.v1i1.33

Haney, C., Banks, C., & Zimbardo, P. (1973). Interpersonal dynamics in a simulated prison. *International Journal of Criminology and Penology*, 1(1), 69–97.

Haugestad, C. A. P., Skauge, A. D., Kunst, J. R., & Power, S. A. (2021). Why do youth participate in climate activism? A mixed-methods investigation of the #FridaysForFuture climate protests. *Journal of Environmental Psychology*, 76, 101647. https://doi.org/10.1016/j.jenvp.2021.101647

Hawlina, H., Gillespie, A., & Zittoun, T. (2019). Difficult differences: A sociocultural analysis of how diversity can enable and inhibit creativity. *The Journal of Creative Behavior*, 53(2), 133–144. https://doi.org/10.1002/jocb.182

Hayes, S. C., & Hofmann, S. G. (2020). *Beyond the DSM: Toward a process-based alternative for diagnosis and mental health treatment*. New Harbinger Publications.

Hayes, S. C., Hofmann, S. G., Stanton, C. E., et al. (2019). The role of the individual in the coming era of process-based therapy. *Behaviour Research and Therapy*, 117, 40–53. https://doi.org/10.1016/j.brat.2018.10.005

Heasman, B., & Gillespie, A. (2017). Perspective-taking is two-sided: Misunderstandings between people with Asperger's syndrome and their family members. *Autism*, 22(6), 740–750. https://doi.org/10.1177/1362361317708287

Hegel, G. W. F. (1807). *Phenomenology of spirit*. Oxford University Press.

Helbing, D. (2012). *Social self-organization: Agent-based simulations and experiments to study emergent social behavior*. Springer.

Henderson, K. A., Ainsworth, B. E., Stolarzcyk, L. M., Hootman, J. M., & Levin, S. (1999). Notes on linking qualitative and quantitative data: The cross cultural physical activity participation study. *Leisure Sciences*, 21(3), 247–255. https://doi.org/10.1080/014904099273138

Hendrick, C. (1977). Social psychology as an experimental science. In C. Hendrick (Ed.), *Perspectives on social psychology* (pp. 1–74). Erlbaum.

Hesse-Biber, S. (2010). Emerging methodologies and methods practices in the field of mixed methods research. *Qualitative Inquiry*, 16(6), 415–418.

Hewstone, M., & Brown, R. (1986). Contact is not enough: An intergroup perspective on the "contact hypothesis." In M. Hewstone & R. Brown (Eds.), *Contact and conflict in intergroup encounters* (pp. 1–44). Basil Blackwell.

Hirschberg, J., & Manning, C. D. (2015). Advances in natural language processing. *Science*, 349(6245), 261–266. https://doi.org/10.1126/science.aaa8685

Ho, P., Chen, K., Shao, A., et al. (2021). A mixed methods study of public perception of social distancing: Integrating qualitative and computational analyses for text data. *Journal of Mixed Methods Research*, 15(3), 374–397. https://doi.org/10/gmggzw

Hogan, B. (2015). From invisible algorithms to interactive affordances: Data after the ideology of machine learning. In E. Bertino & S. A. Matei (Eds.), *Roles, trust, and reputation in social media knowledge markets* (pp. 103–117). Springer.

Holstein, J. A., & Gubrium, J. F. (2013). *Handbook of constructionist research*. Guilford Publications.

Holton, G. (1975). On the role of themata in scientific thought. *Science*, 188(4186), 328–334.

Holton, J. A., & Walsh, I. (2016). *Classic grounded theory: Applications with qualitative and quantitative data*. SAGE.

Hood, K., Robling, M., Ingledew, D., et al. (2012). Mode of data elicitation, acquisition and response to surveys: A systematic review. *Health Technology Assessment*, 16(27), 1–162.

Hoover, J. (2016). *Reconstructing human rights: A pragmatist and pluralist inquiry into global ethics*. Oxford University Press.

Hunter, A. (2018). Towards a framework for computational persuasion with applications in behaviour change. *Argument & Computation*, 9(1), 15–40. https://doi.org/10.3233/AAC-170032

Hussein, A. (2009). The use of triangulation in social sciences research: Can qualitative and quantitative methods be combined. *Journal of Comparative Social Work*, 1(8), 1–12.

Imhoff, R., & Lamberty, P. (2018). How paranoid are conspiracy believers? Toward a more fine-grained understanding of the connect and disconnect between paranoia and belief in conspiracy theories. *European Journal of Social Psychology*, 48(7), 909–926. https://doi.org/10.1002/ejsp.2494

Jaccard, J., & Jacoby, J. (2020). *Theory construction and model-building skills: A practical guide for social scientists*. Guilford Press.

Jäger, K. (2016). Not a new gold standard: Even big data cannot predict the future. *Critical Review*, 28(3–4), 335–355. https://doi.org/10.1080/08913811.2016.1237704

James, W. (1882). On some Hegelisms. *Mind*, 7(26), 186–208.

James, W. (1890). *Principles of psychology*. Harvard University Press.

James, W. (1907). *Pragmatism*. Dover Publications.

James, W. (1912). *Essays in radical empiricism*. Longman Green and Co.

Janasik, N., Honkela, T., & Bruun, H. (2009). Text mining in qualitative research: Application of an unsupervised learning method. *Organizational Research Methods*, 12(3), 436–460. https://doi.org/10.1177/1094428108317202

Joas, H. (1993). *Pragmatism and social theory*. University of Chicago Press.

Johansen, M. B., & Frederiksen, J. T. (2021). Ethically important moments – A pragmatic-dualist research ethics. *Journal of Academic Ethics*, 19(2), 279–289. https://doi.org/10.1007/s10805-020-09377-y

John of Salisbury. (1159). *Metalogicon* (D. McGarry, Trans.). University of California Press.

Johnson, R. B. (2017). Dialectical pluralism: A metaparadigm whose time has come. *Journal of Mixed Methods Research*, 11(2), 156–173. https://doi.org/10.1177/1558689815607692

Johnson, R. B., Onwuegbuzie, A. J., & Turner, L. A. (2007). Toward a definition of mixed methods research. *Journal of Mixed Methods Research*, 1(2), 112–133. https://doi.org/10.1177/1558689806298224

Jovanović, G. (2010). Historizing epistemology in psychology. *Integrative Psychological and Behavioral Science*, 44(4), 310–328. https://doi.org/10.1007/s12124-010-9132-9

Jovchelovitch, S. (2019). *Knowledge in context: Representations, community and culture*. Routledge.

Jovchelovitch, S., & Hawlina, H. (2018). Utopias and world-making: Time, transformation and the collective imagination. In C. de Saint-Laurent, S. Obradović, & K. R. Carriere (Eds.), *Imagining collective futures* (pp. 129–151). Springer.

Just, D. R. (2019). Is the ban on deception necessary or even desirable? *Food Policy*, 83, 5–6. https://doi.org/10.1016/j.foodpol.2018.12.010

Kafka, F. (1915). *The metamorphosis*. Schocken Books.

Kakutani, M. (2018). *The death of truth: Notes on falsehood in the age of Trump*. William Collins.

Kaposi, D. (2017). The resistance experiments: Morality, authority and obedience in Stanley Milgram's account. *Journal for the Theory of Social Behaviour*, 47(4), 382–401. https://doi.org/10.1111/jtsb.12137

Kauffman, S. (1996). *At home in the universe: The search for the laws of self-organization and complexity*. Oxford University Press.

Kaufman, J. C., & Glăveanu, V. P. (2018). The road to uncreative science is paved with good intentions: Ideas, implementations, and uneasy balances. *Perspectives on Psychological Science*, 13(4), 457–465. https://doi.org/10.1177/1745691617753947

Kaushik, V., & Walsh, C. A. (2019). Pragmatism as a research paradigm and its implications for social work research. *Social Sciences*, 8(9), 255. https://doi.org/10.3390/socsci8090255

Kelly, L. M., & Cordeiro, M. (2020). Three principles of pragmatism for research on organizational processes. *Methodological Innovations*, 13(2), 2059799120937242. https://doi.org/10.1177/2059799120937242

Kerrigan, M. R. (2014). A framework for understanding community colleges' organizational capacity for data use: A convergent parallel mixed methods study. *Journal of Mixed Methods Research*, 8(4), 341–362. https://doi.org/10/f6ngcv

Kessler, J. S. (2017). Scattertext: A browser-based tool for visualizing how corpora differ. *ArXiv*, Preprint ArXiv:1703.00565.

Kilpinen, E. (2009). Pragmatism as a philosophy of action. In S. Pihlström & H. Rydenfelt (Eds.), *Pragmatist perspectives* (pp. 163–179). Societas Philosophica Fennica.

Kim, Y., Russo, S., & Amnå, E. (2017). The longitudinal relation between online and offline political participation among youth at two different developmental stages. *New Media & Society*, 19(6), 899–917. https://doi.org/10.1177/1461444815624181

Knappertsbusch, F. (2020). "Fractal heuristics" for mixed methods research: Applying Abbott's "fractal distinctions" as a conceptual metaphor for method integration. *Journal of Mixed Methods Research*, 14(4), 456–472. https://doi.org/10.1177/1558689819893573

Knight, L. W. (2008). *Citizen: Jane Addams and the struggle for democracy*. University of Chicago Press.

Kordzadeh, N., & Warren, J. (2013). Toward a typology of health 2.0 collaboration platforms and websites. *Health and Technology*, 3(1), 37–50. https://doi.org/10.1007/s12553-013-0043-x

Kowsari, K., Jafari Meimandi, K., Heidarysafa, M., et al. (2019). Text classification algorithms: A survey. *Information*, 10(4), 150. https://doi.org/10.3390/info10040150

Kreuzer, M. (2010). Historical knowledge and quantitative analysis: The case of the origins of proportional representation. *American Political Science Review*, 104(2), 369–392. https://doi.org/10.1017/S0003055410000122

Krippendorff, K. (2019). *Content analysis: An introduction to its methodology*, 4th edition. SAGE Publications.

Krpan, D. (2022). (When) should psychology be a science? *Journal for the Theory of Social Behaviour*, 52(1), 183–198. https://doi.org/10.1111/jtsb.12316

Kuhn, T. S. (1962). *The structure of scientific revolutions*. University of Chicago Press.

Kvale, S., & Brinkmann, S. (2008). *Interviews: Learning the craft of qualitative research interviewing*. SAGE.

Kyza, E. A., Varda, C., Panos, D., et al. (2020). Combating misinformation online: Re-imagining social media for policy-making. *Internet Policy Review*, 9(4), 1–24. https://doi.org/10.14763/2020.4.1514

LaFollette, H. (1997). Pragmatic ethics. In H. LaFollette (Ed.), *The Blackwell guide to ethical theory* (pp. 400–419). Blackwell.

Lakoff, G., & Johnson, M. (1980). *Metaphors we live by*. University of Chicago Press.

Lakoff, G., & Johnson, M. (1999). *Philosophy in the flesh: The embodied mind and its challenge to Western thought*. Basic Books.

Lakoff, G., & Núñez, R. (2000). *Where mathematics comes from*. Basic Books.

Lamm, C., Decety, J., & Singer, T. (2011). Meta-analytic evidence for common and distinct neural networks associated with directly experienced pain and empathy for pain. *Neuroimage*, 54(3), 2492–2502. https://doi.org/10.1016/j.neuroimage.2010.10.014

Laplace, P. S. (1814). *A philosophical essay on probabilities*. Wiley.

Latour, B. (1993). *We have never been modern*. Harvard University Press.

Law, J. (2004). *After method: Mess in social science research*. Routledge.

Leary, D. E. (1990). *Metaphors in the history of psychology*. Cambridge University Press.

Lee, L. W., Dabirian, A., McCarthy, I. P., & Kietzmann, J. (2020). Making sense of text: Artificial intelligence-enabled content analysis. *European Journal of Marketing*, 54(3), 615–644. https://doi.org/10/gmt7m3

Leeson, W., Resnick, A., Alexander, D., & Rovers, J. (2019). Natural language processing (NLP) in qualitative public health research: A proof of concept study. *International Journal of Qualitative Methods*, 18, 1609406919887021. https://doi.org/10.1177/1609406919887021

Leonelli, S. (2016). Locating ethics in data science: Responsibility and accountability in global and distributed knowledge production systems. *Philosophical Transactions of the Royal Society A: Mathematical, Physical and Engineering Sciences*, 374(2083), 20160122. https://doi.org/10.1098/rsta.2016.0122

Levinas, E. (1991). *On thinking-of-the-other: Entre nous*. The Athlone Press Ltd.

Lewandowsky, S., Ecker, U. K., & Cook, J. (2017). Beyond misinformation: Understanding and coping with the "post-truth" era. *Journal of Applied Research in Memory and Cognition*, 6(4), 353–369. https://doi.org/10.1016/j.jarmac.2017.07.008

Lewandowsky, S., Ecker, U. K., Seifert, C. M., Schwarz, N., & Cook, J. (2012). Misinformation and its correction: Continued influence and successful debiasing. *Psychological Science in the Public Interest*, 13(3), 106–131. https://doi.org/10.1177/1529100612451018

Lewandowsky, S., Oberauer, K., & Gignac, G. E. (2013). NASA faked the moon landing—therefore,(climate) science is a hoax: An anatomy of the motivated rejection of science. *Psychological Science*, 24(5), 622–633. https://doi.org/10.1177/0956797612457686

Lewin, K. (1943). Psychology and the process of group living. *Journal of Social Psychology*, 17(1), 113–131. https://doi.org/10.1080/00224545.1943.9712269

Lieber, E. (2009). Mixing qualitative and quantitative methods: Insights into design and analysis issues. *Journal of Ethnographic & Qualitative Research*, 3(4), 218–227.

Linell, P. (2009). *Rethinking language, mind, and world dialogically: Interactional and contextual theories of human sense-making*. Information Age Publishing.

Liu, C. (2014). *The three-body problem* (Vol. 1). Macmillan.

Locke, J. (1847). *An essay concerning human understanding*. Kay & Troutman.

Love, H. R., & Corr, C. (2022). Integrating without quantitizing: Two examples of deductive analysis strategies within qualitatively driven mixed methods research. *Journal of Mixed Methods Research*, 16(1), 64–87. https://doi.org/10/gpdcq2

Ludwig, K. (2007). The epistemology of thought experiments: First person versus third person approaches. *Midwest Studies in Philosophy*, 31(1), 128–159.

Luria, A. R. (1968). *The mind of a mnemonist: A little book about a vast memory.* Harvard University Press.

Mach, K. J., Lemos, M. C., Meadow, A. M., et al. (2020). Actionable knowledge and the art of engagement. *Current Opinion in Environmental Sustainability*, 42, 30–37. https://doi.org/10.1016/j.cosust.2020.01.002

Macnab, N., Visser, J., & Daniels, H. (2007). Desperately seeking data: Methodological complications in researching "hard to find" young people. *Journal of Research in Special Educational Needs*, 7(3), 142–148. https://doi.org/10.1111/j.1471-3802.2007.00091.x

Madison, G. (2005). Habermas, psychoanalysis, and emancipation. *Existential Analysis*, 16(2), 209–220.

Malafouris, L. (2019). Mind and material engagement. *Phenomenology and the Cognitive Sciences*, 18(1), 1–17. https://doi.org/10.1007/s11097-018-9606-7

Manikandan, S. (2010). Preparing to analyse data. *Journal of Pharmacology & Pharmacotherapeutics*, 1(1), 64–65.

Mannell, J., Davis, K., Akter, K., et al. (2021). Visual participatory analysis: A qualitative method for engaging participants in interpreting the results of randomized controlled trials of health interventions. *Journal of Mixed Methods Research*, 15(1), 18–36. https://doi.org/10.1177/1558689820914806

Mantelero, A. (2018). AI and Big Data: A blueprint for a human rights, social and ethical impact assessment. *Computer Law & Security Review*, 34(4), 754–772. https://doi.org/10.1016/j.clsr.2018.05.017

Markie, P. (2004). Rationalism vs. empiricism. *The Stanford Encyclopaedia of Philosophy*. https://plato.stanford.edu/entries/rationalism-empiricism

Marková, I. (1982). *Paradigms, thought and language.* Wiley.

Marková, I. (2016). *The dialogical mind.* Cambridge University Press.

Marshall, M. N. (1996). Sampling for qualitative research. *Family Practice*, 13(6), 522–526. https://doi.org/10.1093/fampra/13.6.522

Martin, J. (2006). Reinterpreting internalization and agency through GH Mead's perspectival realism. *Human Development*, 49, 65–86.

Martin, J., & Gillespie, A. (2013). Position exchange theory and personhood: Moving between positions and perspectives within physical, socio-cultural, and psychological space and time. In J. Martin, & M. H. Bickhard (Eds.), *The psychology of personhood* (147–164). Cambridge University Press.

Martin, J., & Gillespie, A. (2020). Position exchange theory. In V. Glaveanu (Ed.), *The Palgrave Encyclopedia of the Possible* (pp. 1–9). Springer International Publishing. https://doi.org/10.1007/978-3-319-98390-5_111-2.

Martin, J., & Sugarman, J. (2001). Interpreting human kinds: Beginnings of a hermeneutic psychology. *Theory & Psychology*, 11(2), 193–207. https://doi.org/10.1177/0959354301112003

Martin, K. (2019). Ethical implications and accountability of algorithms. *Journal of Business Ethics*, 160(4), 835–850. https://doi.org/10.1007/s10551-018-3921-3

Masson, M. E. J. (2011). A tutorial on a practical Bayesian alternative to null-hypothesis significance testing. *Behavior Research Methods*, 43(3), 679–690. https://doi.org/10.3758/s13428-010-0049-5

Mayer-Schönberger, V., & Ramge, T. (2022). The data boom is here-it's just not evenly distributed. *MIT Sloan Management Review*, 63(3), 7–9.

McCain, K. W. (2015). "Nothing as practical as a good theory" Does Lewin's maxim still have salience in the applied social sciences? *Proceedings of the Association for Information Science and Technology*, 52(1), 1–4. https://doi.org/10.1002/pra2.2015.145052010077

McCloskey, D. N. (1995). Metaphors economists live by. *Social Research*, 62(2), 215–237.

McCrudden, M. T., Marchand, G., & Schutz, P. A. (2021). Joint displays for mixed methods research in psychology. *Methods in Psychology*, 5, 100067. https://doi.org/10.1016/j.metip.2021.100067

McGuire, W. J. (1997). Creative hypothesis generating in psychology: Some useful heuristics. *Annual Review of Psychology*, 48(1), 1–30.

McIntyre, A. (2008). *Participatory action research*. SAGE Publications.

McIntyre, L. (2018). *Post-truth*. MIT Press.

McNamee, S. (1988). Accepting research as social intervention: Implications of a systemic epistemology. *Communication Quarterly*, 36(1), 50–68. https://doi.org/10.1080/01463378809369707

Mead, G. H. (1903). The definition of the psychical. *Decennial Publications of the University of Chicago*, 1(3), 77–112.

Mead, G. H. (1912). The mechanism of social consciousness. *The Journal of Philosophy, Psychology and Scientific Methods*, 9(15), 401–406.

Mead, G. H. (1913). The social self. *Journal of Philosophy, Psychology and Scientific Methods*, 10(14), 374–380.

Mead, G. H. (1917). Scientific method and individual thinker. In J. Dewey, A. W. Moore, H. C. Brown, G. H. Mead, B. H. Bode, H. W. Stuart, J. H. Tufts, & H. M. Kallen (Eds.), *Creative intelligence: Essays in the pragmatic attitude* (pp. 176–227). Henry Holt and Co.

Mead, G. H. (1925). The genesis of self and social control. *International Journal of Ethics*, 35(3), 251–277.

Mead, G. H. (1926). The objective reality of perspectives. In S. Brightman (Ed.) *Proceedings of the Sixth International Congress of Philosophy* (pp. 75–85). Longmans, Green, and Co.

Mead, G. H. (1932). *The philosophy of the present*. Open Court.

Mead, G. H. (1934). *Mind, self & society from the standpoint of a social behaviorist*. University of Chicago Press.

Mead, G. H. (1936). *Movements of thought in the nineteenth century* (M. H. Moore, Ed.). University of Chicago Press.

Mead, G. H. (1964a). *On social psychology: Selected papers*. University of Chicago Press.

Mead, G. H. (1964b). *Selected writings* (A. J. Reck, Ed.). Bobbs-Merrill.

Mearns, K., Kirwan, B., Reader, T. W., et al. (2013). Development of a methodology for understanding and enhancing safety culture in Air Traffic Management. *Safety Science*, 53, 123–133. https://doi.org/10.1016/j.ssci.2012.09.001

Mede, N. G., Schäfer, M. S., Ziegler, R., & Weißkopf, M. (2021). The "replication crisis" in the public eye: Germans' awareness and perceptions of the (ir)reproducibility of scientific research. *Public Understanding of Science*, 30(1), 91–102. https://doi.org/10.1177/0963662520954370

Melles, G. (2008). An enlarged pragmatist inquiry paradigm for methodological pluralism in academic design research. *Artifact: Journal of Design Practice*, 2(1), 3–13.

Merchant, C. (2015). *Autonomous nature: Problems of prediction and control from ancient times to the scientific revolution*. Routledge.

Merleau-Ponty, M. (1945). *Phenomenology of perception*. Routledge.

Mertens, D. M. (2007). Transformative paradigm: Mixed methods and social justice. *Journal of Mixed Methods Research*, 1(3), 212–225. https://doi.org/10/bn9hm3

Merton, R. K. (1936). The unanticipated consequences of purposive social action. *American Sociological Review*, 1(6), 894–904.

Midgley, M. (2003). The myths we live by. *Taylor & Francis*. https://doi.org/10.4324/9780203480922

Milgram, S. (1969). *Obedience to authority: An experimental view*. Harper Torchbooks.

Milgram, S. (1992). Cyranoids. In S. Milgram, J. E. Sabini, & M. E. Silver (Eds.), *The Individual in a social world* (pp. 337–345). McGraw-Hill.

Miller, G. A. (1956). The magical number seven, plus or minus two: Some limits on our capacity for processing information. *Psychological Review*, 63(2), 81.

Miller, R. (2010). Embracing complexity and using the future. *Ethos*, 10(10), 23–28.

Mitchell, A. (2018). A review of mixed methods, pragmatism and abduction techniques. *The Electronic Journal of Business Research Method*, 16(3), 103–116.

Molina-Azorin, J. F., & Fetters, M. D. (2022). Books on mixed methods research: A window on the growth in number and diversity. *Journal of Mixed Methods Research*, 16(1), 8–16.

Montiel, C. J., & Uyheng, J. (2022). Foundations for a decolonial big data psychology. *Journal of Social Issues*, 78(2), 278–297. https://doi.org/10.1111/josi.12439

Moore, H., & Gillespie, A. (2014). The caregiving bind: Concealing the demands of informal care can undermine the caregiving identity. *Social Science & Medicine*, 116, 102–109. https://doi.org/10.1016/j.socscimed.2014.06.038

Moran-Ellis, J., Alexander, V. D., Cronin, A., et al. (2006). Triangulation and integration: Processes, claims and implications. *Qualitative Research*, 6(1), 45–59. https://doi.org/10.1177/1468794106058870

Moretti, F. (2013). *Distant reading*. Verso Books.

Morgan, D. L. (2007). Paradigms lost and pragmatism regained: Methodological implications of combining qualitative and quantitative methods. *Journal of Mixed Methods Research*, 1(1), 48–76. https://doi.org/10.1177/2345678906292462

Morgan, D. L. (2014a). Pragmatism as a paradigm for social research. *Qualitative Inquiry*, 20(8), 1045–1053. https://doi.org/10.1177/1077800413513733

Morgan, D. L. (2018). Living within blurry boundaries: The value of distinguishing between qualitative and quantitative research. *Journal of Mixed Methods Research*, 12(3), 268–279. https://doi.org/10/gdtbrn

Morgan, M. (2014b). The poverty of (moral) philosophy: Towards an empirical and pragmatic ethics. *European Journal of Social Theory*, 17(2), 129–146. https://doi.org/10.1177/1368431013505016

Morse, J. M. (1991). Approaches to qualitative-quantitative methodological triangulation. *Nursing Research*, 40(2), 120–123. https://doi.org/10.1097/00006199-199103000-00014

Morse, J. M. (2010). "Cherry picking": Writing from thin data. *Qualitative Health Research*, 20(1), 3. https://doi.org/10.1177/1049732309354285

Moscovici, S. (1987). The conspiracy mentality. In C. F. Graumann & S. Moscovici (Eds.), *Changing conceptions of conspiracy* (pp. 151–169). Springer-Verlag.

Moscovici, S. (1991). Experiment and experience: An intermediate step from Sherif to Asch. *Journal for the Theory of Social Behaviour*, 21(3), 253–268.

Moscovici, S. E., Mucchi-Faina, A. E., & Maass, A. E. (1994). *Minority influence*. Nelson-Hall Publishers.

Mulej, M. (2007). Systems theory: A worldview and/or a methodology aimed at requisite holism/realism of humans' thinking, decisions and action. *Systems Research and Behavioral Science* 24(3), 347–357. https://doi.org/10.1002/sres.810

Mulhall, A. (2003). In the field: Notes on observation in qualitative research. *Journal of Advanced Nursing*, 41(3), 306–313. https://doi.org/10.1046/j.1365-2648.2003.02514.x

Mullen, B., Johnson, C., & Salas, E. (1991). Productivity loss in brainstorming groups: A meta-analytic integration. *Basic and Applied Social Psychology*, 12(1), 3–23.

Nasie, M., Bar-Tal, D., Pliskin, R., Nahhas, E., & Halperin, E. (2014). Overcoming the barrier of narrative adherence in conflicts through awareness of the psychological bias of naïve realism. *Personality and Social Psychology Bulletin*, 40(11), 1543–1556.

Nastasi, B. K., Hitchcock, J., Sarkar, S., et al. (2007). Mixed methods in intervention research: Theory to adaptation. *Journal of Mixed Methods Research*, 1(2), 164–182. https://doi.org/10.1177/1558689806298181

Neuman, Y. (2016). *Computational personality analysis: Introduction, practical applications and novel directions*. Springer International Publishing. https://doi.org/10.1007/978-3-319-42460-6

Newell, A. (1973). You can't play 20 questions with nature and win: Projective comments on the papers of this symposium. In W. G. Chase (Ed.), *Visual information processing* (pp. 283–308). Academic Press.

Niculae, V., Kumar, S., Boyd-Graber, J., & Danescu-Niculescu-Mizil, C. (2015). Linguistic harbingers of betrayal: A case study on an online strategy game. ArXiv Preprint ArXiv:1506.04744.

Nisbett, R. E., & Cohen, D. (1996). *Culture of honor: The psychology of violence in the south*. Routledge.

Noort, M. C., Reader, T. W., & Gillespie, A. (2019a). Speaking up to prevent harm: A systematic review of the safety voice literature. *Safety Science*, 117, 375–387. https://doi.org/10.1016/j.ssci.2019.04.039

Noort, M. C., Reader, T. W., & Gillespie, A. (2019b). Walking the plank: An experimental paradigm to investigate safety voice. *Frontiers in Psychology*, 10. https://doi.org/10.3389/fpsyg.2019.00668

Noort, M. C., Reader, T. W., & Gillespie, A. (2021a). Cockpit voice recorder transcript data: Capturing safety voice and safety listening during historic aviation accidents. *Data in Brief*, 39, 107602.

Noort, M. C., Reader, T. W., & Gillespie, A. (2021b). Sounds of silence: Data for analysing muted safety voice in speech. *Data in Brief*, 37, 107186. https://doi.org/10.1016/j.dib.2021.107186

Noort, M. C., Reader, T. W., & Gillespie, A. (2021c). The sounds of safety silence: Interventions and temporal patterns unmute unique safety voice content in speech. *Safety Science*, 140, 105289. https://doi.org/10.1016/j.ssci.2021.105289

Norman, D. A. (1967). Temporal confusions and limited capacity processors. *Acta Psychologica*, 27, 293–297. https://doi.org/10.1016/0001-6918(67)90071-6

Norton, J. (1991). Thought experiments in Einstein's work. In T. Horowitz & G. J. Massey (Eds.), *Thought experiments in science and philosophy* (Vol. 1991). Rowman & Littlefield Publishers. http://philsci-archive.pitt.edu/archive/00003190/01/8_norton.pdf

Nosek, B. A., Beck, E. D., Campbell, L., et al. (2019). Preregistration is hard, and worthwhile. *Trends in Cognitive Sciences*, 23(10), 815–818. https://doi.org/10.1016/j.tics.2019.07.009

Nzabonimpa, J. P. (2018). Quantitizing and qualitizing (im-)possibilities in mixed methods research. *Methodological Innovations*, 11(2), 1–16. https://doi.org/10.1177/2059799118789021

Obradović, S., & Sheehy-Skeffington, J. (2020). Power, identity, and belonging: A mixed-methods study of the processes shaping perceptions of EU integration in a prospective member state. *European Journal of Social Psychology*, 50(7), 1425–1442. https://doi.org/10.1002/ejsp.2691

O'Halloran, K. L., Pal, G., & Jin, M. (2021). Multimodal approach to analysing big social and news media data. *Discourse, Context & Media*, 40, 100467. https://doi.org/10.1016/j.dcm.2021.100467

O'Halloran, K. L., Tan, S., Pham, D.-S., Bateman, J., & Vande Moere, A. (2018). A digital mixed methods research design: Integrating multimodal analysis with data mining and information visualization for big data analytics. *Journal of Mixed Methods Research*, 12(1), 11–30. https://doi.org/10.1177/1558689816651015

O'Neil, C. (2016). *Weapons of math destruction*. Crown.

Onwuegbuzie, A. J., & Johnson, R. B. (2021). *The Routledge reviewer's guide to mixed methods analysis*. Routledge.

Onwuegbuzie, A. J., & Leech, N. L. (2005). On becoming a pragmatic researcher: The importance of combining quantitative and qualitative research methodologies. *International Journal of Social Research Methodology*, 8(5), 375–387. https://doi.org/10.1080/13645570500402447

Open Science Collaboration. (2015). Estimating the reproducibility of psychological science. *Science*, 349(6251), aac4716. https://doi.org/10.1126/science.aac4716

Page, S. E. (2015). What sociologists should know about complexity. *Annual Review of Sociology*, 41, 21–41. https://doi.org/10.1146/annurev-soc-073014-112230

Paluck, E. L., Green, S. A., & Green, D. P. (2019). The contact hypothesis re-evaluated. *Behavioural Public Policy*, 3(2), 129–158. https://doi.org/10.1017/bpp.2018.25

Parker, I. (1998). *Social constructionism, discourse and realism*. SAGE.

Paschalides, D., Stephanidis, D., Andreou, A., et al. (2020). Mandola: A big-data processing and visualization platform for monitoring and detecting online hate speech. *ACM Transactions on Internet Technology (TOIT)*, 20(2), 1–21. https://doi.org/10.1145/3371276

Patterson, D. M. (1990). Law's pragmatism: Law as practice & narrative. *Virginia Law Review*, 76(5), 937–996. https://doi.org/10.2307/1073154

Peirce, C. S. (1878). How to make our ideas clear. *Popular Science Monthly*, 12(January), 286–302.

Peirce, C. S. (1894). What is a sign? In R. T. Craig & H. L. Muller (Eds.), *Theorizing communication: Readings across traditions* (pp. 177–182). SAGE.

Peirce, C. S. (1955). *Philosophical writings of Peirce*. Dover Publications, Inc.

Peirce, C. S. (1974). *Collected papers of Charles Sanders Peirce*. Harvard University Press.

Peirce, C. S. (1992). *The essential Peirce: Selected philosophical writings* (Vol. 2). Indiana University Press.

Perlstadt, H. (2018). How to get out of the Stanford prison experiment: Revisiting social science research ethics. *Journal of Social Sciences and Humanities*, 1(2), 45–59.

Pettigrew, T. F. (1998). Intergroup contact theory. *Annual Review of Psychology*, 49(1), 65–85. https://doi.org/10.1146/annurev.psych.49.1.65

Phillips, D. C. (1995). The good, the bad, and the ugly: The many faces of constructivism. *Educational Researcher*, 24(7), 5–12. https://doi.org/10.3102/0013189X024007005

Piaget, J. (1977). *The development of thought: Equilibration of cognitive structures*. Viking.

Pinfield, S., Salter, J., Bath, P. A., et al. (2014). Open-access repositories world-wide, 2005–2012: Past growth, current characteristics, and future possibilities. *Journal of the Association for Information Science and Technology*, 65(12), 2404–2421. https://doi.org/10.1002/asi.23131

Pokhrel, P., Herzog, T. A., Muranaka, N., & Fagan, P. (2015). Young adult e-cigarette users' reasons for liking and not liking e-cigarettes: A qualitative study. *Psychology & Health*, 30(12), 1450–1469. https://doi.org/10.1080/08870446.2015.1061129

Poli, R. (2017). *Introduction to anticipation studies*. Springer.

Popper, K. (1934). *The logic of scientific discovery*. Routledge.

Popper, K. (1969). *Conjectures and refutations: The growth of scientific knowledge*. Routledge & Kegan Paul.

Poth, C. N. (2018). *Innovation in mixed methods research: A practical guide to integrative thinking with complexity.* SAGE.

Poth, C. N., Bulut, O., Aquilina, A. M., & Otto, S. J. G. (2021). Using Data mining for rapid complex case study descriptions: Example of public health briefings during the onset of the COVID-19 pandemic. *Journal of Mixed Methods Research*, 15586898211013924. https://doi.org/10.1177/15586898211013925

Power, S. A. (2018). The deprivation-protest paradox: How the perception of unfair economic inequality leads to civic unrest. *Current Anthropology*, 59(6), 765–789. https://doi.org/10.1086/700679

Power, S. A., Velez, G., Qadafi, A., & Tennant, J. (2018). The SAGE model of social psychological research. *Perspectives on Psychological Science*, 13(3), 359–372. https://doi.org/10.1177/1745691617734863

Power, S. A., Zittoun, T., Akkerman, S., et al. (2023). Social psychology of and for world-making. *Personality and Social Psychology Review*, 10888683221145756. https://doi.org/10.1177/10888683221145756

Prasad, A. (2022). Anti-science misinformation and conspiracies: COVID–19, post-truth, and science & technology studies (STS). *Science, Technology and Society*, 27(1), 88–112. https://doi.org/10.1177/09717218211003413

Preissle, J., Glover-Kudon, R., Rohan, E. A., Boehm, J. E., & DeGroff, A. (2015). Putting ethics on the mixed methods map. In S. Hesse-Biber & B. R. Johnson (Eds.), *The Oxford handbook of multimethod and mixed methods research inquiry* (pp. 144–166). Oxford University Press.

Psaltis, C., & Duveen, G. (2006). Social relations and cognitive development: The influence of conversation type and representations of gender. *European Journal of Social Psychology*, 36(3), 407–430.

Psaltis, C., & Duveen, G. (2007). Conservation and conversation types: Forms of recognition and cognitive development. *British Journal of Developmental Psychology*, 25(1), 79–102.

Putnam, H. (1974). Meaning and reference. *The Journal of Philosophy*, 70(19), 699–711. https://doi.org/10.2307/2025079

Putnam, H. (1995). *Words and life.* Harvard University Press.

Qu, S. Q., & Dumay, J. (2011). The qualitative research interview. *Qualitative Research in Accounting & Management*, 8(3), 238–264. https://doi.org/10.1108/11766091111162070

Rawls, J. (1971). *A theory of justice.* Belknap Press.

Reader, T. W., & Gillespie, A. (2021). Stakeholders in safety: Patient reports on unsafe clinical behaviors distinguish hospital mortality rates. *Journal of Applied Psychology*, 106(3), 439–451. http://dx.doi.org/10.1037/apl0000507

Reader, T. W., & Gillespie, A. (2022). Developing a battery of measures for unobtrusive indicators of organisational culture: A research note. *Journal of Risk Research*, 0(0), 1–18. https://doi.org/10.1080/13669877.2022.2108116

Reader, T. W., Gillespie, A., Hald, J., & Patterson, M. (2020). Unobtrusive indicators of culture for organizations: A systematic review. *European Journal of Work and Organizational Psychology*, 29(5), 633–649. https://doi.org/10.1080/1359432X.2020.1764536

Reader, T. W., Gillespie, A., & Roberts, J. (2014). Patient complaints in health-care systems: A systematic review and coding taxonomy. *BMJ Quality & Safety*, 23(8), 678–689. https://doi.org/10.1136/bmjqs-2013-002437

Reeve, C. D. (2004). *Plato: Republic.* Hackett Publishing Company.

Renz, S. M., Carrington, J. M., & Badger, T. A. (2018). Two strategies for qualitative content analysis: An intramethod approach to triangulation. *Qualitative Health Research*, 28(5), 824–831. https://doi.org/10.1177/1049732317753586

Rice, J. A. (2007). *Mathematical statistics and data analysis.* Cengage Learning.

Rodriguez, M. Y., & Storer, H. (2020). A computational social science perspective on qualitative data exploration: Using topic models for the descriptive analysis of social media data. *Journal of Technology in Human Services*, 38(1), 54–86. https://doi.org/10/gg2wrw

Roots, E. (2007). Making connections: The relationship between epistemology and research methods. *Special Edition Papers*, 19(1), 19–27.

Rorty, R. (1981). *Philosophy and the mirror of nature.* Princeton University Press.

Rorty, R. (1982). *Consequences of pragmatism: Essays, 1972-1980.* University of Minnesota Press.

Rorty, R. (1989). *Contingency, irony, and solidarity.* Cambridge University Press.

Rorty, R. (1998). *Truth and progress: Philosophical papers.* Cambridge University Press.

Rorty, R. (1999). *Philosophy and social hope.* Penguin.

Rose, N. (1998). *Inventing our selves: Psychology, power, and personhood.* Cambridge University Press.

Rosenbaum, P. J., & Valsiner, J. (2011). The un-making of a method: From rating scales to the study of psychological processes. *Theory & Psychology*, 21(1), 47–65. https://doi.org/10.1177/0959354309352913

Ross, W., & Vallée-Tourangeau, F. (2021). Rewilding cognition: Complex dynamics in open experimental systems. *Journal of Trial and Error.* https://doi.org/10.36850/e4

Rozin, P. (2001). Social psychology and science: Some lessons from Solomon Asch. *Personality and Social Psychology Review*, 5(1), 2–14. https://doi.org/10.1207/S15327957PSPR0501_1

Rozin, P. (2009). What kind of empirical research should we publish, fund, and reward? A different perspective. *Perspectives on Psychological Science*, 4(4), 435–439. https://doi.org/10.1111/j.1745-6924.2009.01151.x

Rubin, H. J., & Rubin, I. S. (2005). The first phase of analysis: Preparing transcripts and coding data. In H. J. Rubin & I. S. Rubin (Eds.), *Qualitative interviewing: The art of hearing data* (pp. 201–223). SAGE.

Rubin, M., & Donkin, C. (2022). Exploratory hypothesis tests can be more compelling than confirmatory hypothesis tests. *Philosophical Psychology*, 0(0), 1–29. https://doi.org/10.1080/09515089.2022.2113771

Runco, M. A. (2010). *Divergent thinking, creativity, and ideation.* Ablex Publishing Corporation.

Said, E. W. (1978). *Orientalism: Western conceptions of the Orient.* Penguin.

Sale, J. E., Lohfeld, L. H., & Brazil, K. (2002). Revisiting the quantitative-qualitative debate: Implications for mixed-methods research. *Quality and Quantity*, 36(1), 43–53. https://doi.org/10/bczskd

Salganik, M. (2019). *Bit by bit: Social research in the digital age*. Princeton University Press.

Sandelowski, M., Voils, C. I., & Knafl, G. (2009). On quantitizing. *Journal of Mixed Methods Research*, 3(3), 208–222. https://doi.org/10.1177/1558689809334210

Sanderson, I. (2002). Evaluation, policy learning and evidence-based policy making. *Public Administration*, 80(1), 1–22. https://doi.org/10.1111/1467-9299.00292

Sandoval, C. (2013). *Methodology of the oppressed*. University of Minnesota Press.

Saussure, F. (1916). *Course in general linguistics*. Open Court.

Schaffner, B. F., & Luks, S. (2018). Misinformation or expressive responding? What an inauguration crowd can tell us about the source of political misinformation in surveys. *Public Opinion Quarterly*, 82(1), 135–147. https://doi.org/10.1093/poq/nfx042

Scheel, A. M., Tiokhin, L., Isager, P. M., & Lakens, D. (2020). Why hypothesis testers should spend less time testing hypotheses. *Perspectives on Psychological Science*, 16(4), 744–755. https://doi.org/10.1177/1745691620966795

Schegloff, E. A. (1992). Repair after next turn: The last structurally provided defence of intersubjectivity in conversation. *The American Journal of Sociology*, 97(5), 1295–1345.

Schegloff, E. A. (2007). *Sequence organization in interaction: A primer in conversation analysis*. Cambridge University Press.

Schilbach, L., Timmermans, B., Reddy, V., et al. (2013). Toward a second-person neuroscience. *Behavioral and Brain Sciences*, 36(04), 393–414.

Schoonenboom, J., & Johnson, R. B. (2017). How to construct a mixed methods research design. *KZfSS Kölner Zeitschrift Für Soziologie Und Sozialpsychologie*, 69(2), 107–131. https://doi.org/10.1007/s11577-017-0454-1

Schrag, Z. M. (2011). The case against ethics review in the social sciences. *Research Ethics*, 7(4), 120–131. https://doi.org/10.1177/1747016111100700402

Schratz, M., & Walker, R. (2005). *Research as social change: New opportunities for qualitative research*. Routledge.

Schuetz, A. (1945). On multiple realities. *Philosophy and Phenomenological Research*, 5(4), 533–576.

Seale, C. (1999). *The quality of qualitative research*. SAGE Publications.

Searle, J. R. (1982). The Chinese room revisited. *Behavioral and Brain Sciences*, 5(2), 345–348. https://doi.org/10.1017/S0140525X00012425

Seawright, J. (2016). *Multi-method social science: Combining qualitative and quantitative tools*. Cambridge University Press.

Senghor, A. S., & Racine, E. (2022). How to evaluate the quality of an ethical deliberation? A pragmatist proposal for evaluation criteria and collaborative research. *Medicine, Health Care and Philosophy*, 1–18.

Senteio, C., Adler-Milstein, J., Richardson, C., & Veinot, T. (2019). Psychosocial information use for clinical decisions in diabetes care. *Journal of the American*

Medical Informatics Association, 26(8–9), 813–824. https://doi.org/10.1093/jamia/ocz053

Serra, J. P. (2010). What is and what should pragmatic ethics be? Some remarks on recent scholarship. *European Journal of Pragmatism and American Philosophy*, 2(1–15).

Shabou, B. M., Tièche, J., Knafou, J., & Gaudinat, A. (2020). Algorithmic methods to explore the automation of the appraisal of structured and unstructured digital data. *Records Management Journal*, 30(2), 175–200.

Shahin, S. (2016). When scale meets depth: Integrating natural language processing and textual analysis for studying digital corpora. *Communication Methods and Measures*, 10(1), 28–50. https://doi.org/10.1080/19312458.2015.1118447

Shannon-Baker, P. (2016). Making paradigms meaningful in mixed methods research. *Journal of Mixed Methods Research*, 10(4), 319–334. https://doi.org/10/f84htc

Shehzad, W. (2011). Outlining purposes, stating the nature of the present research, and listing research questions or hypotheses in academic papers. *Journal of Technical Writing and Communication*, 41(2), 139–160. https://doi.org/10.2190/TW.41.2.c

Shergill, S. S., Murray, R. M., & McGuire, P. K. (1998). Auditory hallucinations: A review of psychological treatments. *Schizophrenia Research*, 32(3), 137–150. https://doi.org/10.1016/S0920-9964(98)00052-8

Shrout, P. E., & Rodgers, J. L. (2018). Psychology, science, and knowledge construction: Broadening perspectives from the replication crisis. *Annual Review of Psychology*, 69(1), 487–510. https://doi.org/10.1146/annurev-psych-122216-011845

Shweder, R. A. (1996). Quanta and qualia: What is the "object" of ethnographic method. In R. Jessor, A. Colby, & R. A. Shweder (Eds.), *Ethnography and human development: Context and meaning in social inquiry* (pp. 175–182). University of Chicago Press.

Simpson, B., & den Hond, F. (2022). The contemporary resonances of classical pragmatism for studying organization and organizing. *Organization Studies*, 43(1), 127–146. https://doi.org/10.1177/0170840621991689

Sinclair, S., & Rockwell, G. (2016). Text analysis and visualization. In S. Schreibman, R. Siemens, & J. Unsworth (Eds.), *A new companion to digital humanities* (pp. 274–290). John Wiley & Sons, Ltd. https://doi.org/10.1002/9781118680605.ch19

Skinner, B. F. (1989). The origins of cognitive thought. *American Psychologist*, 44(1), 13.

Smagorinsky, P. (1995). The social construction of data: Methodological problems of investigating learning in the zone of proximal development. *Review of Educational Research*, 65(3), 191–212. https://doi.org/10.3102/00346543065003191

Smith, R. J., Grande, D., & Merchant, R. M. (2016). Transforming scientific inquiry: Tapping into digital data by building a culture of transparency and consent. *Academic Medicine: Journal of the Association of American Medical Colleges*, 91(4), 469. https://doi.org/10.1097/ACM.0000000000001022

Stadnick, N. A., Poth, C. N., Guetterman, T. C., & Gallo, J. J. (2021). Advancing discussion of ethics in mixed methods health services research. *BMC Health Services Research*, 21(1), 1–9. https://doi.org/10.1186/s12913-021-06583-1

Stahl, C. C., & Literat, I. (2022). # GenZ on TikTok: The collective online self-Portrait of the social media generation. *Journal of Youth Studies*, 1–22. https://doi.org/10.1080/13676261.2022.2053671

Stainton Rogers, W. (2011). *Social psychology*. McGraw-Hill Education (UK).

Stebbins, R. A. (2001). *Exploratory research in the social sciences*. SAGE.

Stein, M. I. (1953). Creativity and culture. *The Journal of Psychology*, 36(2), 311–322. https://doi.org/10.1080/00223980.1953.9712897

Stewart, I., & Cohen, J. (1997). *Figments of reality: The evolution of the curious mind*. Cambridge University Press.

Stinson, C. (2022). Algorithms are not neutral: Bias in collaborative filtering. *AI and Ethics*, 2, 763–770.

Swami, V., Voracek, M., Stieger, S., Tran, U. S., & Furnham, A. (2014). Analytic thinking reduces belief in conspiracy theories. *Cognition*, 133(3), 572–585. https://doi.org/10.1016/j.cognition.2014.08.006

Swedberg, R. (2020). Using metaphors in sociology: Pitfalls and potentials. *The American Sociologist*, 51(2), 240–257. https://doi.org/10.1007/s12108-020-09443-3

Tanggaard, L. (2007). The research interview as discourses crossing swords: The researcher and apprentice on crossing roads. *Qualitative Inquiry*, 13(1), 160–176. https://doi.org/10.1177/1077800406294948

Tavory, I., & Timmermans, S. (2014). *Abductive analysis: Theorizing qualitative research*. University of Chicago Press.

Teddlie, C., & Tashakkori, A. (2009). *Foundations of mixed methods research: Integrating quantitative and qualitative approaches in the social and behavioral sciences*. SAGE.

Tenner, E. (1996). *Why things bite back: Technology and the revenge effect*. Fourth Estate.

Thaler, R. H., & Sunstein, C. R. (2009). *Nudge: Improving decisions about health, wealth, and happiness*. Penguin.

Thompson, N. A., & Byrne, O. (2022). Imagining futures: Theorizing the practical knowledge of future-making. *Organization Studies*, 43(2), 247–268. https://doi.org/10.1177/0170840621105322

Toulmin, S. (1973). *Human understanding, Vol. I: The collective use and evolution of concepts*. Clarendon Press.

Toulmin, S. (1992). *Cosmopolis: The hidden agenda of modernity*. University of Chicago Press.

Tourish, D. (2020). The triumph of nonsense in management studies. *Academy of Management Learning & Education*, 19(1), 99–109. https://doi.org/10.5465/amle.2019.0255

Trafimow, D. (2022). Generalizing across auxiliary, statistical, and inferential assumptions. *Journal for the Theory of Social Behaviour*, 52(1), 37–48. https://doi.org/10.1111/jtsb.12296

Trochim, W. M., & Donnelly, J. P. (2021). *Research methods knowledge base* (Vol. 2). https://conjointly.com/kb/

Trott, C. D. (2019). Reshaping our world: Collaborating with children for community-based climate change action. *Action Research*, 17(1), 42–62. https://doi.org/10.1177/1476750319829209

Tukey, J. W. (1977). *Exploratory data analysis* (Vol. 2). Addison-Wesley Publishing Company.

Tukey, J. W. (1980). We need both exploratory and confirmatory. *The American Statistician*, 34(1), 23–25.

Tynes, R. (2021). Democracy's savior or citizen spy? *Surveillance & Society*, 19(3), 350–353. https://doi.org/10.24908/ss.v19i3.15015

Valsiner, J. (1998). *The guided mind*. Harvard University Press.

Valsiner, J. (2006). Developmental epistemology and implications for methodology. In R. M. Lerner (Ed.), *Handbook of child psychology* (pp. 166–209). John Wiley & Sons.

Valsiner, J. (2014). *An invitation to cultural psychology*. SAGE.

Van Dael, J., Gillespie, A., Reader, T., et al. (2021). Getting the whole story: Integrating patient complaints and staff reports of unsafe care. *Journal of Health Services Research & Policy*, 13558196211029324. https://doi.org/10.1177/13558196211029323

Van den Bossche, P., Gijselaers, W., Segers, M., Woltjer, G., & Kirschner, P. (2011). Team learning: Building shared mental models. *Instructional Science*, 39(3), 283–301. https://doi.org/10.1007/s11251-010-9128-3

van der Duin, P. (2019). Toward "responsible foresight": Developing futures that enable matching future technologies with societal demands. *World Futures Review*, 11(1), 69–79. https://doi.org/10.1177/1946756718803721

Van Dijk, J. (2020). *The digital divide*. John Wiley & Sons.

van Huizen, L. S., Dijkstra, P., Halmos, G. B., et al. (2019). Does multidisciplinary videoconferencing between a head-and-neck cancer centre and its partner hospital add value to their patient care and decision-making? A mixed-method evaluation. *BMJ Open*, 9(11), e028609. https://doi.org/10.1136/bmjopen-2018-028609

van Velzen, J. H. (2018). Students' general knowledge of the learning process: A mixed methods study illustrating integrated data collection and data consolidation. *Journal of Mixed Methods Research*, 12(2), 182–203. https://doi.org/10.1177/1558689816651792

Verkuyten, M. (2022). The meanings of tolerance: Discursive usage in a case of "identity politics". *Journal for the Theory of Social Behaviour*, 52(2), 224–236. https://doi.org/10.1111/jtsb.12339

Vermeule, C. A., & Sunstein, C. R. (2009). Conspiracy theories: Causes and cures. *Journal of Political Philosophy*, 17(2), 202–227.

Vogeley, K. (2017). Two social brains: Neural mechanisms of intersubjectivity. *Philosophical Transactions of the Royal Society B: Biological Sciences*, 372(1727), 20160245. https://doi.org/10.1098/rstb.2016.0245

Vogl, S. (2019). Integrating and consolidating data in mixed methods data analysis: Examples from focus group data with children. *Journal of Mixed Methods Research*, 13(4), 536–554. https://doi.org/10.1o/gd4twk

Voigt, K., Gottschall, M., Köberlein-Neu, J., et al. (2016). Why do family doctors prescribe potentially inappropriate medication to elderly patients? *BMC Family Practice*, 17(1), 93. https://doi.org/10.1186/s12875-016-0482-3

Von Uexküll, J. (1982). The theory of meaning. *Semiotica*, 42(1), 25–79.

Voros, J. (2003). A generic foresight process framework. *Foresight*, 5(3), 10–21. https://doi.org/10.1108/14636680310698379

Vygotsky, L. S., & Luria, A. (1994). Tool and symbol in child development. In R. Van de Veer & J. Valsiner (Eds.), *The Vygotsky reader* (pp. 99–174). Blackwell.

Wagoner, B., & Valsiner, J. (2005). Rating tasks in psychology: From static ontology to dialogical synthesis of meaning. In A. Gulerce, A. Hofmeister, I. Staeuble, G. Saunders, & J. Kaye (Eds.), *Contemporary theorizing in psychology* (pp. 197–213). Captus Press.

Webb, E. J., Campbell, D. T., Schwartz, R. D., & Sechrest, L. (1966). *Unobtrusive measures: Nonreactive research in the social sciences* (Vol. III). Rand McNally Chicago. www.ncjrs.gov/App/Publications/abstract.aspx?ID=48508

Wee, L. E., Cher, W. Q., Sin, D., Li, Z. C., & Koh, G. C.-H. (2016). Primary care characteristics and their association with health screening in a low-socioeconomic status public rental-flat population in Singapore-a mixed methods study. *BMC Family Practice*, 17(1), 1–14. https://doi.org/10.1186/s12875-016-0411-5

Wegener, C., Meier, N., & Maslo, E. (2018). *Cultivating creativity in methodology and research*. Springer.

Weiss, D. J. (2001). Deception by researchers is necessary and not necessarily evil. *Behavioral and Brain Sciences*, 24(3), 431. https://doi.org/10.1017/S0140525X01544143

Wenzel, M. (2022). Taking the future more seriously: From corporate foresight to "future-making". *Academy of Management Perspectives*, 36(2), 845–850. https://doi.org/10.5465/amp.2020.0126

Werner, H. (1957). The concept of development from a comparative and organismic point of view. In D. B. Harris (Ed.), *The concept of development* (pp. 125–147). University of Minnesota Press.

Wertsch, J. V. (1998). *Mind as action*. Oxford University Press.

West, C. (1989). *The American evasion of philosophy*. Springer.

Whittaker, L., & Gillespie, A. (2013). Social networking sites: Mediating the self and its communities. *Journal of Community & Applied Social Psychology*, 23(6), 492–504. https://doi.org/10.1002/casp.2148

Wicherts, J. M., Veldkamp, C. L. S., Augusteijn, H. E. M., et al. (2016). Degrees of freedom in planning, running, analyzing, and reporting psychological studies: A checklist to avoid p-hacking. *Frontiers in Psychology*, 7. https://doi.org/10/gc5sjn

Wicks, A. C., & Freeman, R. E. (1998). Organization studies and the new pragmatism: Positivism, anti-positivism, and the search for ethics. *Organization Science*, 9(2), 123–140. https://doi.org/10.1287/orsc.9.2.123

Wiedemann, G. (2013). Opening up to big data: Computer-assisted analysis of textual data in social sciences. *Historical Social Research / Historische Sozialforschung*, 38(4 (146)), 332–357.

Wight, C. (2018). Post-truth, postmodernism and alternative facts. *New Perspectives*, 26(3), 17-29,177. https://doi.org/10.1177/2336825X1802600302

Wilson, N. L., Just, D. R., Swigert, J., & Wansink, B. (2017). Food pantry selection solutions: A randomized controlled trial in client-choice food pantries to nudge clients to targeted foods. *Journal of Public Health*, 39(2), 366–372.

Wise, A. F., & Shaffer, D. W. (2015). Why theory matters more than ever in the age of big data. *Journal of Learning Analytics*, 2(2), 5–13. https://doi.org/10.18608/jla.2015.22.2

Wolfle, D., Likert, R., Marquis, D. G., & Sears, R. R. (1949). Standards for appraising psychological research. *American Psychologist*, 4(8), 320–328. https://doi.org/10.1037/h0057345

World Medical Association. (2022). *Declaration of Helsinki – Ethical principles for medical research involving human subjects*. World Medical Association. www.wma.net/policies-post/wma-declaration-of-helsinki-ethical-principles-for-medical-research-involving-human-subjects/

Wright, E. O. (2010). *Envisioning real utopias*. Verso.

Yao, Q., & Tong, H. (1994). On prediction and chaos in stochastic systems. *Philosophical Transactions: Physical Sciences and Engineering*, 348(1688), 357–369. https://doi.org/10.1098/rsta.1994.0096

Yaqoob, I., Hashem, I. A. T., Gani, A., et al. (2016). Big data: From beginning to future. *International Journal of Information Management*, 36(6), 1231–1247. https://doi.org/10.1016/j.ijinfomgt.2016.07.009

Yardley, L., & Bishop, F. (2017). Mixing qualitative and quantitative methods: A pragmatic approach. In C. Willig & W. Stainton Rogers (Eds.), *The SAGE handbook of qualitative research in psychology* (pp. 398–413). SAGE Publications.

Zeller, R. A., Zeller, R. A., & Carmines, E. G. (1980). *Measurement in the social sciences: The link between theory and data*. Cambridge University Press.

Zittoun, T., & Gillespie, A. (2015). *Imagination in human and cultural development*. Routledge.

Zittoun, T., & Gillespie, A. (2018). Imagining the collective future: A sociocultural perspective. In C. de Saint-Laurent, S. Obradović, & K. R. Carriere (Eds.), *Imagining collective futures* (pp. 15–37). Palgrave. https://doi.org/10.1007/978-3-319-76051-3_2

Zittoun, T., & Gillespie, A. (2020). Metaphors of development and the development of metaphors. *Theory & Psychology*, 30(6), 827–841. https://doi.org/10.1177/0959354320939194

Zydney, J. M., & Warner, Z. (2016). Mobile apps for science learning: Review of research. *Computers & Education*, 94, 1–17. https://doi.org/10.1016/j.compedu.2015.11.001

Index

For EU product safety concerns, contact us at Calle de José Abascal, 56–1°,
28003 Madrid, Spain or eugpsr@cambridge.org.

www.ingramcontent.com/pod-product-compliance
Ingram Content Group UK Ltd.
Pitfield, Milton Keynes, MK11 3LW, UK
UKHW020354140625
459647UK00020B/2461